The Coughlin-Fahey Connection

American University Studies

Series VII
Theology and Religion
Vol. 102

PETER LANG
New York · San Francisco · Bern
Frankfurt am Main · Paris · London

Mary Christine Athans

The Coughlin-Fahey Connection

Father Charles E. Coughlin, Father Denis Fahey, C.S.Sp., and Religious Anti-Semitism in the United States, 1938-1954

PETER LANG
New York · San Francisco · Bern
Frankfurt am Main · Paris · London

Library of Congress Cataloging-in-Publication Data

Athans, Mary Christine
 The Coughlin-Fahey connection : Father Charles E.
Coughlin, Father Denis Fahey, C.S.Sp., and religious
anti-Semitism in the United States, 1938-1954 / Mary
Christine Athans.
 p. cm. — (American university studies. Series VII,
Theology and religion ; v. 102)
 A revision of the author's thesis (Ph.D.—Graduate
Theological Union, 1982) published under the title: The
Fahey-Coughlin connection.
 Includes bibliographical references.
 1. Coughlin, Charles E. (Charles Edward), 1891-1979.
2. Fahey, Denis, 1883-1954. 3. Christianity and
antisemitism—History—20th century. 4. Antisemitism—
United States—History—20th century. I. Title. II. Series.
BX4705.C7795A75 1991 261.2'6'0922—dc20 91-3821
ISBN 0-8204-1534-0   CIP
ISSN 0740-0446

Die Deutsche Bibliothek-CIP-Einheitsaufnahme

Athans, Mary Christine:
The Coughlin-Fahey connection : Father Charles E.
Coughlin, Father Denis Fahey, C.S.Sp., and religious
anti-semitism in the United States, 1938-1954 / Mary
Christine Athans.—New York; Berlin; Bern;
Frankfurt/M.; Paris; Wien: Lang, 1991
 (American university studies : Ser. 7, Theology and
religion ; Vol. 102)
 ISBN 0-8204-1534-0
NE: American university studies / 07

Photo of Fr. Coughlin reprinted with the
permission of The Religious News Service

The paper in this book meets the guidelines for permanence and durability
of the Committee on Production Guidelines for Book Longevity of the
Council on Library Resources.

© Peter Lang Publishing, Inc., New York 1991

Printed in the United States of America.

Acknowledgments

Permission is gratefully acknowledged for the use of the following material:

Fahey Papers, Kilmore: Mr. and Mrs. Denis Fahey, County Tipperary.

Fahey Papers, Archives of the Irish Province of the Holy Ghost Congregation, Dublin: Reverend Brian McLaughlin, C.S.Sp., Provincial.

Published writings of Denis Fahey, C.S.Sp.: Smurfit Communications Division (Browne and Nolan), Regina Publications, Holy Ghost Missionary College, Kimmage.

Goldstein Papers: John J. Burns Library of Rare Books and Special Collections, Boston College, Chestnut Hill, Massachusetts, Robert O'Neill, Archivist.

Rabbi Abraham Gudansky letters: Mrs. Sybil Good, Dublin.

The Gerald L. K. Smith Letters: Charles Robertson, Literary Executor, The Gerald L. K. and Elna Smith Estate.

Abbreviations

ADL	Anti-Defamation League of B'nai B'rith
APVM	*Apologia Pro Vita Mea*
CCTPA	Catholic Cinema and Theatre Patrons Association
CEG	Cinema Educational Guild
CF	*The Church and Farming*
FP-HGP	Fahey Papers, Holy Ghost Provincialate Archives, Dublin
FP-Kilmore	Fahey Papers, Fahey homestead, Kilmore, Golden, County Tipperary
HGP	Holy Ghost Provincialate, Dublin
IER	*Irish Ecclesiastical Record*
JJB-BC	John J. Burns Library, Boston College, Chestnut Hill, Massachusetts
KCCJN	*The Kingship of Christ and the Conversion of the Jewish Nation*
KCON	*The Kingship of Christ and Organized Naturalism*
KCPSTA	*The Kingship of Christ According to the Principles of St. Thomas Aquinas*
MBCMW	*The Mystical Body of Christ and the Modern World*
MBCRS	*The Mystical Body of Christ and the Reorganization of Society*
MMSO	*Money Manipulation and the Social Order*
MPPSTA	*Mental Prayer According to the Principles of St. Thomas Aquinas*
NUSJ	National Union for Social Justice
RISS	*Revue Internationale de Sociétés Secrètes*
RR	*The Rulers of Russia*

Contents

Preface

Irish influence in the Roman Catholic Church in the United States for the most part has been in the persons of the immigrants who left Ireland, chiefly in the nineteenth century, hoping to find a better life in America. Irish Catholics have exerted unusual influence (some would say undue influence) on the American Catholic Church in the past two hundred years. We need only look at the surnames of the Roman Catholic hierarchy to be assured of that fact.

Irish culture and piety have been held in renown by the American Irish for over a hundred years. The "theological grounding" for the clerical attitudes held acceptable in many an Irish family was: "Ah—sure, if he's a good Irish Catholic priest, what he's sayin' can't be all that wrong." Certainly that was the response of many in the Irish American Catholic community to the formidable figure of Father Charles E. Coughlin, influential "radio priest" of the pre-World War II period. The subject of this study is the relationship between Coughlin and "the good Irish Catholic priest" whom he invoked to help support his attitudes, conscious or unconscious, of anti-Semitism in the second quarter of the twentieth century—Denis Fahey of the Irish Province of the Holy Ghost Congregation, Professor of Philosophy and Church History at the Holy Ghost Missionary College, Kimmage, Dublin.

Prior studies on Coughlin have not explored the theological framework out of which he was operating, nor have they been able to explain why the "radio priest" became so rabidly anti-Semitic in 1938. An exploration of Fahey's relationship to Coughlin points to the Irish priest as a major influence on Coughlin, and also a channel for the dissemination of French and Roman conservative Catholic thought between Europe and America in that era. Coughlin publicized Fahey's work in the United States, and made the writings of the Irish theologian available to notable Protestants who also used Fahey's books as a partial rationale for their anti-Semitic crusades.

Efforts to interview Father Coughlin before his death, October 27, 1979, were unsuccessful. In a letter of January 15, 1979, he explained that he was sorry he could not be of assistance, but that the doctors would not permit it. He added: "This I can understand and you will too if you reach my age of eighty-seven."[1] Letters and papers which were in Coughlin's possession have been destroyed.[2] Taped interviews of Coughlin by Sheldon Marcus from April 1970 are available in the Special Collections Division of the Deering Library, Northwestern University, Evanston, Illinois. The Archives of the Archdiocese of Detroit contains Coughlin's correspondence with Bishop Michael Gallagher and Archbishop Edward Mooney but there is only secondary material on Denis Fahey.[3] Coughlin's letters in other collections, such as the Roosevelt Papers, are related to political issues and not germane to the theological focus of this study.

An unusual set of circumstances allowed me to be the first person, along with the archivist, to sort through a trunk-like box of papers of Denis Fahey, C.S.Sp., which was discovered upon my inquiry at the Holy Ghost Missionary College, Kimmage, Dublin in 1979. It had been stored away shortly after Fahey's death in 1954 when the two priests who were to dispose of Fahey's letters and papers left the task unfinished. Ten months later, a cabinet containing another substantial collection of Fahey's correspondence was found in the basement of the seminary, necessitating a second research trip to Ireland.[4] In addition to this material, I was fortunate to be able to interview members of Fahey's family both in Dublin and in Tipperary, and a cross section of persons who knew him in various capacities: younger colleagues, former students, committed lay people, admirers and adversaries, and those who appreciated Fahey but did not agree with his ideas. I also had the opportunity to meet members of the Jewish community in Dublin who remember the impact Fahey had in Ireland.

I am particularly grateful to William Jenkinson, C.S.Sp., a former Provincial of the Irish Province of the Holy Ghost Congregation, who facilitated my initial communications regarding the existence of the Fahey Papers, and who recommended that I have access to them; to Enda Watters, C.S.Sp., Provincial during my two research trips, for his aid and insights, and for allowing me to explore the many facets of Fahey's life and work; to Leo Layden, C.S.Sp., Archivist, for his competence, encouragement and good cheer in the entire challenging enterprise. The spirited community at the Holy Ghost Provincialate afforded me joyous hospitality. The Sisters at Our Lady's School, Templeogue, were marvelously supportive, and their convent truly became my home in Ireland. If one has to have cold weather, how wonderful to have warm people!

On the American scene, my first research in Jewish-Christian relations was under the direction of Avery Dulles, S.J. His affirmation was no small part of my decision to continue studies in this area. This work began as a Ph.D dissertation and special gratitude is due to Joseph P. Chinnici, O.F.M., advisor, dissertation director, and friend, who was challenging and demanding and continues to be supportive and encouraging in all my work; to Eldon G. Ernst, Moses Rischin, Daniel O'Hanlon, S.J., and Philipp Schmitz,S.J. who provided wisdom and advice throughout the project; and to the many other persons at the Graduate Theological Union in Berkeley who allowed good scholarship and ecumenical exchange to be a reality within a caring community.

Without the love of my family and friends, this work would never have been completed. I am grateful to my Greek father for his sense of philosophy and politics, and to my Irish mother for her poetry and piety. It was from them that I first experienced ecumenism in the broadest sense of that Greek word. I deeply appreciate the support and encouragement of my religious congregation, the Sisters of Charity of the Blessed Virgin Mary, especially the Sisters at Xavier Convent in Phoenix, Arizona.

This study was made possible in part by the North Phoenix Corporate Ministry, that special group of five Protestant churches, one Catholic church, and two synagogues which worked together in education, social concern, liturgy, and communications in Phoenix, Arizona. It was as the first Executive Director of that ecumenical cluster (1970-1976), an exciting venture in Jewish-Christian relations, that my desire grew to probe the question of the theological roots of anti-Semitism in the United States.

The encouragement I received at the St. Paul Seminary School of Divinity of the University of St. Thomas (St. Paul, MN) has been significant in the completion of this volume. I am deeply grateful to the Reverend Charles Froehle, Rector/Vice-President, to Dean Victor Klimoski, and to Rabbi Max Shapiro of the Center for Jewish-Christian Learning for their personal and professional support in joyful as well as trying times. A revision of the manuscript was prepared while on sabbatical at The Institute for Ecumenical and Cultural Research at Collegeville, MN. The opportunity for interchange in that community of scholars contributed to the refinement of my ideas. I am indebted to Dr. Patrick Henry, Director of the Institute, and to Rev. Gerard Sloyan, Dr. Arthur Zannoni, and Dr. Roy Wortman for reading the manuscript and offering valuable comments. Appreciation is also due to Rev. Phillip Rask, Janet Gould, Scott Hippert and Johanna Baboukis for their technical assistance.

It has not been my purpose to "drag ghosts out of the closet." Individuals and groups in history, however, have too often used Christian theology as a rationale for anti-Semitic crusades. In this day of the resurgence of the Ku Klux Klan, of Neo-Nazi marches, and of synagogue bombings from Paris to San Jose, the theological tenets of religio-political groups need further reflection. This study is presented with the hope and prayer that we will be alerted to the distortions of Christian theology which have periodically evolved, resulting in effects which are the opposite of the Christian message. In learning from the sad events of the past, may we move into the future determined to promote the positive aspects of Jewish-Christian relations which can be enriching to us all.

[1]Charles E. Coughlin to author, January 15, 1979.

[2]Letters and papers which were in Coughlin's possession have been destroyed, according to the Reverend Leonard P. Blair, Archivist of the Archdiocese of Detroit (telephone interview, March 16, 1982) and the Reverend Gerald Brown,S.S. (telephone interview, March 10, 1982), who had interviewed Coughlin when writing his master's thesis in 1969.

[3]Telephone interview with Elizabeth Yakel, Archivist, Archdiocese of Detroit, September 29, 1986.

[4]The Fahey Papers are in the Archives of the Irish Province of the Holy Ghost Congregation, Dublin, Ireland. Approximately 2,700 pages of documents are relevant to this study, including Fahey's *Apologia Pro Vita Mea*, correspondence, notebooks, class notes, papers, clippings, early drafts of books and articles.

FATHER DENIS FAHEY, C.S.Sp.

FATHER CHARLES E. COUGHLIN

CHAPTER I

JEWISH-CHRISTIAN RELATIONS IN THE UNITED STATES BEFORE WORLD WAR II

And to think that this was done *"all in the name of God!"* Francis Gilbert had just read the manuscript of a book on religious prejudice in the United States. The author, Dr. Everett Clinchy, first Executive Director of the National Conference of Christians and Jews, recognized in Gilbert's shocked phrase the title the book needed. *All in the Name of God!*, published in 1934, described Catholic-Protestant and Jewish-Christian relations in America. Gilbert's emotional outburst describes particularly well the anti-Semitism in the United States in the second quarter of the twentieth century .[1]

Jewish-Christian relations in the United States prior to the East European immigration which began in the 1880s can be characterized as basically courteous with occasional moments of confrontation. In the newly independent American colonies there were only about two thousand Jews in a population of three million Protestants and thirty thousand Catholics. After the Napoleonic wars in 1815, with the restoration of church and monarchy to their "rightful" places in European society, Jewish emancipation was viewed as one of the consequences of the French Revolution which should be curtailed. The predominantly German Jewish immigration which flowed to America in the 1820-1880 period consisted largely of those who were seeking opportunities in the New World that had recently been closed off to them in the old. The 1836 Bavarian law limiting the number of Jews who could contract marriages inspired a mass emigration to America. The Jewish population in the United States, approximately fifteen thousand in 1840, reached two hundred and fifty thousand by 1880—the majority coming from a German cultural background.[2]

Whereas the earliest Jewish immigrants in the seventeenth and eighteenth centuries had been both Sephardic and Askenazic, many of them in the merchant class, the nineteenth century arrivals from German lands were often artisans, peddlers or operators of drygoods stores. Most Jews settled in communities rather than on farms, many of them in the growing cities of the Eastern seaboard. They were often accepted as German-Americans who practiced Judaism.

There are examples of discrimination against Jews in the pre-1880 period. North Carolina did not allow Jews to hold high office until 1868, and New Hampshire until 1876.[3] However, there were many positive interactions as well. Congregation Mickve Israel of Savannah, Georgia was erected on land given to the congregation as a gift by the city, and at the dedication on July 21, 1820 the mayor and aldermen marched in the procession and played an important part.[4] Isaac Leeser, a prominent leader in American Judaism in the first part of the century, attended the dedication of many synagogues and was frequently aware of the presence of non-Jews on these occasions.[5] The relationship of Episcopal Bishop John Henry Hobart and Congregation Shearith Israel in New York City was one of warmth and friendliness.[6]

Efforts to proselytise Jews were common, but did not go without challenge from rabbis such as Isaac Mayer Wise.[7] Frequently these crusades were organized by Jews newly converted to Christianity.[8] Leeser stated: "Among the many missionaries whom I have met, the converted Jews were rascals without exception. To my regret, many of these returned later to the Jewish fold. The Christian missionaries I found occasionally companionable and well-meaning."[9] There was great animosity between Protestants and Catholics in the pre-Civil War period, but Jewish-Christian relations were relatively calm.[10]

The East European immigration (1880-1924) was largely

Catholic and Jewish. Languages, costumes, customs, and religious practices hitherto unknown in the United States suddenly flooded the major ports of disembarkation on the East Coast. During this era of the "Gilded Age," and the "Social Gospel," Protestant Americans continued to believe they were the new chosen people in a promised land. Fear that an invasion of foreigners would "pollute" the environment of a "Christian America," contributed to waves of xenophobia culminating in the restriction of immigration in 1924.

Prior to the French Revolution, Jews had been excluded or restricted in many western European countries. With the advent of liberal thought which allowed for religious pluralism Jews found themselves confronted instead by the growth of racial theories following upon Darwin's "survival of the fittest" hypothesis. White superiority over Blacks, Asians, and Eastern Europeans had to be rationalized in a period when Africa, Asia and the Middle East were being divided by the then super-powers. Racial discrimination as distinct from religious discrimination became the crucial issue after 1880. Liberal Jews who no longer believed or practiced their Judaism were not exempt from restrictions.

Methods of exclusion toward Jews differed somewhat from those practiced toward other groups. Even educated and wealthy Jews were not considered for positions for which they were qualified, were not allowed to belong to exclusive clubs, were not permitted to buy homes in "restricted" areas. Allusions to Jewish connections to international monetary conspiracies, Socialism, Communism, and Zionism were common. Stereotypes of the Jew in novels and other popular writings were accentuated in this period.[11]

The immigrants of the middle nineteenth century who had become the "uptown" German Jews found themselves embarrassed by the newly arrived members of their own religio-ethnic groups at the turn of the century. It was painful for them to face the possibility of losing the place they had achieved in society because of the inappropriate behavior of the newcomers. With the pogroms of the early 1900s in Russia, however, a substantial segment of the

Jewish community accepted the necessity of supporting "their own." The American Jewish Committee was founded in 1906 for that purpose. Rabbi Stephen B. Wise, Louis Brandeis, Lillian Wald, Henrietta Szold, Judah Magnes and Abraham Cahan were among an impressive group of Jewish leaders who assisted immigrant Jews at that time.

John Higham in *Strangers in the Land* reflects on American nativism in the period 1860-1925 with the following helpful distinction: "Generically, nativism was a defensive type of nationalism, but the defense varied as the nativist lashed out sometimes against a religious peril, sometimes against a revolutionary peril, and sometimes against a racial peril."[12] In the early twentieth century, Jews probably exceeded other groups in falling into all three categories. Jews were targets of the "100 percent Americanists" because of their race, because of their religion, and because they were frequently identified with liberal revolutionary movements such as socialism and communism.

The idealism surrounding the entrance of the United States into World War I to "make the world safe for democracy" provided a rare instance of Protestant-Catholic-Jewish cooperation. The united efforts of the Federal Council of Churches, the National Catholic War Council, and the Joint Distribution Committee representing the various Jewish groups, was an example to all of the beneficial effects of cooperative endeavors. The Interchurch World Movement attempted to carry that spirit forward in the post-war period, but its crusade was short-lived.[13] The Social Action Department of the National Catholic Welfare Conference, and its counterparts in the Federal Council of Churches and the Central Conference of American Rabbis, did make some progress regarding the need for reform in labor.[14] With these efforts, a new era in American ecumenical life had begun. Each of the three major traditions, however, found itself facing an identity crisis as the 1920s wore on. These experiences provide an important backdrop for understanding the growth of anti-Semitism in the 1930s and the decades after.

In the immediate post-World War I period it appeared that

the Protestants were still the culturally dominant force in America as exemplified by the Volstead Act legislating prohibition, the "witch hunts" of Attorney-General A. Mitchell Palmer, and the restriction of immigration in 1924. Isolationism and laissez-faire capitalism were the hallmarks of the day. Government's willingness to assist industry resulted in some of the highest protective tariffs in American history. The consequences of its reluctance to support labor were the social evils which followed upon industrialization when voiceless workers were often at the mercy of employers who were concerned only with profits.

The outstanding crisis in American Protestantism was the Fundamentalist-Modernist controversy which culminated in the Scopes Trial in 1925. Modernists found themselves backed into a humanistic-secularistic corner, and yet even there they were attacked by naturalist philosophers. Liberal theology may have won the battle, at least for the time being, regarding the Bible and evolution, but it had lost the war. Journalists made a mockery of the "monkey trial." To many, religion was becoming irrelevant.[15]

By 1925, Social Gospelites and liberal theologians were suffering from what Robert T. Handy termed "The American Religious Depression."[16] The establishment of prohibition which was supposed to be the great triumph of a Puritan culture had become a sorry experience of the decade. The "roaring twenties," bootlegging and "immorality" all proved that many a preacher was not being heard. Increasingly, Protestants blamed World War I for "the end of American innocence."[17] The American dream no longer seemed viable. "The errand into the wilderness" had gone astray. "Manifest Destiny" wasn't very manifest any more. Fear of "foreigners" who appeared to be taking control of politics became irrational with the reaction to the nomination of Al Smith in 1928.[18]

The Protestant churches were approaching a low ebb in both financial and personal resources. Contributions were down. The status and numbers of ministers were declining, and indicative of an ominous trend, the Student Volunteer Missionary groups which had received twenty-seven hundred young persons in 1920, had only two hundred and fifty applicants in 1928. Peace movements had not been successful, the Ku Klux Klan, a largely Protestant organization, was in full operation, and the Social Gospel appeared to be dead. With the stock market crash of 1929, and the crisis that followed, there was only further "depression" in the churches. Earlier periods of economic hardship had often caused Christians to return to the church to pray for divine assistance; the response on this occasion was otherwise. Handy suggests that it was because America was "religiously depressed" even before the crash.[19]

The whole experience resulted in soul-searching which was not without fruit. Influenced by European theologians, primarily Karl Barth, a small group of Protestant leaders began to reflect on major questions. Had the Church become so involved in American culture that it had "sold its soul" and failed to genuinely be the Church? In 1933 John Coleman Bennett wrote "After Liberalism —What?"[20] Reinhold Niebuhr published *Moral Man and Immoral Society* in the previous year.[21] The challenge emerged to return to a biblically based, Reformation type theology which had been watered down too long by liberal theologians. The Neo-Orthodox movement which was often to the "right" in theology, and to the "left" in politics, believed original sin was a reality which liberals in their unwarranted optimism had neglected. The Church, they believed, must not lose her independence when being prophetic about the social and political concerns of the day. It was important to "let the Church be the Church."[22]

Fundamentalists did not see the Neo-Orthodox position as a solution. Some Protestants experienced fear as they realized that their established position in the United States was being questioned. They could no longer take for granted that America was a "Protestant nation." The emergence of groups such as the Catholic War Veterans and the Jewish War Veterans only emphasized the Protestant character of the American Legion.[23] Catholic and Jewish voices became more vocal as the decade progressed.

If Protestants saw themselves in a period of decline after World War I, Catholics were willing to step forward with a new blueprint for American Christendom. A revitalized confidence in "the truth" as it was expounded by the Catholic Church in the cogent rational natural law framework allowed many Catholics to look upon their Protestant brothers and sisters embroiled in the Fundamentalist-Modernist controversy with a patronizing smile. With the Neo-Thomistic revival, a new "Catholic" view of every discipline was encouraged. Catholic societies for every field of study grew apace.

The image of "the thirteenth—the greatest of centuries"[24] not only contributed to an emphasis on guilds and sodalities, but provided a crusade mentality which spoke out on censorship of books and films, immodest dress, and the infiltration of Communists and their atheistic values into society. Scholars such as Jacques Maritain and Etienne Gilson, novelists among whom were Francois Mauriac and Georges Bernanos, and urbane essayists epitomized by G. K. Chesterton and Hilaire Belloc gave Catholics a new sense of identity and a conviction that they had a heritage both ancient and true that could be a creative contribution to American culture.[25]

The experience of the election of 1928 had given Catholics a new sense of identity. Although the episodes of bigotry sharply divided Protestants from Catholics and left many open wounds, Catholics realized that they were not without power in the Democratic Party and in the nation.

With the Bolshevik Revolution of 1917, the question of the relationship of Jews to Communism was sharpened. In the early 1920s, the famous forged document *The Protocols of the Elders of Zion* was published by Henry Ford in *The Dearborn Independent* (later reprinted in book form under the title *The International Jew*). Fear of sinister Jewish plots was further implanted in the minds of both Catholics and Protestants who shared an apprehension of the Communist menace in America.[26]

The identity crisis among Jews in the United States was perhaps the most overt. Although many became "Americanized" in a radical way, leaving behind the traditions and obligations of their parents, old/new questions once again came to the surface. What did it mean to be a Jew? Was it religious membership? Was it racial identification? Was it a cultural entity? Mordecai Kaplan attempted to give an answer in his 1934 classic *Judaism as a Civilization*.[27] He believed it was in being "a people," a "religious civilization" akin to an organism which was supported by the active participation of Jews in community observing the customs which they shared. Although Reconstructionism, Kaplan's particular branch of Judaism, has had limited success, the impact of his ideas influenced many Jews, particularly in the Conservative movement.

Even Reform Judaism retreated from its ultra-liberal position as expressed in the Pittsburgh Platform of 1885. The Central Conference of American Rabbis meeting in Columbus, Ohio in 1937, adopted a new statement of principles more in keeping with traditional norms.[28] The treatment of the Jews in Hitler's Germany could not be ignored. Many Jews found it difficult to believe, however, that Germany, a nation of great culture and promise, would ultimately harm their people.

Cooperative efforts did evolve in the late 1920s to aid in alleviating interracial and interreligious strife. The formation of the National Conference of Christians and Jews (NCCJ) in 1928 was a direct corollary of a political campaign in which anti-Catholic bigotry had reached a new height. The activities of the Ku Klux Klan, aimed at Blacks, Catholics and Jews, hardly contributed to a positive image of religious and racial pluralism in America. The institution of the Religious News Service by the NCCJ, with its goal of presenting objective reports, was an effort to close the communication gap. Panels of a priest, minister and rabbi who traveled to various communities to discuss the nature of current problems came into vogue. "Brotherhood Week" became an annual event.[29] While none of these activities were earthshaking, they were a beginning in calling people to examine the destructive elements of racial and religious prejudice that had surfaced through the years, particularly in the decade of the twenties.

Protestants, Catholics and Jews moved into the 1930s, therefore, searching for a deeper understanding of their own religious heritages, coupled with the desire to retain religious identity in a nation that professed religious pluralism. If it had not been for the crash of 1929, the severe depression that followed, the rise of Fascism in Europe (particularly Nazism in Germany), and the advent of war, it is possible that the American experience of the "triple melting pot" might have evolved in the 1930s instead of after World War II.[30]

A period of economic depression, however, is always a time to search for scapegoats. The bankers, whom most people assumed to be Jewish, became prime candidates. Fear of a Communist take-over was also heightened, and once again the Jews were a target. It was in such an atmosphere that Father Charles E. Coughlin, the Reverend Gerald L. K. Smith, and other religio-political figures sowed the seeds of hate, suspicion, fear and distrust regarding Jews. They were to find the writings of an Irish priest named Father Denis Fahey useful to them. Little did Fahey dream when he wrote his volumes that he would be hailed as a scholar and authority by the famous "radio priest" of Royal Oak, Michigan on a Sunday afternoon in November 1938.

[1]Everett Ross Clinchy, *All in the Name of God* (New York: The John Day Co., 1934), Preface, p.3.

[2]Nathan Glazer, *American Judaism*, 2nd. ed. rev. (Chicago: University of Chicago Press, 1972), p. 23.

[3]Joseph L. Blau and Salo W. Baron, *The Jews in the United States, 1790-1840: A Documentary History* (New York: Columbia University Press, 1966), I, 17. See also Rufus Learsi, *The Jews in America: A History* (New York: KTAV Publishing House, 1972), p. 49.

[4]Blau and Baron, III, pp. 686-687.

[5]Jacob Rader Marcus, *Memoirs of American Jews, 1775-1865* (Philadelphia: The Jewish Publication Society of America, 1955), II, p. 67.

[6]Blau and Baron, III, pp. 691-694.

10

[7]James G. Heller, *Isaac Mayer Wise: His Life, Work, and Thought* (New York: Union of American Hebrew Congregations, 1965), p. 144.

[8]Blau and Baron, III, pp. 701-773.

[9]Marcus, II, p. 108.

[10]See letter of Rebecca Gratz to her brother Benjamin Gratz, July 12, 1844 regarding the Catholic-Protestant riots in Philadelphia, *American Jewish Archives* V, 2 (June 1953), p. 114.

[11]John Higham, "Social Discrimination Against Jews in America, 1830-1930," *Jewish Experience in America* V. ed. Abraham J. Karp (New York: KTAV Publishing House, 1969), p. 351.

[12]John Higham, *Strangers in the Land: Patterns of American Nativism 1860-1925* (New York: Atheneum, 1974), Preface to the Second Edition, n.p. [p. 2].

[13]Eldon G. Ernst, *Moment of Truth for Protestant America: Interchurch Campaigns Following World War I* (Missoula, Montana: Scholar's Press, 1972), p. 24.

[14]Glazer, p. 139. In 1923 they issued a joint statement attacking the seven-day week, twelve-hour day in the steel industry.

[15]H. Shelton Smith, Robert T. Handy, and Lefferts A. Loetscher, *American Christianity: An Historical Interpretation with Representative Documents, Volume II: 1820-1960* (New York: Charles Scribner's Sons, 1963), pp. 220-221. See also Martin E. Marty, *Righteous Empire: The Protestant Experience in America* (New York: Dial Press, 1970), pp. 220-228.

[16]Robert T. Handy, "The American Religious Depression, 1925-1935," *Church History* 29 (March 1960): 3-16.

[17]Henry F. May, *The End of American Innocence: A Study of the First Years of Our Time, 1912-1917* (New York: Franklin Watts, 1964).

[18]Gustavus Myers, *History of Bigotry in the United States* (New York: Capricorn Books, 1960). See especially Chapter 27, "Campaigning on Religious Lines."

[19]Handy, p. 4.

[20]John Coleman Bennett, "After Liberalism—What?" *Christian Century* 50 (November 8, 1933): 1403-1406.

[21]Reinhold Niebuhr, *Moral Man and Immoral Society* (New York: Charles Scribner's Sons, 1932).

[22]Slogan of the Life and Work Conference, Oxford, England, 1937.

[23]Will Herberg, *Protestant—Catholic—Jew: An Essay in American Religious Sociology*, rev. ed. (Garden City, New York: Doubleday and Company, 1960), pp. 234 ff.

[24]The expression was popularized by James J. Walsh in his volume *The Thirteenth, Greatest of Centuries* (New York: Catholic Summer School Press, 1907).

[25]See William H. Halsey, *The Survival of American Innocence: Catholicism in an Era of Disillusionment, 1920-1940* (Notre Dame, Indiana: University of Notre Dame Press, 1980).

[26][Henry Ford], *The International Jew* (Dearborn, Michigan: *The Dearborn Independent*, 1920-1921), 2 vols.

[27]Mordecai Kaplan, *Judaism as a Civilization* (New York: T. Yoseloff, 1957).

[28]Glazer, pp. 103-104.

[29]*Judaism*, Special Issue: "Interfaith at Fifty," (Summer 1978), Vol. 27, No. 3.

[30]Herberg, pp. 32 ff., popularized Ruby Jo Kennedy's thesis of the "triple melting pot" which she had published in the *Journal of Sociology* (January 1944).

CHAPTER II

THE LIFE AND TIMES OF DENIS FAHEY,C.S.Sp.

Early Years in Ireland

Denis Fahey was born July 2, 1883 in Kilmore, Golden, County Tipperary, the youngest of the three sons of Timothy Fahey and Brigit Clery. The Clerys are remembered as "the quiet ones," with a tradition of literature and music.[1] By contrast, Timothy Fahey is distinctly recalled as a fiery spirit. He attended at least five schools in his youth, loved horses, and never found it easy to settle down. In later years, he was always involved in controversies. On one occasion the local parish priest, Father Matt, announced to him after an argument, that he would not even come to Fahey's funeral. Timothy replied hotly: "I don't care because I will have a *bishop* at my funeral!" When Timothy died in 1935, he had two bishops at his funeral, both relatives of the clan.[2]

John Fahey, the middle son of Timothy and Brigit, died at an early age. It was expected that the care of the family home and farm would eventually fall to his brothers, Thomas and Denis. Denis received his early education in primary schools in Knockavilla and Thomastown. In personality Thomas was more like his father, while Denis resembled his mother. One story is that when Denis was young he liked to study under a tree, and would hide from his father so that he could continue reading. The fiery spirit of his father, however, was not entirely lost in him.

At the age of twelve Denis entered Rockwell College, and was a boarder during his five years as a student there (1895-1900). Rockwell had been established by the Holy Ghost Fathers near

Cashel in County Tipperary in 1864. The town, still referred to as "The Cashel of the Kings," is dominated by Cormac's Chapel, an impressive structure, the first of the Irish Romanesque churches, built in 1127-1134 by Cormac McCarthy, King of Munster. Rockwell boys took periodic excursions there to explore the ruins.

Driving a short distance south of Cashel on the highway, one moves up what was known to generations of Rockwell students as "Misery Hill." When that meager summit was reached it was clear that holiday time was over, and the regimen of student life had to be resumed. James Joyce's description in *A Portrait of the Artist as a Young Man* is certainly not the only interpretation of life as experienced by college lads at that time in Ireland, but it does provide a few clues.[3]

Rockwell itself is a commanding structure, surrounded by extensive playing fields, and having a sizable lake for rowing and water sports. St. Patrick's Chapel where Denis prayed was built in the 1880s. The hallway which joins the chapel to the main building is lined with portraits of notables associated with Rockwell including Patrick Hillary, President of Ireland, who was an alumnus, and Eamon De Valera, Prime Minister and later President of Ireland, who had been a member of the faculty. The next hall is lined with student pictures. The first on the left is a photograph of the cast of an 1899 production of Shakespeare's *Richard II*, with "D. Fahey" in an Elizabethan costume in the first row.[4]

Denis distinguished himself in his academic pursuits, but sports were also important to him attested to by a large picture of the Rockwell Rugby Team which still hangs over the piano in the Fahey homestead in Kilmore. Just a year before Fahey's death he received a letter from Father Tim B. Walsh, a classmate from Rockwell days, who reminisced: "I have a very vivid recollection of you flitting down the line with a ball safely tucked under your arm making for a try for the old school."[5]

Summers and holidays were spent helping on the farm at Kilmore. Although his home was only six miles from Rockwell, these were different worlds. The experience of the land would always be "in his blood." While he tended to emphasize the rational aspects of life, his love of the earth, and a certain simplicity of spirit were never lost to him. The Fahey boys Thomas and Denis socialized with other families in the area, especially the Kelly family, which included ten boys and four girls. Denis was a good friend of Mary Ann Kelly, and according to one account, she was the first one to whom he confided his decision to be a priest.[6]

Timothy Fahey was anything but pleased about the decision. It was not that it would bring economic hardship. A series of land acts from 1870 on had restricted the landlords' right to evict, and had provided for the buying out of the landlords by the tenants.[7] Timothy Fahey was proud of his land, and the family could live comfortably. The reason for Timothy's response could well have been the fact that he had only one other son, and if anything happened to Thomas, the family heritage would be lost.[8]

Ireland at the turn of the century had hardly solved her problems. Some of her most trying days were still ahead. The Land League, under the leadership of the Protestant Charles Stewart Parnell, elected to the House of Commons in 1875, had given Irish Catholics a new lease on life and land. With the fall and death of Parnell in 1891, however, many in Ireland had lost the hope of achieving their aims constitutionally. Some were bitter about the stand of the Irish Catholic hierarchy who declared that the proceedings of the divorce case involving Parnell and "Kitty" O'Shea had made him "unfit to be an Irish leader."[9] Some of those who grew up idolizing Parnell decided to turn to more aggressive means of pursuing their goals. In face of this, Timothy Fahey was not happy that his son wanted to be a priest. However, Denis entered the novitiate of the Holy Ghost Congregation at Grignon-Orly near Paris in the autumn of 1900.

Novitiate in France

France at the turn of the century was attempting to recover from another revolution, this time a social and emotional revolution referred to as the Dreyfus Affair. The eventual result of this revolution was a radical change in the relationship of church and state which became etched into law in 1905. During this important year in France, Denis Fahey imbibed some of these influences, despite his sheltered life as a novice.

Church-state relationships in France had been fragile for centuries, but from 1789 on the roles of the clergy and religious orders were under scrutiny. In the 1790s, religious congregations were suppressed, property confiscated, and nuns and priests sent to the guillotine. In the hope of using the church to restore peace and order to France, Napoleon initiated the Concordat of 1801 with Pope Pius VII. Napoleon's determination to dominate the church in France, and to control Rome as well, contributed to the ongoing struggle between Ultramontane and Gallican forces.

With the Congress of Vienna in 1815, and the restoration of the monarchs after the Napoleonic era, the themes of legitimacy and balance of power were primary. The Roman Catholic Church was reestablished as the state church, and a long-standing alliance between the royalists and the church was sealed. In the eyes of the church, all republican forms of government were suspect, espoused by deists, atheists, socialists, or radicals who questioned the traditional church-state relationship which the Roman Catholic Church had considered to be her rightful inheritance. An outrageous experiment such as religious pluralism in the United States was barely tolerated by Rome.

Pius IX, through the publication of the *Syllabus of Errors* (1864), alienated not only those who proclaimed scientific, modern and liberal ideas, but confirmed the attitudes of most liberals regarding church-state policy. Separation of church and state was unthinkable to Pius IX, as it had been to his predecessors, at least since medieval times.

When Leo XIII ascended to the papacy in 1878 there was hope that a more liberal attitude would evolve. With his encyclical *Immortale Dei* of November 1, 1885, *rapprochement* between church and state in France seemed possible.[10] This movement toward reconciliation was aptly termed *ralliement* and might have had more success if it were not for the Dreyfus Affair.

No event polarized all factions and groups in France in the late nineteenth century so much as the emotion-laden Dreyfus Affair. It was not simply a charge of treason made in October 1894 against Captain Dreyfus, an Alsatian Jew in the French Army, for selling military secrets to the Germans. It was the means of unleashing anger and hostilities pent up in France since her humiliating defeat in the Franco-Prussian War in 1871, and her loss of Alsace-Lorraine in the treaty negotiations. The spirit of revenge was very close to the surface in France during those years, permeating the atmosphere in various degrees until after World War I. It took only one such incident for emotions to boil over.

In addition to hostility against Germany, the influence of nationalism and of Darwinian thought had cultivated a milieu in France not dissimilar to that in Nazi Germany in the 1930s. There was an unquestioned presupposition by many that the "purity" and superiority of French culture must not be contaminated by inferior types who, if left unchecked, would "pollute" the nation. Eduard Drumont in *La Libre Parole* led the movement identifying the Jews as the contaminating force. Albert Monnier, a sometime contributor to the same periodical, wrote violent tracts declaring that Prussia's victory in 1871 was the result of Jewish espionage.[11] Conspiratorial theories supposedly identified Jews and Freemasons as members of international groups which were manipulating money and influence in an effort to take over the government of France. Publication of the famous forged document *The Protocols of the Elders of Zion* contributed to the fears of people. The Dreyfus Affair seemed to provide evidence that such a takeover might be possible.

Basic to the stance of the Dreyfusards and the Anti-Dreyfusards was the attitude of each toward the French Revolution. It was only with that event that the Jews as a group were given civil rights and a claim to a share in "liberty, equality, and fraternity." Their emancipation as a people was clearly tied to a positive view of the Revolution and a republican form of government. They had never before experienced the rights of citizenship and equality in a Christian monarchical system. Tolerance, perhaps; but rights, no. The Roman Catholic Church, however, regarded the French Revolution as the antithesis of all order and stability, and the diminishment of the position she had enjoyed. In contrast to the Jews, the large majority of Catholics tended to be sympathetic to royalist causes.

The Dreyfusards believed that the army was orchestrating the whole affair in an effort to overthrow the Third Republic and take control of the government. They saw an alliance of army, royalists, and clericalists working together. The Anti-Dreyfusards believed that their opponents were marshalled by socialists, radicals, liberals, republicans and intellectuals, many of whom were Jews. Ultimately, they believed, the seeds of destruction of France lay in the conspiracy of these groups controlled by Jews and Freemasons. Some members of the press convinced patriotic French citizens that "outside forces" were taking over.

The influence of the Dreyfus Affair extended from 1894-1899, but was not actually laid to rest until 1906. In 1899 it seemed nearly impossible for any leader to form a Cabinet in France. Eventually Pierre Waldeck-Rousseau formed a government, but to get the necessary majority he agreed to work with the Left, with Alexandre Millerand and others whose anti-clericalism was hardly a secret. Because of the involvement of high ecclesiastical officials and a goodly number of Catholics on the side of the Anti-Dreyfusards, the question of church-state relations was again a vital one. Waldeck-Rousseau agreed to tackle the controversial issue of the status of religious congregations. These institutions were seen as having immense power. On the one hand they controlled an enormous amount of property; on the other, they controlled the education system, the minds of the young. Supervision must be exercised by the government if a conversion from monarchism to republicanism was to take place at all.

Under Waldeck-Rousseau's leadership, the Associations Bill, which required that a religious congregation had to be authorized by the government before it could legally exist, became the law of the land on June 28, 1901. In its original form there was nothing really new in this, though the stated principles and regulations had not been upheld by the Old Regime. In 1901 the government was determined to enforce its law.[12]

When Denis Fahey arrived at Grignon-Orly near Paris to begin his novitiate in 1900 there is no doubt that the French atmosphere was still clouded by the Dreyfus Affair. The first efforts of Waldeck-Rousseau to pass the Associations Law were in process. The principal debates took place in the spring of 1901, and final passage was effected in June of that year. Even though traditional novitiates allowed for very little communication with "the outside world," it is quite unlikely that novices would have been unaware of so grave a threat to the life of the religious congregation.[13]

The effect of the French Revolution on the later writings of Denis Fahey, his attitudes toward the separation of church and state, and his emphasis on Jews and Freemasons as forces attempting to dismantle the church, suggest that the crucial year 1900-1901 in France had more than a little influence on this young Irish seminarian.

The Congregation Fahey Entered

The congregation which Denis Fahey entered was definitely French. Appropriately, the Holy Ghost Congregation was founded on Pentecost Day 1703 by Claude Francis Poullart des Places (1679-1709). His major objective was not only to work with the poor, but more specifically to provide seminaries to train men for the priesthood who were themselves poor, allowing them to work with poverty-stricken members of society.[14]

Poullart des Places received his theological and spiritual training under the Jesuits at the College of Louis the Great in Paris. It was Cardinal de Noailles, Archbishop of Paris, who gave Poullart des Places permission to establish a religious institute. Although Poullart was only thirty years old when he died two years after his ordination, his dream would survive the crises of the French Revolution and Napoleon.[15]

The Holy Ghost Seminary, operated by members of the congregation sometimes called "Spiritans," was not without problems. It was attacked by Gallicanists irked by its attachment to the Holy See, and by Jansenists, because its students seemed to avoid their doctrines. Legal and political battles ensued, and it was not until 1734 that the new Archbishop of Paris, Charles de Vintimille, granted in writing the first official ecclesiastical approbation of the Society. In that same year, legal recognition was extended by the French government.[16] These documents were to serve the congregation well in the years to come.

Between 1703-1789, the Holy Ghost Congregation had educated and trained 1600 priests in their seminary in Paris alone. After the fall of Napoleon, there was special need for clergy in the extended French colonies. In 1816 the Holy Ghost Congregation was reestablished and officially charged with that task. On February 7, 1824 the Holy See approved the Rule of the congregation, and its status was changed from diocesan congregation to that of pontifical institute.[17]

Some priests trained at the Holy Ghost Seminary considered themselves "Spiritans" although they were not formally members of the Congregation. In the 1840s the problem of delineating authority regarding missionary priests in the French colonies, and their specific relationship to Rome and to the Holy Ghost Congregation, came to the fore. One plan was to incorporate all the colonial clergy into the Congregation. Dialogue also developed with a group desirous of serving the missions—particularly abandoned slaves. This newly-projected congregation was under the leadership of Francis Libermann, a convert from Judaism, who according to Koren, had a poor press in ecclesiastical circles as "an ambitious Jew"—although he was an extraordinarily serene and gentle spirit.[18]

With a new threat of suppression after the Revolution of 1848, and faced with multiple concerns, the greatly diminished Holy Ghost Congregation elected Father Alexander Monnet as Superior General. He was able to deal with the political crisis, and it was under his administration that Libermann's Congregation of the Holy Heart of Mary became one with the Holy Ghost Congregation. Many Spiritans were anything but elated at the prospect of such a union; some were vehemently against it. [19]

Father Libermann had an extraordinary history. He was born Jacob Libermann on April 12, 1808, the son of Rabbi Libermann of Saverne, Alsace. His father hoped that he would become a rabbi. With his conversion to Catholicism in 1826 he took the name Francis Mary Paul. He entered the seminary at St. Sulpice, but was unable to be ordained because of attacks of epilepsy. However, he was allowed to stay on at the Sulpician seminary at Issy, and was sought after as a spiritual director. From 1837-1839 he served as the Novice Master of the Eudist Fathers, although he was only in minor orders. About that time Libermann became convinced that he should join a project launched by some of his associates from St. Sulpice on behalf of the slaves in the French colonies. It was this group which eventually became the Congregation of the Holy Heart of Mary with Libermann as its head.[20]

Many obstacles had to be overcome, but with the encouragement of Propaganda Fide, the two groups met in informal session on Pentecost, June 10, 1848 and accepted the union in principle. Because the Holy Ghost Congregation had been raised to the status of a pontifical institute in 1824, and because it had been legally recognized in France since 1734, it was the opinion of those negotiating the merger that it would be to the advantage of all for Libermann's congregation to dissolve itself, and for the entire group to join the Holy Ghost Congregation. It was also agreed that Father Libermann was the person to bring creative leadership to the combined congregations, and Father Monnet—whose heart had always been in the missions—was named Vicar General of Madagascar, where the Congregation had missions.

Initially members of both congregations felt that they had been slighted, but in time, particularly because of Libermann's sensitivity to the situation, the union was accepted and affirmed. The converted Jew brought a unique spirituality to the Holy Ghost Congregation, and is revered as its "Second Founder." He died on

February 2, 1852. His cause for canonization was set forth in 1868 and in 1910, while Fahey was a student in Rome, Libermann was declared "Venerable." It is significant that Libermann's process was the first one ever introduced in favor of a Jew since the founding of the Congregation of Rites in the Middle Ages.[21]

About the time of Fahey's entrance into the Spiritans a major question was: "Who is the real founder of the Holy Ghost Congregation?" With the threat of suppression in 1899, and the introduction of the Associations Bill by Waldeck-Rousseau, Archbishop LeRoy, then Superior-General of the Holy Ghost Congregation, explored more carefully the documents of the "union" and discovered that the congregation truly dated from 1703, not 1848. Many had apparently understood that with the merger a new religious congregation had been formed. The documents proved that, as has been discussed above, the Congregation of the Holy Heart of Mary dissolved itself, and joined the already existing Holy Ghost Congregation.[22]

This "awakening" to the earlier history which took place during Fahey's formative years in the Congregation was the impetus for a group under LeRoy to restore Claude Poullart des Places to his rightful place as founder of the congregation. There emerged the "Libermannists" and the "Placists." The latter group was reinforced by the commitment of Father Henri L'Floch, C.S.Sp., then Director of the Senior Seminary of the congregation at Chevilly. The controversial L'Floch became Superior of the *Séminaire Française* in Rome where Fahey lived as a student from 1908-1912. The Pontifical French Seminary had been founded in Rome in 1853 by the Spiritans at the express invitation of Pope Pius IX in an effort to stamp out Gallicanism in France. In the period 1853-1953, three thousand priests and one hundred bishops received their training there.[23] To be Rector of the *Séminaire Française* in Rome was to hold real power in that day.

L'Floch had substantial influence on Fahey.[24] As a person of immense authority and prestige, the rector was an exponent of conservative right-wing French and Italian Catholic thought in those anti-Modernist years.[25] He was later removed from his position as Rector because of his relationship to the controversial and anti-Semitic *Action Française* movement, which was finally condemned by Pius XI in 1926. In that same period, another acknowledged mentor of Fahey's, Louis Cardinal Billot, S.J., professor at the Pontifical Gregorian University, met a similar fate. Fahey's exposure to the French experience during his pre-ordination years both in France and in Rome was to imprint itself on the young seminarian, and was later reflected in his own writings.

Continuing Education: Home to Ireland—Return to France

With his novitiate year completed, Fahey returned to Dublin. A new cultural nationalism was evolving during this period which had strong political and economic overtones. The era 1890-1910 in Ireland has been known as the time of "killing Home Rule by kindness."[26] Parnell was dead. Gladstone's second Home Rule Bill, the last valiant effort of a very old man, had been defeated in 1893. To keep the Irish quiet, the Tory policy hoped to redress economic grievances.[27]

A new sense of Irish identity came to the fore with the formation of the Gaelic League by Douglas Hyde in 1893. The National Literary Society, and the theatre which was to become the Abbey, were founded by William Butler Yeats and Lady Gregory in 1899. These groups and Arthur Griffith's self-reliance movement Sinn Fein ("Ourselves") participated in a kind of romantic nationalism. F. S. L. Lyons describes the period:

To the dedicated nationalist, benevolent reforms conceded by the British parliament were ultimately no substitute for the reassertion of a separate national identity. And in the same decade of disenchantment with constitutionalism there began to appear the faint but unmistakable signs of such a reassertion, a reassertion not through heroic or hopeless violence, but through a steady and

relentless emphasis on the need to resurrect the idea
of "Irish Ireland."[28]

Ireland in these two decades may have been growing quietly
prosperous, even "somnolent."[29] But Irish identity was not to be
wooed away. The Catholic hierarchy walked the fine line between
decrying revolution and promoting the Irish and Catholic cause.

Though Fahey had completed his novitiate year at Grignon-
Orly, he did not pronounce his vows at that time, as would have
been usual, because of a serious illness. He returned to Ireland to
recuperate and continue his studies. He was assigned to "The
Castle" at Blackrock College to begin his university course in
1901.[30]

Higher education had not been available to the majority of
Catholics in Ireland. An impetus was given to seminaries and
colleges by the Act of 1879, in which the Royal University was
established. Accordingly, the State agreed to pay for "the results
of secular education wherever given," even in denominational
colleges.[31] The Royal University from which Fahey received his
degree, therefore, was in reality only an examining and degree-
granting body related to the various colleges and universities which
participated in its program.[32]

The Holy Ghost Congregation had grown rapidly in Ireland.
Blackrock College (founded 1860), in the Dublin area, and
Rockwell College near Cashel were both leading secondary schools
in the nineteenth century. With the Act of 1879, a university
college participating in the Royal University program was added at
Blackrock.[33]

By 1902 Fahey's health must have improved because he was
assigned as a "Prefect" at St. Mary's College, Rathmines, another
Holy Ghost secondary school in the Dublin area. Seminarians were
involved in supervising the younger students in various capacities,
sometimes taking university courses themselves.[34] Still, Fahey did
not make his vows. However, it appears that Fahey did not go to
France at that time, but probably continued at St. Mary's,
Rathmines. The dates on his record card are inconclusive, but it

seems that in 1904 he returned to Blackrock. From his own *Apologia Pro Vita Mea* it is clear that he spent most of the period 1904-1906 devoted to his studies. In this document written about 1948, Fahey stated: "From 1904-1906 I studied for a degree in Civil and Constitutional History, Political Economy, etc. I loathed the anti-Catholic spirit and doctrine of a number of the books I had to study."[35] He received his degree from the Royal University in 1906 "with the highest honors in civil and constitutional history, political economy and general jurisprudence."[36]

Denis Fahey's relationship to the Holy Ghost Congregation had yet to be clarified. Anticipating his degree, he wrote to the Superior-General, Archbishop LeRoy, about his future profession. A letter from the Motherhouse in Paris to the Irish Provincial, written March 18, 1906 stated that since Fahey had done his twelve months novitiate in 1900-1901 there was no need for him to repeat it. However, he should return to Chevilly for a period of preparation before vows.

Fahey headed for Paris again, probably sometime in the summer of 1906. Irish Province records indicate that Fahey professed his vows at Grignon-Orly in Paris on February 2, 1907—undoubtedly a happy day for him, and the conclusion of an extended discernment as to whether he was indeed able to live the religious life as a Spiritan.

Making vows in 1907 was significant. It was the year of the proclamation of Pope Pius X's encyclical *Pascendi Dominici Gregis* condemning Modernism, and the accompanying decree *Lamentabili*. It was also the year of the excommunication of George Tyrrell, "Modernism's prophet, apostle and most conspicuous martyr."[37] Tyrrell was an Irishman from Dublin who had been reared in the Church of Ireland, had converted to Catholicism, and joined the Jesuits. These papal pronouncements and Tyrrell's excommunication made the question of authority the key issue of the day. Fahey would prove to be one of the Pope's loyal adherents. No doubt he was excited about the possible prospect of studying in Rome.

Unexpectedly, however, Fahey was to spend another year in France. A letter from Fr. Fraisse in Paris to the new Irish Provincial, Father Edward Crehan, on October 17, 1907 explained that only one student could be sent to Rome for studies at that time, and although Fahey would probably be disappointed, he would have to wait until the following year.[38]

Poor health was to plague Denis Fahey a good part of his life. In the summer of 1908, Fahey had not even received minor orders, and judging from the lengthy process which he had experienced before receiving permission to make vows, and the delay in pursuing his studies in Rome, it seems likely that he was learning patience in his extended journey toward the priesthood.

Rome: 1908-1912

Finally Fahey received word that he would go to study in Rome. Although Fahey returned to France to receive tonsure at Chevilly on December 7, 1908, the years 1908-1912 were definitely centered in Rome.

During those years Vatican orthodoxy was in style. Any gains liberals had made during the pontificate of Leo XIII had been crushed with the decrees against Modernism. The Ultramontanists had gained the ascendancy with a vengeance. Alfred Loisy, the French Catholic biblical scholar, had been excommunicated by name on March 7, 1908, and followed Tyrrell as one of the casualties of the era. Scholars who had hoped to reconcile scriptural and doctrinal interpretations with modern methods of study had no place to go except underground.

Among those who were "above ground" and who exercised immense influence on students residing at the *Séminaire Française* were Cardinal Louis Billot, S.J., then Professor at the Gregorian University where Fahey did his doctorate in theology, and Henri L'Floch, the Rector of the Pontifical French Seminary. Both were related to the Integralist Movement, to the *Action Française*, and were removed from their respective positions by Pope Pius XI at a later date.

Troubled by some of the more liberal ideas to which he had been exposed in the curriculum of the Royal University (Dublin), Fahey went for counsel to Père Marc Voegtli, C.S.Sp., the Director of the Holy Ghost scholastics in Rome. Fahey tells us in his *Apologia* that as a result of this conference, books were assigned for table reading in the refectory as antidotes: *Les Origines de la Civilisation Moderne* (2 vols.) by the Belgian historian Godefroid Kurth, and *Les Sociétés Secrètes et la Société* by Père Nicholas Deschamps, S.J. Fahey later reflected: "My reaction against the disgusting books of my B.A. course was strengthened by the fact that I lived in Rome during the struggle against Modernism with its naturalistic separation of the historian and the believer."[39]

In addition to studying under Billot and imbibing the authors mentioned above, Fahey immersed himself in the writings of St. Thomas Aquinas while studying for a doctorate in philosophy at the Angelicum. He also diligently studied the writings of Popes Pius IX, Leo XIII and Pius X. Because the latter was a great admirer of Cardinal Pie of Poitier, Fahey, too, became enamored of this influential French hierarchical figure. The specific influences of these ecclesiastics on Fahey's thought will be considered in the following chapter, but there is no doubt that they contributed to his tenacious allegiance to the Holy See. He wrote in his *Apologia Pro Vita Mea*:

When in Rome I began to realize more fully the real significance of the history of the world, as the account of the acceptance and rejection of Our Lord's Programme for order. I used to ask permission to remain at the Confession of St. Peter, while the other scholastics went around the Basilica. I spent the time there going over the history of the world and I repeatedly promised St. Peter that if ever I got the chance, I would teach the truth about his Master in the way that he and his successors, the Roman Pontiffs, wanted it done.[40]

Fahey's ten years of preparation culminated in his ordination to the priesthood September 24, 1910 conferred by Cardinal Respighi at the Basilica of St. John Lateran in Rome. Denis Fahey is always remembered first and foremost as a priest. Even those who vehemently disagreed with his ideas recalled his devotion to, and his gratitude for his priesthood.[41]

Ordination, important as it was for Denis Fahey, did not allow much respite from studies. If he was going to proclaim the Kingship of Christ, he knew that he had to be prepared. The one evidence of an enjoyable working holiday is a letter to his parents from San Valentino, Perugia, Italy on July 21, 1911, written on *Séminaire Française* stationery:

> My dear Father and Mother,
> At last I can send you a few lines after a prolonged silence. I don't think I have ever enjoyed the air of the mountains so much as this year, and the country around is much fresher and greener than in former years, probably on account of the quantity of rain which has fallen this year. Though I have had to work very hard these past few months, I am quite myself again after two days rest, thanks be to God.[42]

He then relates the experiences he has enjoyed with "Frs. Jerry, Dan and George" and how happy he is that they will be able to give a first-hand report to his family in Ireland. "Of course," he states, "you will get Fr. Jerry to say mass at the house." He adds: "This time next year, I expect that you will no longer have to remain content with hearing about me from others for I am almost sure to be home in the last days of July, if not before."[43]

Regarding his stay in San Valentino, Denis relates: "I teach catechism as usual and on Sunday week I am to preach a sermon in Italian." His only request is: "Kindly send me a pair of garters when you have time, as these I have are almost worn and garters in the Sabine Mountains are too great a luxury to think of getting them here." He concludes: "Love to all. Thomas forgets that all news about families in the neighborhood interests me." Apparently his brother Thomas was not the best correspondent, and Denis was eager to hear about his friends at home. The letter is signed: "Your affectionate son, Denis."

The tone of this letter and the accomplishments of these years indicate that Denis Fahey had grown as a person and as a priest. The theology and the philosophy to which he had been exposed profoundly impressed him. The conservative environment of anti-Modernism in Rome undoubtedly affected his perception of the world for the rest of his life. But life was just beginning for Denis Fahey, and at the age of twenty-nine, now "Father Denis Fahey, C.S.Sp.," with a Doctor of Philosophy (D.Phil.) from the Angelicum in 1911, and a Doctor of Divinity (D.D.) from the Gregorian University in 1912, he returned home to Ireland.[44]

1912-1919: Professor, Patient, Chaplain

In 1911, the Irish novitiate, and the junior seminary at Castlehead in England were moved to Kimmage Manor, one of the Shaw mansions, an estate on the outskirts of Dublin. It was to this growing seminary environment that Fahey returned in 1912. He was appointed Professor of Philosophy, and Director of the recently opened Senior Scholasticate at Kimmage.[45]

The demands of those years seem to have been intense. Fahey taught Church History and Philosophy, and had administrative duties as well. In the *Bulletin de la Congrégation* for April 1920, there is reference to Father Fahey as having arrived in Switzerland in February 1916 to recover his health.[46] The Holy Ghost Congregation had built a senior seminary in Fribourg in 1904 when anti-clericalism in France was at its height. It also served as a residence for students who were attending the university, and became an interprovincial house of studies for the congregation. In 1913, the Spiritans also rented a villa nearby where tubercular victims could recuperate in the mountain air. It is not clear what Fahey's ailment was, or whether he was at the rest sanitarium at that time. Students, colleagues and family recall that he was always plagued with intense headaches, and some believe that to have been the major cause of his difficulties.[47]

After he recuperated, he was able to act as chaplain to prisoners of war in Berner-Oberland during World War I. Although little is known about this period in his life, a collection of typed sermon notes having his signature, includes the following:

> After Mass, I intend to distribute to the new men the medals sent by the Holy Father to the interned in Switzerland as a token of his love for His children. You know He is the successor of St. Peter to whom our Lord addressed these sublime words: "Feed my lambs" and "Feed my sheep" and as such loves each member of the vast fold committed to his care, loves him for Jesus our Saviour and in Jesus. As common Father of the Faithful the Pope exercises an authority that is not confined by national boundaries, but is coextensive with the Church and he reckons millions of his children in the opposing armies and in the belligerent countries.[48]

There are indications in the text that Fahey was ministering to English P.O.W.s. The prisoners had apparently sent the Pope an album for which they received the medals and a note in which Peter Cardinal Gasparri, Vatican Secretary of State, tells of the gratitude of Pope Benedict XV. Fahey concluded his sermon:

> These little medals then, will help to remind you of your obligation to be faithful Catholics. Nothing would delight the Pope's heart more than that. May the Sacred Heart of Jesus grant that you may give this consolation to His Vicar on earth![49]

Fahey made every effort to live out the promise to St. Peter that he had made as a student in Rome.

It was at this time that Fahey met the English writer Sir Arnold Lunn, and had some important conversations with him which apparently contributed to his conversion to Catholicism.[50] With the termination of the war, Fahey attended lectures at the University of Fribourg. Bernard Kelly, C.S.Sp., believes that experience made him a totally committed Thomist.

In later years he reflected back upon this period as a happy time in his life. Father John Chisholm, C.S.Sp., who had known Fahey as a student, and who returned to Kimmage as a young professor in the early 1950s, recalls taking walks with Fahey after evening prayers as part of the recreation period. Basically, he remembers Fahey as pessimistic, but whenever he spoke of "mountaineering in Switzerland" he would seem happy.[51]

One cannot help conjecturing about two significant events which occurred during Fahey's sojourn in Switzerland. The *Bulletin* indicated that he arrived in Switzerland in February 1916. He was not, therefore, in the Dublin area at one of the most volatile times in Irish history, the Easter Monday Rising, 1916; nor was he there for the traumatic executions of James Connelly, Padraic Pearse, Tom Clarke and Roger Casement that followed. The years 1916-1919 were crucial for the future of Ireland. It is very likely that Fahey missed all the events which led to the assembly of the first Dail Eirann which met on January 21, 1919. His lack of immediate experience during these trying years did not make him less loyal to Ireland, but it may have inclined him to a more "Roman" allegiance through the years, particularly on the issue of church and state. Whether his presence in Ireland during those years would have made a difference cannot be determined.

Secondly, Fahey's experience of World War I in Switzerland was in ministering to prisoners of war. This was also the period of turmoil in Russia, and the revolutions in that country about which he was to write so prolifically in the years ahead. One can only speculate as to the influence of these events on his later writings about war, finance, and revolution.

Now thirty-six years old, Fahey returned to Ireland in 1919 to live the rest of his years as priest, professor, author, spiritual director to clergy and laity, and religio-political activist. In his later years, he was not content to eschew the challenges of political life, and there were some who thought that, like his father Timothy, he was "a contrary man."

Ireland to the End: 1919-1954

No person can be compartmentalized, and no one exists in a vacuum. It is in reflecting on Fahey's relationships that the distinctiveness of his personality becomes apparent. The following categories provide us with helpful insights into the man who was Denis Fahey.

Author Fahey

Friend and foe alike would probably agree that Fahey's main thesis was set out in his small book, *The Kingship of Christ according to the Principles of St. Thomas Aquinas* (1931) and everything else is commentary.[52] An analysis of his key ideas will be the subject of the following chapter, but the question might be asked here—what was there about the person of Denis Fahey that affected his role as author?

To his admirers he had convincingly presented a view of the world which was desperately needed; it seemed so obvious to them that diabolical forces were overwhelming the earth, and people had to be alerted to this if the Kingship of Christ was going to survive. To his critics, he was a fundamentalist, particularly regarding papal documents, and his supporting material was of inferior quality selected with blinders on. To state, as he did, that he did not know whether *The Protocols of the Elders of Zion* was a forgery or not, and then to have used it extensively to prove points in discussion, was scarcely a method acceptable to the historian or theologian, even in Fahey's day.

Shortly after Fahey's death, Michael Troy, C.S.Sp. wrote an article attempting to evaluate Fahey's writings apart from his person. He claimed:

> Many of those who never knew Father Fahey personally, too easily fell into the fallacy of identifying the man with his books. As a result, those who agreed with his views too easily idealized him as a saint or a seer; while those who disagreed, often went to the extreme of overlooking even his personal integrity.[53]

Troy then expands on the fact that he was "a very holy priest, a faithful religious, a good confrere, a man selflessly devoted to the service of Christ." But, he adds, "That is not exactly the same as giving a favourable verdict of his published works."

One factor has been reflected upon by both opponents and adherents of Fahey. He was an extremely hypersensitive person, and any criticism of his work was viewed in an intensely personal way. Troy wrote:

> During Fahey's life-time, a cautious reserve was the only prudent attitude in this delicate matter, as many of his cherished opinions were of a highly controversial nature and he himself was not an easy man to criticize or oppose. He was very sensitive about his views and, never having developed a power of self-criticism, was prone to identify conscientious disapproval with malicious misinterpretation.[54]

An avowed admirer of Fahey, Father Frank Comerford, C.S.Sp. eulogized his mentor after his death in an essay published in the *Tipperary Star*. In a concluding section he stated that he could not complete his brief portrait of the great Irishman and great priest without adding:

> It was generally admitted that he was hypersensitive where his work and the opposition it aroused were concerned. To ideas that ran counter to the teaching of Christ and His Vicars on earth Fr. Fahey was opposed with the fiery zeal of a Crusader. Such opposition hurt him personally even to the extent of making him physically ill. So fully was his mind attuned (by long years of study and meditation) to that of Christ, so closely was his heart identified with the Sacred Heart of Christ the King, that any opposition to the interests of Christ caused him intense pain. Where ideas were concerned he was certainly very sensitive, much as a trained musician is sensitive to and shudders at the slightest discordant note.[55]

Several Holy Ghost Fathers agreed that Fahey so completely identified the plan of Christ with his own interpretation of that plan that he saw criticism of his description as somehow criticism of Christ himself. This wounded Fahey deeply because he believed that it wounded Christ. It was therefore impossible, because of his temperament, to criticize his published works. His horizons as an author were, as a result, severely limited. He asked for approbation only from those who agreed with him, and if it was not forthcoming, he—at least in one instance—exerted a kind of "moral pressure" to wring out agreement for a favorable review.[56]

Fahey continued to be controversial even after his death. A.K. Chesterton summed up the convictions of those who would defend Fahey by stating: "...he had immense erudition, a quiet and judicial mind, complete fearlessness and no bees buzzing in his bonnet."[57] Those who opposed Fahey's approach would highly question the one-sided accumulation of evidence which he used, and would completely deny "the quiet and judicial mind." There is no question, however, that he was a committed author and a prolific writer.

Professor Fahey

Every Irish Holy Ghost seminarian who studied at the Holy Ghost Missionary College from 1920-1954 was in some way exposed to Denis Fahey, and there are almost as many stories as there were seminarians. Fahey taught philosophy and church history at Kimmage. In addition, he also gave weekly lectures which the seminarians were expected to attend; therefore, even if a student was taking philosophy courses at University College, Dublin, he would still have the opportunity to learn about Fahey's "theology of history" and to reflect on his diagram of order during one of the weekly sessions. Frank Comerford,C.S.Sp. gave this description:

> It was as a teacher of Philosophy that most of us first encountered Fr. Fahey. His fame had of course preceded him and he was something of a fable before we ever met him. He was not a teacher in the Quintillian sense that he succeeded in making his matter, logic and metaphysics, palatable to the untrained mind. He did not possess, as the "born teacher" does, the art of putting his ideas across with clarity, at least in English. English is not the language of philosophy and Father Fahey was often cumbersome in his efforts to clothe in the English idiom those philosophical concepts that are so happily couched in Latin as their native setting.[58]

Comerford hastened to add regarding his mentor:

> He was, however, a teacher in the higher sense that his mere presence exercised over all who were unbiased a strange charm and fascination. He radiated a very real quality, difficult to describe and

impossible to define, and which many would call
holiness. We felt we were in the presence of one
who was great because he was good with the
goodness of God. He had a rare sense of humour
which found expression often at his own expense
but never at the expense of others.[59]

Fahey was best remembered for "the grasp of order." The
concept of order was essential to his entire scheme. Even the
smallest item had to be seen in that context. Eating white bread
from which the nutrients had been removed was a violation of the
natural order. Professors and students alike remember him in the
refectory eating his brown bread, cheese and yogurt. To this day
Holy Ghost members recall that brown bread at the seminary was
known as "the grasp." "Please pass me 'the grasp'!" was not an
uncommon request among students at the dinner table in obvious
reference to Fahey's class.[60] An ecologist ahead of his time, Fahey
believed that living an ordered life required respect for the natural
law even in its less conspicuous forms.

Seminarians complained, however, that each time Fahey
came to a class lecture he would begin by drawing his diagram of
world order on the blackboard and rarely proceed beyond a certain
point. Fahey's former students will never forget his favorite
authors, especially Cardinal Pie of Poitiers.[61] Papal encyclicals were
always the last word on any issue. When questioned on a papal
statement he was known to defend himself encyclical in hand, by
a parody on the Irish comedian Jimmy O'Dea's then famous
question: "Will ye hit me now with a baby in me arms?" In his
high-pitched voice Fahey would ask: "Will ye hit me now with the
Pope in me arms?!"[62] His particular eccentricities made him
lovable to many students though they might not have agreed with
what he taught them.

As a professor Fahey also had his students involved in his
various projects—sometimes as part of their assigned duties,
sometimes on a volunteer basis. Thomas Mackin remembers riding
a bicycle back and forth between Kimmage and the Jesuit

theologate at Milltown Park carrying books which Fahey and Father Edward Cahill,S.J. were exchanging. Desmond Byrne recalls delivering letters and papers to Tom Agar, a leader in the Fahey-inspired *Maria Duce* movement. John Chisholm took books and leaflets of Fahey's on summer holidays, passed them on to friends, and encouraged them to purchase or subscribe. Other students typed and did research and translations for him.[63]

Many tell stories about the pranks they played on Fahey in the classroom. One such was Peter Nolan, C.S.Sp., who then added that he would also remember Fahey as a kind and holy man who never wanted material things for himself. He was often cited for his simplicity, and his helpfulness to students who might otherwise have failed.[64] Students delighted in imitating his high-pitched voice. He was not without wit and humor. On one particularly warm day, after an unexciting class, as he made his way to the door to leave, the seminarian in the first seat rose to open the door for him, as was customary in those days. Fahey said to him in a loud whisper as he was moving out: "Tell the others that I was here!"[65] As a professor of philosophy he was also available to the larger Dublin community. A Study Circle under the auspices of the Central Catholic Library, founded in 1923, announced its twelfth course for the Spring Session 1933 as a series of ten lectures titled: "Course on Thomistic Philosophy" by the Reverend Denis Fahey,D.D., D.Ph., C.S.Sp., Professor of Philosophy, Blackrock College." The third lecture was on "Opposition to God's Plan in the Jewish Nation and the Roman Empire. Jewish rejection persevered in down the centuries. Consequences of that rejection."[66] The Jewish community in Dublin in the 1930s felt pain and fear as they became aware of Fahey's teaching. As will be discussed later, not all who knew of his ideas glimpsed in them the love of God.

Spiritual Director Fahey

When Fahey returned from Switzerland to Dublin in 1919, the Senior Scholasticate of the Irish Province had been relocated at St.

Mary's College, Rathmines, during the period when that institution was closed as a day school (1919-1924). He continued there in his role as Professor of Philosophy, and in 1921 was appointed Professor of Church History as well. During his years as a professor in a seminary community it was often difficult to distinguish where the role of teacher ended and the role of spiritual director began. Fahey was always willing to give time to his students. He was available for confession and spiritual guidance, although one usually had to wend one's way through stacks of books to reach his chair or prie-dieu.

One of the few documents of Fahey's of a more spiritual nature from this period is a notebook in his handwriting, with "Rev. D. Fahey, St. Mary's College, Rathmines" on the cover. It consists of spiritual notes, with a table of contents. It would appear that these notes were matter for the giving of retreats. They give us a clue to his interior life during this time. A peculiarity of his style was that of enclosing in parentheses words or phrases he had considered, rather than crossing them out. Ideas similar to those in his notes were no doubt communicated in spiritual direction:

Now, my dear [a title of address and affection which Fahey was known for using constantly], descend into your own conscience, question yourselves in the light of the principles I have (explained to) laid before you. If your soul is the theatre of troubles and conflicts which rend it, do not be deceived, it is because your will (refusing) refuses to subject itself to God, and is thus divided against itself. Your instincts, claiming autonomy (local "Home Rule") are in revolt against reason. Reestablish order in your interior life, allow God to dispose of all your life and action, regulate your desires according to His precepts and the objective order of your Rules, cling to Him above as your last end and you will taste the happiness of a secret

peace which though resembling only from afar off
the peace of the Blessed, is nevertheless beyond
compare.[67]

Fahey believed it imperative that he warn students regarding
moral and spiritual dangers. Seamus Galvin, C.S.Sp. recounts
that as a seminarian his room was next to Fahey's; when Fahey's
books started spilling out of his own room, he started storing them
in Galvin's. At one point Fahey left a bundle of Communist
newspapers in Galvin's closet, securely tied and labelled: "Father
Fahey says it is a mortal sin if you read these." Galvin used to joke
about "living in a proximate occasion of sin." He also recalled two
or three occasions when he was sick in bed with the flu; Fahey
would arrive at his door in the afternoon with an orange. Vitamin
C was important! Fahey's concern extended beyond the spiritual
and intellectual realms.[68]

Those outside the seminary environs sometimes appreciated
Fahey more than his confreres in his own community. He got
support and affirmation from Sisters to whom he occasionally gave
conferences, and lay people to whom he ministered in a variety of
ways. The following letter to an unknown Sister gives us a
glimpse of his concern for others, and also of the way in which his
spiritual direction flowed from his world view and concept of
order. Dated February 17, 1941, it reads:

> Dear Sister,
> This will only be a short letter, but I cannot
> allow the children's lovely letters, by which I have
> been deeply touched, to go without some sort of
> answer. I want to help you to help them to live for
> Our Lord not only during the passing crisis of the
> war but all their lives. We are all members of our
> Dear Lord, you and I and the children and their
> parents and friends. We are all meant to live our
> lives lovingly and calmly allowing Him to act
> through us. That means we are meant to think out

what the order of life, family life and school life, demand from us daily and accomplish it lovingly and calmly as if our hands, our eyes, our tongues were prolongations of Jesus. Some sacrifices, therefore, in fact: the vast majority of them, are simply the expression of our acceptance of the order of our lives from our parents, our time-table (drawn up by those over us) and our surroundings.[69]

Fahey's strictness with himself in terms of discipline and self-sacrifice is further expressed in the conclusion of the letter:

Other sacrifices are not precisely demanded by the order of our lives here and now, but if we do not accustom our bodies and our souls to regular refusals of gratifications they will not readily accept order, they will not be disciplined and they will rise up and demand selfish satisfaction against Jesus later on, sometimes very quickly. So then in order not to be weak and feeble members, we must discipline ourselves. That is the meaning of the second group of sacrifices.[70]

This letter, while not atypical for the period in which it was written, is also indicative of the goals Fahey set for himself, and his own attitudes regarding penance and sacrifice.

As will be discussed in the following section, Fahey inspired a group of bright and enthusiastic young Irish men and women to commit themselves to Christ and in the spirit of crusaders to live their lives totally for Jesus. They found in Fahey a kind of spiritual direction that continued to be important in their lives. One such person was Michael O'Toole, an active member of the *Maria Duce*. At Father Fahey's suggestion, he and his fiancee Kathleen Byrne pledged themselves to one another in an espousal ceremony in the chapel at Kimmage on November 1, 1953. At Our Lady's altar, Michael and Kathleen exchanged the promise(s) composed by Father Fahey for the occasion. Father Fahey presided at the ceremony and blessed the engagement ring. The following is the text of Michael's promise:

> In the presence of Our Lord Jesus Christ, of His Blessed Mother, of my Guardian Angel and of the whole court of Heaven, I, Michael O'Toole, promise to wed Kathleen Byrne, and to enable us both to prepare worthily for the reception of the Holy Sacrament of Matrimony, we ask them to deepen in us a reverence for such sublime dignity as members of Christ.[71]

Michael O'Toole added: "After the ceremony, Father Fahey gave Kathleen a photo of himself and told her to keep it 'well dusted.'"[72] The O'Tooles were only one such couple who felt their lives enriched by Father Fahey and were convinced that they knew Christ better for having such a relationship. It is interesting to note that in this period of the early 1950s when liturgical ceremonies such as the Easter Vigil, espousal ceremonies, etc. were being restored in the Church, Fahey took the initiative to suggest that they participate in such a ceremony. In this matter, he may be considered liturgically *avant garde*.

Activist Fahey

A scholarly treatise will no doubt be written in time on the organization *Maria Duce* ("under Mary's leadership").[73] This movement grew out of a study circle conducted by Fahey in the 1940s. It began as an organization in 1942, and in August 1945 introduced its periodical, *Fiat*. This was never dated, but was published about every six weeks. The initial issue was run off on a duplicating machine, but later issues became more sophisticated in style. It announced that its program was based on the Catholic social principles as outlined in the papal encyclicals. Point 1 read: "The Catholic Church is the One True Church and ought to be acknowledged as such by States and Nations." One of the battles waged by *Maria Duce* was against Article 44 of the Irish Constitution which stated instead: "The State recognizes the special position of the Holy, Catholic, Apostolic and Roman Church, as the guardian of the faith professed by the great majority of its citizens."[74] It pained Fahey greatly that the Irish Catholic hierarchy accepted this latter version.

Fahey was the unquestioned catalyst of *Maria Duce*. He was with the group for monthly meetings, and frequently presented inspirational talks. He carried on an extended correspondence and communication with Tom Agar, and others who were leaders in the organization. These young Catholic laymen sought his approval for all of their projects and publications, attested to by the correspondence that survives.[75] Part of a front page editorial of *Fiat*, No. 42, provides something of the spirit of the group:

> In the field of Catholic journalism, FIAT endeavors to advance the reign of Christ the King and to repel the plan of Satan. It attempts therefore, to be altogether Catholic, to marshall Catholics along a front unbroken to evil anywhere, to be strong, most closely-knit and—above all else—united when pitted against the Organized Naturalism of Freemasonry and the Jewish Nation. FIAT, therefore, is vocal when others are silent, uncompromising where others waver, courageous, it is humbly hoped, where only pusillanimity abounds.[76]

In the early 1950s, Fahey and his group were leaders in the formation of the "Catholic Cinema and Theatre Patrons Association" which was rabidly anti-Hollywood.[77] It picketed charity performances of film stars in Dublin, and was against such "anti-supernatural" films as *The Song of Bernadette* and *The Keys of the Kingdom*. In this, Fahey was in league was Myron C. Fagan of the Cinema Educational Guild in Hollywood, and others who were convinced that Jews and Communists were corrupting the "Christian morality" of the western world through the media.

Sympathy and concern for Senator Joseph McCarthy and for other right-wing conservative political groups in the U.S.A. is evident on the pages of *Fiat*. J. H. Whyte asserts:

> ... Maria Duce cannot be dismissed as of trivial importance. Its core of full members numbered only about one hundred, but it had a much larger number of associate members—perhaps five or six thousand. Its associated periodical *Fiat* had a circulation, I am told, that went well into five figures, and its rallies in Dublin sometimes attracted attendance of thousands.... Perhaps it was only a lunatic fringe, but it was still of interest as a symptom.[78]

His earlier years of study and publishing had built in Fahey the conviction that he must help to save the world from the corruptive forces of Organized Naturalism as led by Jews and Freemasons. The desire to implement programs which would accomplish these ends took firm hold. With the enthusiasm and affirmation of the young Irish conservatives who idolized him, and who believed that he had a blueprint for the future—Fahey became more and more involved in the political scene. Something of the spirit of his father, Timothy, had come to the fore.

Fahey—Friend

After Fahey's death, Frank Comerford, C.S.Sp. wrote of a visit in Kilmore with his former professor in the course of a summer in the 1940s: "He greeted me with a warmth of affection that I shall never forget. I felt, not without a touch of pride, that I was more than a student now. I was a friend."[79] Yet later in the same article he describes Fahey as follows:

Few knew Father Fahey, knew him as a friend
knows a friend, with that understanding and insight
that is quick to appreciate greatness even amid the
more sombre setting of what is merely human....
Father Fahey had many admirers, men and women,
priests and religious, in whose hearts his zeal for the
social reign of Christ the King awakened a
responsive echo. Such followers were legion, but his
friends were few. The fault, if fault there were, was
largely his own.[80]

Comerford then analyzed this quality of Fahey's which was a
source of frustration to many:

He never sought friendship, as most men do, for its
own sake. Even the handful, who, like the present
writer, claim to have had the key to the mind and
heart of this great priest, will admit that he
maintained a strange reserve that was often misinterpreted as indifference.

Fahey's former student believed that it was his focus on
Christ which created something of a barrier in his relationships:

To us of lesser clay, the merely human element, the
heart-to-heart exchanges of views and the exclu-
sivism that normally accompanied such an exchange,
are of the essence of friendship. With Father Fahey
it was totally different. His personal love for his
Divine Master dominated everything and is the
ultimate explanation of the charm of his personality
and power of his influence. That intense attachment
to Christ begot in its turn a love for his
fellow-members that was necessarily detached and
impersonal because wholly spiritual. Indeed his
preoccupation with Christ and His interests was

almost frightening at times. It was something so
utterly unearthly, so sincerely supernatural that many
felt ill-at-ease.[81]

Even Fahey's admirers admitted that it was difficult to maintain a
friendship with him. He was hurt so easily, and misinterpreted
comments that were part of any healthy relationship.

Earlier it was mentioned that the *Maria Duce* enthusiasts
provided Fahey with a support group, and many of these became
friends, but the chasm between clergy and laity certainly did not
allow for the friendship of equals. Fahey also had a huge correspondence with persons all over the world who became attached to
him, although they never met him in person. One such person was
Thomas J. Kavanagh, who as a young lawyer in New York City in
the 1940s wrote to Fahey frequently, sharing concerns, seeking
advice, and attempting to publicize Fahey's work in America. It
was through Father Coughlin that Kavanagh became acquainted
with Fahey, and it was Kavanagh who arranged the Requiem High
Mass for "The American Friends of Father Denis Fahey, C.S.Sp."
at St. Patrick's Cathedral in New York in January 1954.[82]

Fahey and His Foes

Did Fahey have any foes? That can be answered by interviews with some persons who believed that Fahey was writing and
teaching views that were dangerous. Frank Duff, founder of the
Legion of Mary in 1921, had set up a branch of the Legion in 1936
called "Our Lady of Israel" for the conversion of the Jews. Duff
did not believe in attacking Jews, and the Legion was responsible
in the years 1940-1941 for the establishment of the "Pillar of Fire"
group for Jewish-Catholic dialogue, which was patterned on the
Mercier Society, a group developed for Protestant-Catholic
dialogue. Both of these groups were discontinued by Archbishop
John Charles McQuaid, C.S.Sp. of Dublin in 1943. It was the
belief of some people, including Duff, that McQuaid was a disciple
of Fahey's, and that Fahey's influence was somehow responsible

for that action. Fahey had been McQuaid's professor, and McQuaid wrote the preface to Fahey's first book, *The Kingship of Christ according to the Principles of St. Thomas Aquinas.* McQuaid's position regarding Fahey, however, tended to be ambiguous.[83]

Duff recounted how some of the *Maria Duce* people tried to capitalize on the similarity of their title with that of the Legion of Mary. Indeed, at one point, two branches of the Legion became "infiltrated" with *Maria Duce* adherents. It was learned that Legionaries from these groups who were making home visitations were attacking the Jews, and that the "book barrows" set up by the Legion operated by these two groups placed "Maria Duce" signs above them, and were giving out anti-Jewish literature. Duff recalled:

> I happened to be the President at that time, and I was deputed to send for the two presidents of those two branches, and to ask them to desist. They must not do that under the auspices of the Legion.... we regarded that as a very incorrect procedure on their part. They were two very fine fellows, you know; of course, that was the trouble. They were trained to believe that all evil was proceeding from the Jews.[84]

The two claimed that they were acting according to their consciences, and that they regarded this as a vital matter. Duff said that if they could not comply with the Legion, they must be asked to leave. They did indeed leave, but at a later time after Fahey's death returned to the Legion, and Duff commented that they proved to be superb Legionaries.

When asked directly if Duff had had any conversations or communications with Fahey, he replied:

> No, I never did. And one of the reasons for that would be that I would know exactly what would

take place and I wouldn't want that to take place. That is—you could not reason with him—and that was Father Fahey. With regard to the question of their saying it was their consciences. That would be completely due to him. He assured them that they were in the right, even under our auspices, and contrary to our instructions, in adopting that plan.[85]

Gabriel Fallon, former actor of the Abbey Theatre and literary critic for *The Standard* of Dublin, was more actively involved in confrontation with Fahey. He described the relationship of the *Maria Duce* to the Legion of Mary, as did his friend Frank Duff, seeing the former as growing out of the latter because some members of the Legion did not believe that their organization was aggressive enough. Fallon mentioned that Tom Agar, who later became President of the *Maria Duce*, had been a Vice-President of the group ("presidium") of the Legion to which Fallon belonged.

Hollywood was the issue on which Fallon and Fahey most violently clashed, but ultimately it was on the question of whether the Jews and the Communists controlled the media. When American actors Orson Welles and Danny Kaye visited Dublin, both were picketed by the "Catholic Cinema and Theatre Patrons' Association," and a war of words began. Eventually both Fallon and Fahey were demanding apologies of each other, while Peter O'Curry, editor of *The Standard*, and Archbishop McQuaid occupied a middle position.[86]

Fallon pointed up the fact that the title *Maria Duce* in the 1940s had definite political implications à la Mussolini. The *Maria Duce* symbol depicted Mary standing upon the world which was held up by an arm clad in armor, and holding a sword. This was offensive to many. In an effort to be anti-Communist, a pro-Fascist image had emerged.

In opposition to Duff, Fallon never believed that McQuaid was a Faheyite. He was convinced that the Archbishop, whom he admired very much, was able to manage the *Maria Duce* in his own way. It is interesting to note that with the death of Father

Fahey in January 1954, McQuaid asked the group to change its name. In January 1955, it became known as *Firinne* (the Irish word for "truth"). The followers of Fahey not only mourned their leader, but their title and symbol as well.

Fahey's relationship with the Jewish people is the most difficult phase of his personality to understand. His very first article published in the *Missionary Annals of the Holy Ghost Fathers*, entitled "Father Libermann's Faith," provides us with the enigma that Fahey, in a congregation which revered as its "Second Founder" a convert from Judaism, could write such biased statements regarding the Jews.[87] (The role of the Jews in Fahey's "theology of history" will be discussed in detail later.) Fahey's personal attitude is reflected in the seven letters exchanged with Rabbi Abraham Gudansky of the Dublin Hebrew Congregation in May-June 1937. The Rabbi desired to meet Fahey to present to him, as he said, "facts which might alter your views regarding Jewish influence."[88] Fahey wrote to Gudansky, May 24, 1937:

> Now, the Jewish nation, as an organized entity, refuses to acknowledge that our Lord Jesus Christ was God, the Source of Supernatural Life and the True Messias, and they look forward to another Messias who must of necessity be natural. Hence, the influence of the Jewish nation is diametrically opposed to our Lord Jesus Christ and to the Super-natural Life of Grace. That being so, I am completely puzzled to understand in what sense you wish me "to alter my views regarding Jewish influence."[89]

In a third letter in which Fahey refused to meet with Gudansky, he claimed: "I am animated with a special charity toward the Jews as members of Our Lord Jesus Christ's own nation according to the flesh," but he concluded, "Accordingly I beg to be excused from an interview which would be [the word "extremely" is crossed out on the copy] painful for me."[90] Rabbi Gundansky's reply stated: "I deeply regret your inability to have a few minutes private talk with me, which might have led us to a clearer and better understanding." After responding to specific remarks in Fahey's previous letter, Gudansky concluded, quoting the prophet Malachi (2:10):

> In the meantime, let all right-thinking men and women walk in the light of the Prophet's exclamation, "Have we not one Father? Has not one God created us?" helping thus to dispel the shadows of hatred and prejudice which bedarken the human horizon. The French Rabbi, who with a cross in his hand, administered the last rites to a dying Christian soldier, acted by no means in a contradictory manner and I myself do not feel guilty of any inconsistency by seeing that my Christian maid attends to her religious duties. Again I affirm that believing as we do that "the pious of the gentiles are assured of Eternal Bliss" (Tos.S.Ch. 13) we are animated by the one and only desire to live in perfect friendship with our neighbors and work harmoniously and whole-heartedly together for the common good of the nation to whom we are attached by bonds of loyal citizenship.
> I am Rev. and Dear Sir,
> Yours faithfully
> A. Gudansky[91]

These letters, exchanged in the spring of 1937 when "shadows of hatred and prejudice" were indeed to "bedarken the human horizon," are painful to read. Fahey seemed genuinely convinced that the Jews had diabolical goals, and that if he should grant an interview, he might indeed be murdered. More than one of his former students has stated, "Fahey always thought there was a Jew in the bushes ready to kill him."[92]

In a letter to Archbishop McQuaid August 21, 1948, Fahey described in great detail a visit he received from a man from Chicago "who called to see me some time ago on false pretenses." Fahey claimed that he had learned that the man was a paid spy for the Anti-Defamation League of B'nai B'rith. Fahey continued: "This league is known in the U.S.A. as the Jewish Gestapo. It has a vast network of paid spies and specializes in what Americans call 'character-assassination' and 'smear-work.'" After describing the A.D.L. further, Fahey concluded:

> The spy insisted on taking my photo in front of the chapel here, so when the time comes to pass from "character-assassination" to more effective action, they will not mistake their man. If that does come, I want Your Grace to know that I died for the Kingship of Christ. I am begging the Immaculate Heart of Our Blessed Mother to keep me faithful to the end.[93]

In discussing Fahey's writings in the following chapter, particularly those relating to the Jews, it is necessary to realize that he had a genuine fear of what he understood as "the forces of Organized Naturalism" which were aimed at destroying Christianity (and Fahey) in the process. Even convert Jews were suspect. This paranoia never left Fahey, and in the period 1934-1954 his statements were a source of pain to Jewish people living in Ireland and other parts of the world.

Fahey and His Family

If concern for his family in the last twenty-five years of his life is indicative of an earlier spirit—family was always important to Denis Fahey. The death of his mother in 1922, just three years after his return from Switzerland, and of his older brother Thomas in 1923, were certainly difficult for him. His father Timothy thus mourned a wife and two sons before his own death in 1935.

Thomas' wife, Johanna (O'Connor) had preceded her husband in death. "Father Denis" was the one to whom his brother's seven children looked as a parent figure. In many ways, he became the patriarch of the clan.[94]

Father Fahey truly loved his home and his family. His oldest nephew, Denis, married Nellie McGrath, and lived in the family homestead. It was there that Father Fahey stayed for a few weeks every summer, enjoying the fresh air and the invigorating spirit of his beloved Tipperary. In one of his many letters to Nellie, dated December 21, 1943, he wrote:

> I am ever so glad that you are happy in Kilmore, and I can assure you that I was happy there during the summer. I am very grateful to Denis and yourself for having made me so welcome. As I am growing older, I am getting fonder of the old place and the surroundings, and I love everybody and everything.[95]

Each year, even to his seventieth, he brought his bicycle with him when he came for his summer visits. He rose at 6:00 each morning, and took a swim in the Multeen River nearby. After that, he rode his bike to the Church of the Immaculate Conception at Knockavilla to say Mass. Oftentimes after Mass he took Communion to the sick and the elderly, still fasting from food and water, as was the custom in those days.

When breakfast was completed, he would spread out his material in the parlor. It was there that he wrote some of his books. About three o'clock or after, he would take off on his bicycle and visit family and friends in the neighborhood. He made an effort to spend time with each.

Mary Jo Fahey, a grandniece of Father Denis, remembers one afternoon when he arrived unexpectedly. Her father was out in the meadow. At fifteen and the oldest in the family, she got on her bike and rode along with him three miles to find her father. There they all had tea together. She had been baptized by Father

Denis, who later sent her a picture for her first Holy Communion. Mary Jo has the relic of Thérèse of Lisieux which belonged to him. He was thus an important person in her life, and in those of her cousins. The younger generation also identified their great-uncle with calcium tablets which they took daily "because Father Denis said so!" Mary Jo recalled, however, that he always seemed sad and worried, though he never expressed it in words, but would rather ask others about their problems. Very sensitive to moral questions, he was concerned about secularism and materialism, and somehow communicated a deep spirituality.[96]

Josie, the youngest of Thomas and Johanna's children, now Mrs. Josie Fahey Tuohy of Ballinaclough, was a favorite of Father Denis. She remembers that he kept them too long at Mass, and often they didn't know what he was preaching about. Now, she admits, many older people in the parish say that what he preached has come to pass.[97] He was not insensitive, however, to the need for short sermons on important days in the life of the community. Frank Comerford's description bears this out:

> The locals spoke of "Father Denis" with an affection and respect not untinged with legitimate pride. His sermons on the Sundays of his brief annual sojourn in his native parish were eagerly looked forward to. He knew his audience—none better. That is why perhaps one of his listeners would pay him a tribute and make an important distinction at the same time: "He's a Tipperary man, is Father Denis, and hurling is in his blood. He never delays us on the Sunday of the Munster Final and thinks nothing of cycling the twenty-five odd miles to be present himself."[98]

The Fahey homestead in Kilmore was the one place of joy and respite in his life and he tried to respond with gratitude, doing them little favors and sometimes sending them tea or cocoa. One of the more unusual situations is described in his letter of August 18, 1943, to Nellie regarding the scarcity of tires during World War II:

> I saw John Reynolds for the first time since I came back, last evening. He has applied for two tyres for Tim and will get them, but it will take time. As you are in a bad way for tyres, he says that he has been offered tyres at 12/6 each. You need not send on the old tyres, but simply let me know the size of tyres you need. This I am afraid is "black market" dealing, not that John Reynolds has anything to do with it but, of course, he knows about it. Because you need the tyres badly, you are justified in accepting. He will see if he can get tubes also.[99]

Although nothing more was at stake than bicycle tires, it is interesting to note that there was the need for moral justification. He wrote frequently to Nellie, his nephew Denis' wife, giving her encouragement at the times of her pregnancies and advising her to take vitamins.

Father Denis also warned her of the dangers of the insecticide D.D.T., encouraged her to give the children milk and not tea, and sent a device for grinding their own whole wheat flour. He had them eating yogurt as well. In his concern for health foods he was ahead of his time. More than externals, however, a sense of warmth and love for the family is reflected in the more than ninety letters addressed to her. Denis and Nellie's son Tom remembers how, when he was very small, Father Denis would take him for walks, saying his Office on the way. Nellie recalls that he would push the baby about in the pram with one hand, a prayer book in the other.[100] Denis Fahey was indeed a family man, and to this day he is remembered with love by his family.

Father Fahey, C.S.Sp., Priest

Fahey ministered to others and gave them spiritual care. How did he exercise his priesthood specifically: (a) as an officiant of the Roman Catholic Church; (b) as a member of the Holy Ghost Congregation; (c) as one who "did liturgy" for people mostly in Ireland, both in and out of the seminary?

As was indicated earlier, Denis Fahey's final preparation for ordination in Rome seems to have made the Vatican a focus for his priestly life. His devotion to the Popes as the successors of Peter was manifested on numerous occasions. Every Vatican pronouncement was interpreted in the light of infallibility. If a group, such as the *Action Française* in 1926, came under the censure of the Pope, it would be renounced though its earlier impact could scarcely be removed. If a Pope made a statement—any Pope in any era—it was the last word.[101]

Closer to home, however, Fahey sought actively to influence the church in Ireland. He had great hopes when John Charles McQuaid, C.S.Sp. became Archbishop of Dublin in 1940. When in 1949 the *Maria Duce* launched a campaign to amend Article 44 of the Irish Constitution of 1937, he wanted it to state definitely that the Catholic Church was indeed the one true church, and not merely the church of the majority in Ireland. He was deeply saddened when McQuaid and other members of the Irish hierarchy went along with De Valera and did not fight for the stricter interpretation.[102]

McQuaid and Fahey corresponded on various occasions. Generally Fahey sent information or publications to the Archbishop and received a response. McQuaid's several handwritten notes to Fahey illustrate the need Fahey felt for understanding and affirmation. One letter reads:

> My dear Father Fahey,
> I am grateful for your kindness in sending me the *Correspondence* concerning Maritain and

your own Apologia. I shall read all the latter, not
merely the pages you have indicated.

I do not know how or where I have
condemned you. Rather it seems to myself as if I
had spent a deal of time taking your part. What is
one to do in the face of such a statement? I fear it
must be an interpretation of something I said or, as
has so often occurred, of something I am supposed
to *think*. Yet you know how careful I am in speech
even in company that I do not fear to be incautious.
For the worry such a report has caused you, I am
sorry.

With kind wishes, I remain, dear Father
Fahey, yours very sincerely in Xt,

+John C. McQuaid[103]

It would seem that the Archbishop tried to be gentle with his
professor of earlier years.

Fahey communicated with other bishops in Ireland as well,
sending his own publications or other pertinent material. In 1950
he received a note of appreciation from Bishop Brown of Galway
for sending "the very important California Legislature Reports."[104]
A similar note came from Archbishop Kinane of Cashel
acknowledging "the Reports."[105] Archbishop Joseph Walsh of
Tuam also thanked him for "the documents, which throw so much
light on the influence that the cinema world wields in favour of
Communism."[106] That same month Fahey received a handwritten
note from Archbishop McQuaid stating: "I must thank you for your
kindness in sending me the two volumes. Perhaps you would also
thank the Senator."[107] A letter from Dr. McGrath, Archbishop of
Cardiff, begins: "Thank you very much for sending Mr. Fagan's
'Hollywood Reds' which I have read with very much interest."[108]
These letters indicate that Fahey believed it was his duty to educate
the hierarchy. Much of the material was related to Communist
influence in Hollywood, a particular concern of *Maria Duce* at that
time.

In practice Fahey was meticulous about obtaining authorizations. There are copies of letters to and from Archbishop Kinane, his cousin, regarding faculties to say Mass and preach in the church at Knockavilla during his holiday time in Kilmore. Fahey saw himself as the obedient servant, but believed he had a mission to educate as well. Most sensitive was his problem, as the years wore on, of obtaining an imprimatur for his books. He had great difficulty, as will be discussed later, finding any bishop who would agree to lend his name to *The Kingship of Christ and the Conversion of the Jewish Nation.* This, no doubt, hurt Fahey grievously.[109]

Life was never easy for Denis Fahey in the Holy Ghost Congregation, although there were certainly happy times and moments of joy. The considerable probationary period before he was given permission to make vows might have influenced this. His hyper-sensitivity could well have been a result of never being sure he was "totally accepted." More than one confrere has indicated that in his later years Fahey often felt that the Congregation had let him down. "His contemporaries did not go along with him. No one in the Irish Province would have gone on with him, except maybe some students," noted John Chisholm, C.S.Sp.[110] Many recognized that he was a loner, and interaction was sometimes difficult. Father Bernard Kelly stated: "If you could get him away from his hobby-horses, he was a wonderful man, and had a good wit." The problem? "Fahey was really *incapable* of dialogue. If you questioned him, or disagreed with him, he was grieved."[111]

The two occasions at Kimmage when Fahey always officiated at the liturgy were Good Friday, when he emphasized praying for "the perfidious Jews," and the Feast of Christ the King, which had been established by Pope Pius XI in his encyclical *Quas Primas* in 1925. These two occasions allowed Fahey to incorporate into the liturgical life of the community what he taught over the years.[112]

From the time of his ordination in 1910 until his death in 1954 Fahey was first and foremost a priest. He wrote, taught, organized, ministered, and loved his family—all as a priest. The key focus of his life was Christ as Priest and King, and he interpreted his own life as living out the Priesthood of Christ in the world. One cannot easily separate his priestly functioning from his other activities.

As a celebrant of the liturgy, Fahey is remembered as being exceedingly devout. James McGann,C.S.Sp. recalled that he used to serve Mass for Father Fahey on Sunday at St. Joseph Church in Tereneure. Fahey rode over on his bicycle in every kind of weather. The later Masses were a special hardship in those days because of the requirement of fasting from food and water. James remembered him as very approachable and devout. People appreciated his care with the liturgy, and the fact that he could talk to simple people and enjoy them, even though he was an important professor at Kimmage.[113]

His priestliness seems to have communicated itself by his personal simplicity. Even those who disagreed with his ideas such as Michael O'Carroll described him as "a man of personal asceticism and piety."[114] John Chisholm, who admitted to having "Faheyitis" in his younger days, contended that as a spiritual director and confessor Fahey "was the essence of kindness and patience."[115] He arose at 5:00 each morning, earlier than the rest of the community, to take his cold shower so that he could have an extra half-hour of meditation before Mass began. Everyone remembers his special place in the chapel which he occupied regularly.

Dying as He Lived: January 21, 1954

The later years were hard for Denis Fahey. On June 1, 1950 he wrote to Nellie: "I have had a very hard year, the hardest of my life, I think." On December 29, 1950 he refers to "old age" coming upon him. In a letter of August 19, 1952 he stated: "I have had a very bad headache more or less all the time, in fact the worst I have ever had."[116] The conflicts regarding the imprimatur of his last book undoubtedly added to his discomfort. This could well have been the reason for arranging an appointment with the Archbishop of Thurles en route to his holiday visit in Kilmore. The following letter, written on his seventieth birthday, July 2, 1954, which he notes is the "Feast of the Visitation, B.V.M.", reflects something of the person of Fahey just six months before his death.

> Dear Nellie,
>
> I was delighted to get your letter of the 29th June this morning. I did not write, because I do not want to impose extra work on you with all the children to be attended to, but of course, I am delighted to come to you for a change. It enables me to get exercise, and I badly need it. It will take me two or three days to get to be normal, but I expect to revive after that period. Please get Denis to meet me in Thurles at 12:27 p.m. (Railway Time) on Tuesday, 7th July. I want to see His Grace, the Archbishop. If the day is not good, Denis will kindly wait, as I shall be only 20 to 30 minutes with His Grace, but if the day is fine I will make my other calls in Thurles, so as not to have to return there, and then cycle home. I hope this will not put Denis out to have to come to Thurles, but I want to make sure to see His Grace, before he goes away on holidays. If the day is not good, Denis will have to tie on the bicycle.
>
> I shall be delighted to give my blessing to Mary Teresa. I am taking it that I need not bring yogurt with me, as you have it going again. (I shall have a little drop for myself in the train, of course.)
>
> You know that I am grateful to you for being so kind to me. I am 70 today, thanks be to Our

Divine Lord and His Blessed Mother. May God
bless you all.

Yours sincerely in Our Lord Jesus Christ.

D. Fahey,C.S.Sp.[117]

Fahey taught in the fall semester 1953 as usual, but toward
the end of the year he was failing and thought that death might be
near. On his way to class on January 16, 1954 he collapsed. Sur-
gery the next day revealed that nothing could be done, and it was
evident that he would not live long.[118]

Many members of the family came up to see him, and after
bidding them goodby he told them not to return because he needed
the time to prepare for his death.[119] He also said farewell to his
many lay friends, as well as members of his own Congregation.
When Enda Watters visited with his former professor shortly before
he died Fahey said to him: "Pray that Our Blessed Mother will give
me a sign that everything is all right between Her Divine Son and
myself."[120] On January 21, 1954 he expired at Mater Hospital in
Dublin.

Headlines for Fahey's obituary include everything from
"Eminent Catholic Writer Dead" to "The Priest Who Sought
World"s 'Hidden Hand.'"[121] The traditional evening funeral Mass
was attended by the Prime Minister Eamon De Valera who
explained to Enda Watters why he was unable to attend the
morning Mass as well, and asked that his regrets be communicated
to the Superior.[122] On January 22, 1954, Archbishop McQuaid
penned a note to the Holy Ghost Provincial, Patrick O'Carroll:

I am very sorry to hear of the death of
Father Fahey. May he rest in peace! He was one
of the first priests I knew in the Congregation and
had very many proofs of his untiring kindness. It is
with regret that I must be absent tomorrow from his
funeral.[123]

The anniversary of Fahey's death was remembered annually by a special visit of his *Maria Duce* friends to the cemetery at Kimmage where he is buried. Father John Aherne,C.S.Sp. referred to this as the "annual visit to his grave by 'the soldiers of the rear guard.'"[124] At one point there was some concern on the part of the Holy Ghost Congregation that this pilgrimage was associated with groups who were antagonistic to the changes in the church after Vatican II, and people were asked to make small and private visits to the cemetery rather than coming *en masse*.[125] Fahey has continued to be remembered in death as he was in life.

Reflecting upon the totality of Fahey's life, it is clear that some of his goals were admirable: prayer, commitment to the church, social justice and ecology. When Father Bernard Kelly was asked if Jews, Freemasons, Communists, and money manipulators were focal points for Fahey he responded: "No, *the focal point for Father Fahey was always the Kingship of Christ. Communism, money manipulation, etc. were always seen as obstacles to that Kingship.*"[126] It seems, however, that Fahey approached the construction of a world view with tunnel vision which resulted in a sense of darkness. His emphasis on what he saw as the obstacles to the Kingship of Christ would be regarded by many as exaggerated, and therefore as a deterrent to the total vision. This "dark side" of Christian theology as interpreted by Fahey often seemed to dominate his life.

[1]Matthew Hoehn, ed., *Catholic Authors: Contemporary Biographical Sketches* (Newark, New Jersey: St. Mary's Abbey, 1952), II, p. 164. In this volume Fahey's mother's name is listed as O'Cleary.

[2]Interviews with Denis and Nellie Fahey, and Josie Fahey Tuohy, Kilmore, Golden, County Tipperary, September 16, 1980. Denis and Josie are Fahey's nephew and niece, the children of his brother Thomas. The letters and other material they shared with me is hereafter referred to as FP-Kilmore. I also

interviewed Mary Jo Fahey in Dublin, September 17, 1980. Mary Jo's father John was the second eldest son of Father Fahey's brother Thomas.

[3]James Joyce, *A Portrait of the Artist as a Young Man* (London: Granada Publishing Company, 1977). First published in 1916. Interview with Leo Layden,C.S.Sp., September 16, 1980 provided information regarding life at Rockwell and the history of the school.

[4]Visit to Rockwell College and interview with James Hurley,C.S.Sp., Headmaster, September 16, 1980.

[5]Very Rev. Tim B. Walsh to Fahey, January 10, 1953, FP-HGP.

[6]Interview with Therese Moran, a niece of Mary Ann Kelly, Dublin, September 18, 1980.

[7]J.H. Whyte, *Church and State in Modern Ireland, 1923-1970* (New York: Barnes and Noble, 1971), p. 8.

[8]Interview with the Faheys at Kilmore, September 16, 1980.

[9]Whyte, p. 10.

[10]The Pope, partly through Cardinal Lavigerie, Archbishop of Algiers, gave official signals that Catholics would dissociate themselves from the extreme Right and come to terms with the Republic in France. It was the hope of Leo XIII that the Church could, by constitutional means, obtain the repeal of such republican legislation as was hampering her efforts. Cf. David Thomson, ed., *France: Empire and Republic, 1850-1940* (New York: Harper and Row, 1968), pp. 243-246, and Josef L. Altholz, *The Church in the Nineteenth Century* (New York: Bobbs-Merrill, 1967), p. 147.

[11]Malcom O. Partin, *Waldeck-Rousseau, Combes, and the Church: The Politics of Anti-Clericalism, 1899-1905* (Durham, North Carolina: Duke University Press, 1969), p. 46.

[12]Ibid., pp. 15-19, 23. With the elections of 1902, and a sweeping success for the radical republicans, the more objective Waldeck-Rousseau was replaced by Émile Combes, an ex-seminarian who had been refused ordination, and who had become rabidly anti-clerical. The Associations Law thus became a long step toward the Separation Law of 1905.

[13]Because the motherhouse of the Holy Ghost Congregation is located in Paris, Holy Ghost Fathers acknowledge that French life and politics have had powerful influence in their history. The first Irish novitiate was not opened until 1911. Interviews with Enda Watters,C.S.Sp., and Leo Layden,C.S.Sp., HGP, March 1979.

[14]Henry J. Koren,C.S.Sp., *The Spiritans: A History of the Congregation of the Holy Ghost* (Pittsburgh: Duquesne University Press, 1958), pp. 9-11. The diocesan "seminary" of seventeenth century France often consisted of attending theological lectures at a college or university, surviving on a part-time job to make ends meet, and living where one could afford. Financial, moral and spiritual support were not readily available for those who did not join an established religious order but who wanted to be ordained.

[15]Ibid., pp. 8, ii, 23. Pollart des Places is the youngest founder of a religious congregation in the Roman Catholic Church.

[16]Ibid., p. 24.

[17]Ibid., pp. 33, 53-54.

[18]Ibid., pp. 57-61.

[19]Ibid., pp. 106-109.

[20]Ibid., pp. 67-96. See also Adrian Van Kaam,C.S.Sp., *A Light to the Gentiles* (Milwaukee: Bruce Publishing Co., 1959).

[21]See Koren pp. 66, 99, and 134-135.

[22]Ibid., pp. 238-240.

[23]Ibid., p. 198.

[24]Interview with John Daley,C.S.Sp., Assistant General of the Holy Ghost Congregation, Kimmage, Dublin, March 5, 1979. Also in conversations with Holy Ghost Fathers Enda Watters, William Jenkinson, Donal O'Sullivan, and Leo Layden.

[25]Gerald J. O'Brien, "Anti-Modernism: The Integralist Campaign," *Continuum* (1965),III: 190-191. O'Brien included L'Floch on a list of Benigni's "agents" in the secret organization known as the *Sodalitium Pianum* which had

organized a network against those who were not amenable to the Integralist theory of the anti-Modernists.

Some Holy Ghost Fathers, including Donal O'Sullivan and William Jenkinson, believe that L'Floch's influence can also be traced to Archbishop Marcel Lefebvre, a former Superior-General of the Holy Ghost Congregation, founder of the dissident traditionalist movement in the Roman Catholic Church known as the Fraternity of St. Pius X. Cf. Yves Congar, *Challenge to the Church: The Case of Archbishop Lefebvre* (Huntington, Indiana: Our Sunday Visitor, 1976), pp. 16, 88-90.

[26] F.S.L. Lyons, *Ireland Since the Famine* (Great Britain: Collins/Fontana, 1973), p. 31. See also Stephen Gwynn, *The History of Ireland* (Dublin: Talbot Press, 1924), p. 486.

[27]Maire and Conor Cruise O'Brien, *A Concise History of Ireland* (London; Thames and Hudson, 1972), pp. 128-129. "By the Wyndham Act of 1903 most Irish tenants were enabled to buy holdings: the landlords received a generously calculated purchase price from the state, and the tenants were to repay this by their annuities."

[28]Lyons, p. 30.

[29]Ibid., p. 32.

[30]Leo Layden,C.S.Sp. to author, January 8, 1981. This was Layden's conclusion after checking records and correspondence, HGP.

[31]Emmett Larkin, *The Roman Catholic Church and the Creation of the Modern Irish State, 1878-1886* (Philadelphia: The American Philosophical Society, 1975), p. 317.

[32]Fergal McGrath, S.J., "The University Question." *A History of Irish Catholicism*, ed. P.J. Cornish, V (Dublin: Gill and Macmillan, 1971), pp. 110-111.

[33]Koren, p. 207.

[34]File Reference card: "Fahey, Denis," HGP.

[35]Fahey's *Apologia pro Vita Mea* is an unpublished mimeographed document which was circulated among his students and friends. Although it is not dated, there is a letter from Archbishop McQuaid written December 2, 1948 which thanks Fahey for sending a copy. Hereafter APVM.

64

³⁶Hoehn, p. 164 also states: "During the period 1906-1908, Denis Fahey studied philosophy in the houses of the Congregation in England and France...." Exactly when he was in England is unclear. During that period, however, the Congregation rented a large property at Prior Park, Somerset County, which was used as a novitiate for part of the time. Enda Watters,C.S.Sp. stated that Fahey used to speak of doing his philosophy course at Prior Park. Interview, Berkeley, California, January 29, 1981.

³⁷Bernard Reardon, ed., *Roman Catholic Modernism* (Stanford, California: Stanford University Press, 1970), p. 70.

³⁸Alphonse Fraisse,C.S.Sp., Assistant Superior at the Senior Scholasticate at Chevilly, to Edward Crehan, October 17, 1907, HGP.

³⁹Fahey, APVM, p. 1.

⁴⁰Ibid., p. 4 of ms., p. 3 of copy.

⁴¹An exception would be his relationship to and lack of communication with the Jewish people in Dublin. See below to correspondence with Rabbi Abraham Gudansky.

⁴²Fahey to his parents, July 21, 1911, FP-Kilmore.

⁴³Ibid. Father Jerry Kinane was a first cousin whose mother was Katie Fahey. He became bishop of Waterford, and later Archbishop of Cashel, provided imprimaturs for some of Fahey's books and wrote the "Prefatory Letter" to his cousin's first major volume, *The Mystical Body of Christ in the Modern World* (1935).

⁴⁴File Reference Card, "Fahey, Denis," HGP. His family still have his diplomas at the Fahey homestead at Kilmore.

⁴⁵Ibid. There is a notation that he made perpetual vows on February 2, 1915.

⁴⁶*Bulletin de la Congrégation* (Paris: Holy Ghost Congregation, Avril 1920), Tome XXIX, p. 605.

⁴⁷Koren, p. 262. It is the belief of Enda Watters and John Chisholm, younger confreres of Fahey, that he had brain surgery when he was in Switzerland, but there is no direct evidence to prove it.

[48]Fahey, "Sermons" beginning with "Fifth Sunday after Easter," unpublished (n.d.), p. 3. HGP.

[49]Ibid., p. 5.

[50]Arnold Lunn, *Now I See* (New York: Sheed and Ward, 1945), pp. 36-38.

[51]Interview with John Chisholm, Templeogue, Dublin, March 7, 1979.

[52]Michael Troy,C.S.Sp., "Reverend Father Denis Fahey, C.S.Sp.: Towards a Critical Analysis of His Published Works," *Tomorrow's Labourers* (Dublin: Kimmage Manor, 1954), p. 21.

[53]Ibid., p. 17.

[54]Ibid.

[55]Francis J. Comerford,C.S.Sp., "Late Fr. Denis Fahey, C.S.Sp.: An Appreciation" (reprinted from *Tipperary Star*) (n.d.), p. 5, FP-HGP.

[56]Interviews in Dublin with Bernard Kelly,C.S.Sp., Kimmage, March 7, 1979; Michael O'Carroll,C.S.Sp., Blackrock College, March 13, 1979; John Chisholm,C.S.Sp., Templeogue, March 11, 1979. Chisholm related his experience of being asked by Fahey to write a review of *The Kingship of Christ and the Conversion of the Jewish Nation* (Dublin: Regina Publications, 1953). See below, p. 143.

[57]Troy, p. 18.

[58]Comerford, p. 1.

[59]Ibid., p. 2. Comerford's reference to "all who were unbiased" was interpreted by "the biased" as a sign of Comerford's own bias in favor of Fahey. William Jenkinson,C.S.Sp. recalls heated discussions with Comerford when they were both novices regarding Fahey's ideas. Interview with William Jenkinson, Berkeley, California, January 16, 1979.

[60]This was usually the first story related by a Holy Ghost member when he learned that the writer was doing a study on Fahey.

[61]Michael McCarthy,C.S.Sp. recalls that they would wait each day for Fahey to come to a certain point in his famous diagram, but it was rarely achieved. Enda Watters, William Jenkinson, Leo Layden and others recall frequent and eloquent references to Cardinal Pie of Poitiers. Conversations, HGP, March 1979.

[62]Interview with Enda Watters,C.S.Sp., HGP, Templeogue, Dublin, March 26, 1979.

[63]Interviews in Dublin with Thomas Mackin,C.S.Sp., Kimmage, March 19, 1979; Desmond Byrne,C.S.Sp., HGP, March 3, 1979; John Chisholm,C.S.Sp., Templeogue, March 11, 1979.

[64]Interview with Peter Nolan, HGP, September 3, 1980.

[65]Interview with Enda Watters, C.S.Sp., HGP, March 26, 1979.

[66]Flyer advertising the event, FP-HGP.

[67]Notebook, FP-HGP.

[68]Interview with Seamus Galvin,C.S.Sp., HGP, August 30, 1980. Father Bernard Kelly recalls that Fahey was always sympathetic to the students. During the late 1930s and early 1940s Father Edward Leen was Director of the theology students and Father Kelly the Director of the philosophy students. The two did not see eye to eye on discipline. Kelly recalls that when complications arose students frequently went to Fahey.

[69]Copy of letter to Sister from Fahey, Holy Ghost Missionary College, Kimmage, Dublin, February 17, 1941, FP-HGP.

[70]Ibid.

[71]Michael O'Toole to author, December 10, 1980.

[72]Ibid.

[73]Whyte, p. 163. In a copy of a letter from Thomas Agar, President of *Maria Duce*, November 24, 1954, to Archbishop John Charles McQuaid of Dublin he stated: "The title of our association was taken at its inception on St. Patricks' Day 1942. Our membership at present is over 5,000. Having as primary aim the sanctification of the members and as work the promotion of the Kingship of Christ, the name of Maria Duce was to us a happy choice; as Our

Lady, Mediatrix of All Graces, is the Leader of all who strive for God, and only through Her will Our Lord come to reign over society." FP-HGP.

[74]Ibid., pp. 163-165.

[75] FP-HGP. There is extended correspondence from Thomas Agar, Seamus Hurley, Michael O'Toole and others.

[76]*Fiat* (Dublin: Key Publishing Co., n.d.), No. 42, FP-HGP.

[77]Interview with Gabriel Fallon, HGP, March 22, 1979.

[78]Whyte, p. 165. Conversations with former members of the *Maria Duce* confirm Whyte's approximations of persons involved, as well as the circulation of *Fiat*.

[79]Comerford, p.3.

[80]Ibid.

[81]Ibid.

[82]Thomas Kavanagh to Denis Fahey,C.S.Sp., January 13, 1946. There are thirty letters and other related material from Kavanagh to Fahey (FP-HGP). A letter of Kavanagh to Father Patrick O'Carroll, Provincial of the Irish Province at the time of Fahey's death (February 12, 1954) describes the efforts of Kavanagh to provide a fitting tribute for Fahey in America.

[83]Interview with Gabiel Fallon, HGP, Templeogue, Dublin, March 22, 1979. Correspondence in the FP-HGP provides evidence that McQuaid, while accepting of *Maria Duce* while Fahey was alive, required that they curtail their activities after his death.

[84]Interview with Frank Duff, Dublin, March 19, 1979.

[85]Ibid. There are two letters from Frank Duff to Fahey, April 11, and September 12, 1945, FP-HGP.

[86]Interview with Gabriel Fallon, HGP, March 22, 1979.

[87]Denis Fahey, "Father Liebermann's Faith," *The Missionary Annals of the Holy Ghost Fathers* (Dublin: St. Mary's College, Rathmines, February 1923), V. 2:28-30.

[88]Rabbi Abraham Gudansky to Father Denis Fahey, May 20, 1937, FP-HGP.

[89]Fahey to Gudansky, May 24, 1937, FP-HGP.

[90]Ibid., June 3, 1937, FP-HGP.

[91] Gudansky to Fahey, June 10, 1937, FP-HGP. The son of Rabbi Gudansky, Judge Herman Good of Dublin, shared with me something of his father's distress at Fahey's unwillingness to talk with him. Interview, Dublin Hebrew Congregation, March 10, 1979.

[92]Interview with Desmond Byrne,C.S.Sp., HGP, March 3, 1979.

[93]Copy of letter from Fahey to Archbishop John C. McQuaid, August 21, 1948, FP-HGP.

[94]Interview with the Faheys, Kilmore, September 16, 1980, and with Mary Jo Fahey, Dublin, September 17, 1980.

[95]Fahey to Nellie Fahey, December 21, 1943, FP-Kilmore.

[96]Interview with Mary Jo Fahey, Dublin, September 17, 1980.

[97]Interview with Faheys at Kilmore, September 16, 1980.

[98]Comerford, p. 3.

[99]Fahey to Nellie Fahey, August 18, 1943, FP-Kilmore.

[100]Interview with the Faheys at Kilmore, September 16, 1980.

[101]Interviews with Bernard Kelly, Michael O'Carroll, Sean Barry, Farrell Sheridan and others.

[102]See correspondence with leaders of *Maria Duce*, FP-HGP.

[103]Archbishop John C. McQuaid to Fahey, December 2, 1948, FP-HGP.

[104]Bishop Michael Brown to Fahey, January 30, 1950, FP-HGP.

[105]Archbishop Jeremiah Kinane to Fahey, January 23, 1950, FP-HGP.

[106]Archbishop Joseph Walsh to Fahey, January 15, 1950, FP-HGP.

[107]Archbishop John C. McQuaid to Fahey, January 18, 1950, FP-HGP. There is reason to believe that these volumes were from Senator Jack B. Tenny of California.

[108]Archbishop M. McGrath to Fahey, July 30, 1950, FP-HGP.

[109]Interview with John Chisholm,C.S.Sp., March 11, 1979.

[110]Ibid.

[111]Interview with Bernard Kelly,C.S.Sp., March 7, 1979.

[112]Interview with Enda Watters, C.S.Sp. and others.

[113]Interview with James McGann,C.S.Sp., HGP, August 21, 1980.

[114] Interview with Michael O'Carroll,C.S.Sp., March 13, 1979.

[115]Interview with John Chisholm,C.S.Sp., March 11, 1979.

[116]Fahey to Nellie Fahey, June 1, 1950, December 29, 1950 and August 19, 1952, FP-Kilmore.

[117]Fahey to Nellie Fahey, July 2, 1953, FP-Kilmore.

[118]Interview with Enda Watters, C.S.Sp., Berkeley, California, January 29, 1981. See also Comerford, p. 1.

[119]Interview with Mary Jo Fahey, Dublin, September 11, 1980.

[120]Interview with Enda Watters,C.S.Sp., HGP, March 26, 1979.

[121]Irish Independent, January 22, 1954. The second reference appears to be from The Standard, but no indication is on the clipping. Among the Mass cards received at the time of Fahey's death is one from The Standard. FP-HGP.

[122]Interview with Enda Watters, HGP, March 1, 1979.

[123]Archbishop McQuaid to Patrick O'Carroll,C.S.Sp., January 22, 1954. FP-HGP.

[124]Interview with John Aherne,C.S.Sp., Dublin, September 18, 1980.

[125]Interview with William Jenkinson,C.S.Sp., Berkeley, California, January 16, 1979.

[126]Interview with Bernard Kelly,C.S.Sp., Kimmage, March 7, 1979.

Chapter III

FAHEY'S "THEOLOGY OF HISTORY"

Fahey's writing career culminated in a slim volume published shortly before his death entitled *The Kingship of Christ and the Conversion of the Jewish Nation* (1953). In it he exposed his own prejudices beyond the point where many of those who had accepted his ideas (even with qualifications) were willing or able to follow. His efforts to obtain an imprimatur were met with negatives from those among the hierarchy who had previously given their names. The book was eventually published with the imprimatur of the Bishop of Ferns, but it is still unclear as to whether the episcopal approval was actually received. One story is that John English and Company of Wexford, the publishers, presumed the imprimatur. Whatever the case, Bishop James Staunton was summoned for a conversation with Archbishop McQuaid on the issue. Because the book was in circulation, there was little that could be done, but the Archbishop of Dublin let it be known that he did not want any copies sold in the bookstores in his archdiocese because "it would be inopportune."[1]

The most controversial chapter was the final one, entitled "The Coming of Antichrist." In it Fahey stated that it was probable that "the Jews will acclaim Antichrist as the Messias and will help to set up his kingdom."[2] Fahey's admirers might have believed that the Jews were involved in conspiracy and confrontation whether in capitalism or communism or both. They might have agreed that the Naturalistic philosophy of the Jews was contributing to the breakdown of movies, morals, and marriage. But to identify the Antichrist as the Jewish Messias was a theological judgment which only extremists of the worst kind accepted, particularly in the twentieth century when the practical consequences of such a thought had been so recently experienced in Nazi Germany.[3]

How could Fahey's path have led him to this final and frightening conclusion? He was "Professor of Philosophy and Church History" at the Holy Ghost Missionary College, Kimmage, Dublin. He took great pride in his Thomistic training and committed himself to the teachings of the Popes who had elevated the Angelic Doctor to an unusual status in the Catholic Church. In exploring Fahey's "theology of history," and the philosophical/ theological bases of his thought, it becomes clear that his ecclesiology was expressed in his understanding of the doctrine of "the Mystical Body of Christ" in relation to his concept of "Organized Naturalism"—a thesis of particular importance in understanding his teachings on the Jews. Key theologians, as well as four writers on whom he depended for his historical orientation, will be considered.

Fahey's preoccupation with "the Jewish question" affected his entire world view. His fears of "Jewish conspiracy" led him to accentuate the negative dimensions of his earlier work. The result was his radical conclusion of 1953.

Fahey's "Theology of History"

Fahey's world view was constructed as a "theology of history." If philosophy is defined as the science of all things in their ultimate causes as understood in the light of human reason unaided by revelation, the Irish priest believed that it was inadequate to interpret the individual and contingent facts of history.

The world, Fahey believed, had to be viewed from a supernatural perspective. The supernatural was a given without which any picture would be distorted. It worked its way in the world through human reason strengthened by faith which Fahey described as "the acceptance of the information God has given us about the world through His Son and through the Society founded by Him."[4] Attempts to present such a "theology of history" would never be sufficient until one attained the Beatific Vision, but Fahey hastened to add: "The theologian who has the Catholic faith is in touch with the full reality of the world, and can, therefore, undertake to show, however feebly and imperfectly, the interplay of the supreme realities of life."[5] Philosophers, therefore, could not reach conclusions about the reality of the divine life of grace which was lost by Adam and Eve in the fall. They could know nothing about the Mystical Body of Christ. It was clear to Fahey that what was needed was not a philosophy but a "theology of history."

In Fahey's basic presuppositions, philosophical and theological concepts were often interwoven, and from them he drew theological conclusions: (a) that the supernatural life was the only "Real Life" for a human being; (b) that an ordered plan had been given to the world by God, and all conflict stemmed from challenges to that plan on the part of the forces of disorder; (c) that "personality" represented the spiritual component in a human being and was superior to "individuality" which identified only the material dimension. All of these conclusions were based on the Thomistic philosophy and theology to which he had committed himself over the years.

Natural and Supernatural Life

The supernatural was the only "Real Life" for Denis Fahey as attested to by a four-part article with that title which he wrote for the *Irish Ecclesiastical Record* in 1926.[6] A world without the supernatural was unthinkable for him. Human beings enjoyed both sense life which they shared with lower creation, and rational life which made them superior to the animals. "Real Life," however, was supernatural life which had been lost at the time of the Fall, but was available once again as a result of the Incarnation and the Redemption which took place in Jesus.

In the first article he published in the *Irish Ecclesiastical Record* entitled "Nationality and the Supernatural," Fahey stated: "the supernatural is a higher order to which no creature has a natural right."[7] He concluded:

> Though the supernatural does not destroy the
> natural, but, on the contrary perfects it, yet we
> cannot insist too much on the point that sanctifying
> grace raises us to a higher plane to which we can lay
> no claim, and that this favour is due exclusively to
> God's inscrutable goodness.[8]

Supernatural life for Fahey was not only a reality, but also
a necessity. In his most comprehensive volume, *The Mystical Body
of Christ and the Reorganization of Society* (1945) he stated:

> As that Divine Life, infinitely superior to all
> natural life, is, of all, the most real, so the Life of
> Grace is, in the fullest and truest sense, our most
> real life. Divine Grace is life. It is not a mere
> inanimate ornament, like a luminous coating of paint
> but it is life and energy at their highest and
> sublimest.[9]

For a human being, life without the supernatural was not "Real
Life."

Naturalism, the philosophy which denied the supernatural,
was therefore a danger for everyone. Fahey warned that,
weakened by original sin, "our intelligence is darkened, our will is
weakened and our sense-life is inclined to revolt against order."[10]
Each person has within him/her "*unorganized* anti-supernatural or
naturalistic forces" that must be combatted by self-discipline and
social organization."[11]

Organized forces working for *Naturalism* were to be feared
the most. Such groups believed that human nature and human
reason were capable of providing all that was needed for the
fulfillment of humanity. They refused to believe that anything had
been revealed by God, or that God exercised any authority in the
world. Naturalists were not, therefore, just persons who believed
only in the natural; they were inherently *anti-supernatural*. When

they joined with others who had similar philosophies (rationalists, pantheists, etc.), they constituted "Organized Naturalism"—the arch-enemy of the Giver of Life and Grace, Jesus Christ.[12]

Although Fahey accepted Aquinas' thesis of "grace building on nature," he increasingly saw the natural and the supernatural in conflict. This culminated in his emphasis on "Organized Naturalism" as the body of all those forces opposed to the "Real Life" of Christ in the world. Instead of building up or building upon the natural, his vision became one of over-and-against: the Supernaturalists versus the Anti-Supernaturalists who were in league with the forces of Satan.

Fahey developed a schema paralleling "The Programme of Christ" and "The Plans of Satan" which illustrated this confrontational view. The first article of "Satan's Plans for Disorder" states: "Satan aims at preventing the acknowledgement by States and Nations of the Catholic Church as the One Way established by God for ordered return to Him." To accomplish this an effort was mounted to put all religions "including the Jewish religion on the same level as the Catholic Church." Fahey concluded that the "granting of citizenship to the Jews, who, *as a nation*, are engaged in preparing for the natural Messiah, tends in the same direction." This brief description from Fahey's seven points is but one example of his use of juxtaposition to emphasize an adversarial relationship between the program of the Supernatural Messias Jesus Christ, in confrontation with the plans of Satan for a Natural Messias—a campaign he believed was led primarily by the Jews.

Order vs. Disorder in the World

The description above also explicates Fahey's emphasis on order and disorder in the world. Drawing on his Aristotelian-Thomistic roots, the goal of life for Fahey was right order. All creation must follow an ordered path to God: "sense life" was a foundation upon which "natural life" (the rational life of intellect and will) could function; it, in turn, provided the base for the bestowal of "the supernatual life of grace." A human being could only approach God if he/she had the supernatural life of sanctifying grace. The theme of order pervades all of Fahey's writings. In the preface to *The Kingship of Christ according to the Principles of St. Thomas Aquinas* (1931), he stated clearly: "The Author hopes that this work, imperfect though it may be, will contribute in some way to the rebirth of order in the world, by helping Catholics to grasp the integral truth."[13]

The ultimate description of God, for Fahey, was order. "We must never forget that God, the last end of each of us, is the subsistent intellection of that which is—of ordered being."[14] In his magnum opus, *The Mystical Body of Christ and the Reorganization of Society* (1945), he described God as "Subsistent Love of Order:"

God is the Subsistent Act of Intelligence of the infinitely ordered Being that is Himself, so that He may be described, as the Subsistent Grasp of Infinite Order. He is at the same time the Subsistent Act of Love of the Infinite Good that is Himself. He is, therefore, Subsistent Love of Order.[15]

Fahey clung to this concept of God in all his published writings. The center of that order for Fahey was Jesus Christ. Acknowledgement of him was necessary if there were to be harmonious relations in the world.

One of the chief goals of education was to develop "an ordered mind." Fahey claimed: "The primary requisite for an ordered mind is the grasping of the subordination of the natural to the supernatural order, which has been established by God for the crowning and perfection of the natural."[16] In an article in the *Irish Ecclesiastical Record* he stated: "Good conscience, in the last analysis, is an ordered mind."[17] When seminarians capsulized all of Fahey's teachings in his expression "the grasp of order," they were not wrong.

Disorder, therefore, was the disruption of God's plan. Sin was the failure to live according to right order. These presuppositions were familiar to any student of Scholastic philosophy. For Fahey, and other ecclesiologists of his day, right order included not only the belief in God's plan which included the acknowledgement of Jesus as Messias, but also the acceptance of the Catholic Church as the official guardian of the supernatural life to be dispensed by God in the world.[18]

Those who did not accept the Catholic Church were, therefore, living in a state of disorder. Fahey acknowledged the fact that *extra ecclesiam nulla salus* should not be interpreted that "all those who die outside the visible communion of the Catholic Church are damned." He cited Pius IX's Allocution of 1854 regarding those who were kept back from the true church by "invincible ignorance." The condition of such people, however, was "sadly inferior to those who belong to the True Fold."[19] As will be noted later, the degree of lack of acceptance of Jesus as Messiah (or outright rejection of him, as Fahey saw the case of the Jews), became key in discerning who was responsible for the disorder in the world. Fahey exceeded most limits in identifying those he saw as the instigators of disorder.

Personality and Individuality

Fahey was convinced that order could be more quickly established in the world if there were a greater awareness of the Thomistic distinction between "personality" and "individuality."[20] Although a human being is both an individual and a person, individuality, according to Fahey, is based on the material element and is common to all those who have an animal nature. Individuals within a species form social groups such as the family and civil society. Right order required a subordination of these to the common good. An *individual*, therefore, was "directly ordered to society, and through society to God; for society, being God's creature, is bound in the nature of things to acknowledge its due subordination to God."[21]

Personality, the spiritual dimension of a human being, was dependent on the immaterial soul. Because of possessing intellect and will, persons were capable of knowing and loving God, the Supreme Good, and the order of the world subject to Him. As persons, human beings could transcend the material and enter into a direct relationship with God. This conviction, it should be noted, had economic and political consequences for Fahey:

> Every human being, as a *person*, is ordained directly to God and, as such, society exists for him. The political and economic arrangements of society are therefore meant to subserve the spiritual and eternal interests of the human person.... Man as an *individual* is for society, but society is for the *person*.[22]

A human being was a person only to the degree that one's reason and free will dominate over the senses and passions of one's life. Natural life must be subordinated to supernatural life, passion to reason, sense life to rational life, body to soul.[23] Development of one's individuality could lead to a selfish existence because of the emphasis on the material component. Personality, because it was derived from the immaterial soul, allowed the human being to rise above the material to the Supremely Perfect Being, God alone. An understanding of the Trinity as three Persons in one God was enhanced by this distinction, according to the Irish theologian: "Personality in the order of action is this God-centredness in opposition to self-centredness."[24]

Fahey used this distinction between personality and individuality in determining the errors of a variety of groups: Protestants, Liberals, Naturalists, and ultimately the Jews who accepted the individuality but not the personality of Jesus. Individualism was the destructive seed which lured human beings away from the sense of solidarity which they were meant to enjoy as persons in an ordered universe. Fahey concluded: "...since society exists for the development of personality, in and through

Christ, society, on which man as an individual is so dependent, must be organized along the lines dictated by our Lord Himself."[25] Failure to understand the role of the individual in society properly, Fahey was convinced, resulted in massive disorder. The proper ordination was: "...the individual is for society, as the part is for the whole, the hand for the body, but society in its turn is for the development of the person."[26]

Fahey's Ecclesiology

Fahey's theology was largely an ecclesiology. Once God was described as Subsistent Love of Order, and Christ as the Center of that Order, the chief task was to elaborate on how human beings were related to Christ, and how the world should be ordered accordingly. For Fahey, this would only happen through the Catholic Church.

The two images which dominate Fahey's theology are "the Mystical Body of Christ" and "the Kingship of Christ." It is significant that almost all of his books begin with one of these two titles. Fahey described Jesus as "Head of the Mystical Body, the Catholic Church," an equation which was common in his writings. As Head, Jesus was both High Priest and King. Fahey relied on Aquinas' distinction of the "two-fold function of the grace of Headship":

> The head has a twofold influence upon the members: an interior influence because the head submits to other members the power of moving and feeling; and an exterior influence of government, because by the sense of sight and other senses which reside in it, the head directs a man in his exterior actions (III, P.Q. 8, a.6.).[27]

Jesus Christ, therefore, as Head of the Mystical Body, had a twofold influence upon souls: "an interior influence of super-natural life because His Humanity, united to His Divinity has the power of justification; and an exterior influence by His government of His subjects."[28] Fahey pointed to the interior influence as the basis for Christ's role as Priest. Justification and sanctification flowed from this premise. Christ's Spiritual Kingship emerged from the exterior influence which allowed for the second prerogative of government and direction. Fahey hastened to distinguish the Spiritual Kingship of Christ—His primacy in the supernatural order—from the Temporal Kingship of Christ—His primacy in the natural order. In *Quas Primas*, the encyclical of Pius XI on Christ the King, Jesus was acknowledged as having power over all things, but—the Pontiff explained—"He refrained altogether from exercising such dominion and, despising the possession and administration of earthly goods, He left them to their possessors then, as He does today."[29]

Fahey made clear that Christ was a *spiritual* ruler, concerned to redeem people. The Spiritual Kingship was militant in that it involved the struggle against moral evil. In this aspect there was a close relation to Christ's Priesthood, because it was through grace and the sacraments that Christ's Spiritual Kingship would prevail.

In addition to the direct power of Christ's Spiritual Kingship through the organized life of the Mystical Body which functioned in the Catholic Church—there was the thorny doctrine of the Indirect Power of Christ's Spiritual Kingship. Basic to the acceptance of this ecclesiological concept of the Indirect Power, developed by St. Robert Bellarmine and Suarez, was the conviction that the natural and supernatural life must grow together if a person was to attain his/her Divine End. Ultimately, the natural must be subordinated to the supernatural; the temporal must bow to the spiritual. The ruler in the supernatural order, therefore, had the right of intervention in the natural order when there was a concern which affected the supernatural life of the people.[30]

The Indirect Power was not to be confused with the Temporal Kingship of Christ. Fahey readily admitted that the temporal rulers had the right and the task of providing an environment for the pursuit of a temporal end—the common good in the natural order. Temporal rulers received power from God to rule; they should not forget, however, that Christ was the Sovereign and Judge of all kings and rulers. They must render an account "by their acknowledgement of the Indirect Power of the supernatural society founded by Him, the Catholic Church, in temporal affairs."[31] It was not possible for the Spiritual Kingship to be exercised without a permanent body capable of directing souls. Fahey stated clearly: "This mission has been confided only to the Catholic Church."[32] The Church does not have direct power in temporal affairs, but does have "the right of intervening in temporal affairs in order to safeguard the interests of Divine Life."[33] Neither should these distinctions be confused with the temporal sovereignty of the Pope in the Vatican State.

The due subordination of all societies to the one supernatural society in regard to the Indirect Power of the Catholic Church became the acid test for the development of true order in the world:

Accordingly, the history of the world, viewed from the highest standpoint, to which everything else is subordinate, turns around the social acceptance and rejection of the Kingship of Christ, and thus *the attitude of States to the one supernatural society, and to the Indirect Power of the Catholic Church as the keystone of the arch of the world's social order.*[34]

In even stronger language he claimed: "...the attitude of the States to the Indirect Power of the Catholic Church is the *true test* of the world's social progress." He stated further:

The attitude, therefore, of the authority in the State towards the Kingship of Our Lord and the Catholic Church may be spoken of as the spiritual principle or soul of the civilization and is the *real touchstone* of the value of a culture, namely, its capacity to aid in forming true personality resemblance to Our Lord

Jesus Christ (cf. St. Thomas, *De Regimine Princip.*
Lib. 1. c. 15).[35]

If the Indirect Power of the Church was "the keystone of
the arch in the world's social order," "the true test of the world's
social progress," and "the real touchstone of the value of a
culture," then her words should be received without equivocation.
A direct consequence should be the unquestioning acceptance of
papal encyclicals and other statements of the pontiffs such as the
Syllabus of Errors. In *The Mystical Body of Christ in the Modern
World*, Fahey proclaimed:

> ... a Catholic who puts himself fully at the
> point of view of the Church as Christ's Mystical
> Body, continuing his mission of loving guidance,
> will receive every instruction and direction of the
> Sovereign Pontiff as a divinely-guided safeguard of
> weak human reason. This is the only attitude that
> becomes a Catholic, but it means a reaction against
> the world around us.[36]

Fahey believed that Protestant individualism was the greatest culprit
in eroding the concept of the Mystical Body.

Jesus Christ, as Head of the Mystical Body—the Catholic
Church—was Head of a living organism and it was the task of the
church to carry out his mission. Christ as Head was also "Christ as
King," ruling over a kingdom, and wielding authority as an
absolute monarch. As his vicar, the Pope shared that power. The
church as "an absolute monarchy" was dominant in Fahey's
thought. He claimed: "*...the monarchical form has been
determined by our Lord Jesus Christ.*"[37]

With Christ as King, who wielded absolute power, it was
incumbent on all men and women to accept the supernatural, supranatural Catholic Church:

Socially organized, man in the world redeemed by Our Lord is not as God wants him to be unless he accepts the supernatural, supranatural Catholic Church. The modern world has turned aside from order and is suffering for its apostasy and disorder. The great truth needs to be proclaimed unequivocally, so that the interior life with which we celebrate the Feast of the Kingship of Christ may be deepened. It is infinitely better to go down struggling for the integral truth than to win a seeming victory by whittling it down.[38]

The encyclical of Pius XI, *Quas Primas*, promulgated in 1925, which included the establishment of the Feast of Christ the King, was authoritative for Fahey in both his academic and devotional life. Commitment to Christ as King and the Catholic Church as his Kingdom were deeply ingrained in Fahey's very being. Acceptance of the church as a monarchy had vast implications for church/state relations.

Consequences for Society

"Our Lord's Kingdom is meant to come not only in individual souls and in heaven, but on earth through the submission of States and Nations to His rule."[39] This statement of Eduard Cardinal Pie had an immense impact on Fahey's life. As Fahey described in his *Apologia Pro Vita Mea*, it was through the works of this French ecclesiastic that he came to understand the meaning of Jesus' words "Thy Kingdom come!"[40] Pie, a reactionary of nineteenth century revolutionary Europe, believed that only in the union of church and state would a nation be able to proclaim the Kingship of Christ. He took seriously Jesus' injunction to teach all nations:

Remark the last words addressed by Our Lord to His Apostles before He ascended into heaven: "All power is given to me in heaven and on earth. Going therefore, teach ye all nations." Notice that Our Lord Jesus Christ does not say all men, all individuals, all families, but all nations. He does not merely say: Baptize children, teach the catechism, bless marriages, administer the sacraments, give religious burial to the dead. Of course, the mission He confers on the Apostles comprises all that, but it comprises more than that, for it has a public and social character. Jesus Christ is King of peoples and nations.[41]

Fahey believed that the monarchical form of government had been determined by Jesus for his church. Jesus was meant to be King of people and of nations. The political implications favoring monarchy seemed clear to many Catholics of that era who were fearful of liberal, socialist, and democratic movements. A union of church and state, where the one true Church had the Indirect Power to intervene in temporal affairs for the common good, was indeed the desired form of government.

A proper environment was needed, however, if Catholics were to establish the reign of Christ in their nations as well as in their hearts. Fahey, again influenced by Cardinal Pie, believed that only in Catholicizing social institutions would this be possible. He quoted the French theologian on this issue even in the frontispiece of one of his volumes:

So long as Christ does not reign over nations, His influence even over individuals remains superficial and exposed to overthrow.... If the environment is non-Catholic, it prevents him from embracing the faith, or, if he has the faith, it tends to root out of his heart every vestige of belief. If we suppose Catholic social institutions, with our Lord no longer living in the hearts of the individual members of society, then religion is merely a signboard which will soon disappear. *But, on the other hand, try to convert individuals without Catholicizing the social institutions and your work is without stability. The structure you erect in the morning others will tear down in the evening.* Is not the strategy of the enemies of God there to teach us a lesson? They want to destroy the faith in the hearts of individuals, it is true, but they direct still more vigorous efforts to the extirpation of religion from social institutions....[42]

The thirteenth century, according to Fahey, was the ideal. In that period the Mystical Body of Christ came as close to realization as at any other time in the history of the world. Society was established according to right order; the church held a dominant position in religious, social, political and cultural life; the workingmen's guilds provided for the needs of laborers; the laws regarding marriage and the family were determined by the church. Such had been the advantage of social institutions which were indeed Catholic. In *The Kingship of Christ and Organized Naturalism*, Fahey stated:

The Kingdom of God or the rule of Christ the King is present in its integrity only in so far as the whole social life of States, political and economic, is permeated with the influence of the Church. To put it in other terms, Christ fully reigns only when the programme for which He died is accepted as the one true way to peace and order in the world, and social structures in harmony with it are evolved.[43]

In the nineteenth and twentieth centuries, secular state governments attempted to control marriage and divorce laws, education, labor organizations, the arts—even the Church. Primarily, according to Fahey, they were aiming to subvert the Kingship of Christ by de-Catholicizing social institutions.

The most insidious way of undermining the Mystical Body of Christ was the liberal democratic notion, heinous for Fahey, of accepting all religions on the same level by recognizing them in state constitutions. The French Revolution was responsible for the acceptability of religious pluralism, and Fahey cited the distress of Pope Pius VII in 1814 when no mention of the Catholic religion was found in the proposed French Constitution at the time of the restoration of the French monarchy after Napoleon:

> By the fact that the freedom of all forms of worship without distinction is proclaimed, truth is confused with error, and the holy and immaculate Spouse of Christ, outside of which there can be no salvation, is placed on the same level as heretical sects and even as Jewish perfidy.[44]

Fahey examined the writings of innumerable popes on this question, particularly the encyclical *Immortale Dei* ("On the Christian Constitution of the States") 1885, and *Libertas* ("On Human Liberty") 1888, both promulgated by Leo XIII. He concluded: (a) that church and state should not be separated; (b) that some degree of toleration is acceptable, but that error has no rights; and (c) that liberty of worship is a perversion of the truth.

The Irish Constitution of 1937, therefore, was in direct violation of the writings of the Popes. True, Article 44 recognized the "Holy Catholic Apostolic and Roman Church as the guardian of the Faith professed by the majority of the citizens," and as the privileged religion; but it also recognized the Church of Ireland (Anglican), other religious bodies, and even Jewish congregations. Quoting Leo XIII that "error can have no rights," Fahey was convinced that to place all forms of divine worship on the same level was demeaning to Christ the King. The Roman Catholic Church should have been acknowledged not just as privileged because it was the church of the majority—but because it was the one true Church of Jesus Christ given by God for the salvation of the world.[45]

The result of placing all religions on the same level would be conflict, Fahey believed. Jewish and Masonic bankers and industrialists would be taking over:

> Thus it is to be feared that conflict lies ahead of us in Ireland, for the installation of the Natural Messias aimed at by the Jewish nation inevitably leads not only to the elimination of the Supernatural Messias, Our Lord Jesus Christ, but to the subjection of all nations to the Jewish nation. Citizenship of the Irish State can be for the Jews only a means for the attainment of their own national ideal.[46]

It was only a small step to conclude that those who attacked or persecuted the Church of Christ, persecuted Christ himself.[47]

Enemies of Christ: "Organized Naturalism"

"The propagation of Naturalism prior to and since the French Revolution is characterized by *organization*."[48] This statement from one of Fahey's earliest writings is basic to the theme of "Organized Naturalism" which became a battle cry for Fahey, and is unique to him. The Irish theologian brought together his passion for order, and his identification of Naturalism as the most potent anti-supernatural phenomenon. He became convinced that in the organization of Naturalistic forces, a body or entity developed which directly confronted the Mystical Body of Christ—the body of "Organized Naturalism."

Fahey's repudiation of Naturalism was common to many Catholic theologians of the nineteenth and early twentieth centuries. In *The Kingship of Christ and Organized Naturalism*, however, he accentuated the link to organization:

> Naturalism may be defined, therefore, as the attitude of mind which denies the reality of the Divine Life of Grace and of our Fall therefrom by Original Sin.

> It rejects our consequent liability to revolt against
> the order of the Divine Life, when this Life has been
> restored to us by our membership of Christ, and
> *maintains that all social life should be organized on
> the basis of this denial.* We must combat that
> mentality and proclaim the Rights of God.[49]

To support his thesis of "Organized Naturalism," he drew on the writings of the Popes, Cardinal Billot, and the "Angelic Doctor."

Regarding the conspiracy of organized evil forces, Fahey found support in papal statements, particularly Leo XIII's encyclical *Humanum Genus* ("On Freemasonry"), 1884, which he included in its full text in *The Kingship of Christ and Organized Naturalism.*[50] Fahey quoted Pius XI from *Ubi Arcano Dei* on the need for organization: "It is necessary, therefore, that human society be rightly organized, in order that the Church, following its divine mission, be in a position to defend the rights of God towards men, individually as well as collectively."[51] The Church needed to be organized to combat the enemies of the Church who were very well organized.

Louis Cardinal Billot, S.J., whose influence Fahey had experienced at the Gregorian University in Rome, echoed the same cry. Fahey, in his *Apologia*, lauded Volume II of Billot's *De Ecclesia* on the relationship of the church to civil society, which "enabled me to grasp the meaning of the Kingship of Christ and see the horror of the Liberalism of so much of my previous studies," referring to preparation for his undergraduate degree at the Royal University in Dublin.[52] Billot admitted the existence of "impiety" in other eras, but feared the spirit and organized efforts of modern Liberalism: "Impiety has never been absent from the world, and impiety was always a crime, but it has not always had the same character, the same intensity, the same *organization.*[53] Liberals in the modern period wanted not only to organize humankind without God, but—under Satan—militantly aimed to eliminate the influence of God from the world:

Liberty is the pretext; liberty is the idol destined to seduce peoples, an idol which has hands and yet will not feel, which has feet and will not walk, a lifeless deity, under whose aegis Satan is preparing to reduce nations to a state of slavery far worse than that in which he held the ancient world under the material idol of paganism. But religion is the matter at stake. *We want, they proclaim, to organize a humanity that can get on without God.* [54]

Fahey, in all of his volumes, divided the organized evil forces into (1) the invisible organized force—Satan, and (2) the visible organized forces—the Jews and Freemasons. The linchpin for Fahey in terms of developing the concept of Organized Naturalism was the establishment of Satan as the head of all evil men and women. Ultimately there would be the great battle between Christ and Satan: Christ the Head of the Mystical Body, and Satan the head of all evil men and women. To delineate how Organized Naturalism had evolved, it was necessary to understand the struggle around the divinity of Christ from the time of his crucifixion. Fahey discussed this at length in *The Kingship of Christ according to the Principles of St. Thomas Aquinas.* The Irish theologian drew on the *Summa Theologica* of Aquinas regarding the agents of Christ's passion and death (cf. III, Q.41, a.1; Q.42, a.2, Q.47, a.4,5,6.). Thomas listed those involved in Jesus' death in the order of their malevolence and guilt as follows: (1) Satan, (2) the leaders of the Jewish nation, (3) the rank and file of Jews, and (4) the Gentiles, Pilate, and the soldiers who acted as executioners. [55]

It was, therefore, in the context of the crucifixion that Satan was established as "the head and leader of all forces opposed to the supernatural life which comes from Our Lord." [56] Fahey again quoted the *Summa Theologica*: "Inasmuch, therefore, as men are drawn to revolt from God by sinning, they come under the government and direction of the evil one: he is accordingly styled their head." (III a., P.Q. VIII.a.7.). [57] Fahey concluded: "The leader, therefore, against whom we have to struggle for the Kingship of Christ is Satan."[58]

After an extended discussion of the role of the Jews in the death of Jesus, Fahey claimed: "...*all those who reject the supernatural, by refusing to submit to God's order, come under the leadership of Satan*, who was the first to reject the supernatural."[59] Fahey again quoted Aquinas: "It is in this latter fashion [by exterior guidance] that the devil is the head of all men" (cf. IIIa., P.Q. VIII. a.7). The Irish priest gave Satan a new appellation: "Satan was thus the First Naturalist and became the leader, so far as exterior guidance is concerned, of all those who revolt against the supernatural order."[60]

In his later volume, *The Mystical Body of Christ and the Reorganization of Society*, Fahey developed a statement on "The Headship of Satan according to St. Thomas." According to the two-fold function of headship as described earlier in relationship to the Mystical Body of Christ, he quoted Aquinas as stating that although Jesus was head by interior and exterior influence, Satan was influential by exterior guidance alone, which he accomplished by directing the acts of sinners to his own end—that of the destruction of the order by which men return to God.[61] Satan was, therefore, the head of the body of Organized Naturalism. It should be noted here, that Fahey never used the expression "Mystical Body of Satan."

Although Fahey was committed all of his life to exposing the evils of Freemasonry, he frequently did so by establishing its relationship to the Jews. The sequence of chapters in *The Mystical Body of Christ and the Reorganization of Society* is significant: Cbapter VII, "The Invisible Organized Force—Satan and His Fellow Demons;" Chapter VIII, "The First Visible Organized Naturalistic Force—the Jewish Nation;" Chapter IX, "The Second Visible Organized Force—Freemasonry;" and Chapter X, "Links between Organized Anti-Supernatural Forces."[62] This linkage of Satan, Jews and Free-masons as major components in the body of Organized Naturalism is dominant in Fahey's thought.

Fahey believed that Freemasonry had brought into existence *"a naturalistic caricature of the Mystical Body of Christ."*[63] This was blasphemy. The result in Europe and America was "the naturalistic supranationalism of Freemasonry behind which has been looming up the still more strongly organized naturalistic supranationalism of the Jewish Nation."[64] Fahey had no doubts as to the connections between Satan, Jews and Freemasons.

Fahey's Historical Orientation

Fahey was described by one of his younger colleagues, Michael O'Carroll,C.S.Sp., as "an *a priori* historian."[65] He began with very definite Christian theological presuppositions and constructed a system through which he explained all the events of history. Fahey shifted easily from the speculative to the concrete. He came to conclusions in the practical order as if he were doing a syllogism. Fahey not only believed in a master plan revealed by God, but he completely identified that plan with his own explanation of it. His particular deductive approach left no space for other interpretations.

The philosophical/theological presuppositions out of which Fahey operated became, for him, "historical data." His understanding of the supernatural, the struggle between order and disorder, and manifestations of "personality" and "individuality" evolved into "truths" beyond question. His historical presuppositions simply advanced his case further: (1) that all human beings in history are ordained to eternal life according to the Divine Plan for Order; (2) that Satan was the leader of the forces of Organized Naturalism in the world; and (3) that humankind was in a constant struggle between those who accepted the True Supernatural Messias, and those who were awaiting the Natural Messias. In "Our Lord's Programme for Order," and "Satan's Plans for Disorder," Fahey decided—according to his interpretation of church history—which persons or groups belonged on which side of the ledger.

Fahey's undergraduate degree from the Royal University in Dublin included honors in civil and constitutional history. As he admitted in his *Apologia*, he had been repelled by many of the books he had been required to read. This tension was intensified for him while studying in Rome during the Modernism crisis "with its naturalistic separation of the historian and the believer."[66] As mentioned earlier, volumes were assigned for reading in the refectory while he was living at the *Séminaire Française* which became examples for Fahey of how history should be approached, particularly *Les Origines de la Civilisation Moderne* by Godefroid Kurth, and *Les Sociétés Secrètes et la Société* by Nicholas Deschamps, S.J. Fahey stated: "These two books furnished me with the two guiding lines of the Theological and Historical studies which I have pursued ever since."[67] In addition to Kurth and Deschamps, two other authors—Jacques Maritain and Nesta Webster—will be discussed as writers who influenced Fahey's historical orientation.

Godefroid Kurth

Godefroid Kurth (1847-1916), a Knight of the Order of Pius IX, was Director of the Belgian Historical Institute in Rome from 1906-1916, part of which time Fahey was also in the Eternal City. Prior to that, Kurth was Professor of the State University of Liège, Belgium (1872-1906). His specialties included medieval history and the history of Belgium.[68] His second volume of *Les Origines de la Civilisation Moderne* concluded with a chapter on Charlemagne. Fahey described Kurth's work as "...one of the loveliest books ever written." It "showed the Mystical Body of Christ transforming the pagan society of the Roman Empire and preparing the upward movement of acknowledgement of the programme of Our Lord Jesus Christ, Head of the Mystical Body, Priest and King."[69]

More valuable for Fahey's purposes as a teacher was Kurth's *L'Eglise aux Tournants de l'Histoire*, a small volume later translated as *The Church at the Turning Points in History*.[70] In it

Kurth described Christian civilization as "essentially opposed to that of ancient society"—not simply as a matter of degree, "but of a difference of nature." Antiquity would never have been able to solve the problems of existence because its concept of human life was so different. In Christianity, however, "Man is not a child of chance—he is a creature of God." This was the foundation for a new vision of the world.[71]

Roman culture, however, did provide the church with the possibility of expressing herself in social and cultural institutions, a favorite subject of Fahey's. In *Les Origines de la Civilisation Moderne*, Kurth discusses this "Roman link":

> Christianity, as a scheme which was meant to be universal, was obliged to seek its *materia subjecta* in a human culture in itself endowed with a potential universality. The Eastern and Hellenic cultures broke down in the tests of God's laboratory, and it was the Roman culture alone which stood the assay. Christianity must find expression in social and political institutions, stamped with the true character of human social life, if this latter is to be as harmonious as nature postulates, and if it is to make for human progress and development. The Roman culture has wonderfully supplied the potential material for the "informing process" of Christianity....[72]

Rome, although it functioned with a defective philosophy, contributed to the Church the system of Roman Law with its domination of reason over passion. Within that milieu the Church was able to elevate the code and proclaim its own supernatural mission.

The "turning points in history" for Kurth included: (1) the break in relationship between the church and the Jews in the first century; (2) the church and the barbarians; (3) the church and feudalism; (4) the church and neo-Caesarism; (5) the church and the Renaissance; and (6) the church and the French Revolution.[73]

Surprisingly, "the Protestant Revolt" is omitted as a specific topic. With that one exception, Fahey's historical writings follow a similar pattern.

When discussing "The Church and the Jews," Kurth proposed the question, "What were the obstacles to hinder Christianity from becoming a universal religion, and how did she succeed in overcoming them?" He believed that as long as Christianity retained its link to Judaism, the message would not really be available to the wider world. Peter's vision in Acts 10:9-10 was for the purpose of opening up God's revelation in Christ to all humanity. Kurth concluded: "There is nothing now in common between Israel rejected, shut up within her synagogue, and the people of God gathered around the Church."[74]

The struggles that surrounded the Council of Jerusalem led to internal problems in the Church. The destruction of Jerusalem in 70 C.E. was, for Kurth, a decisive revelation: "After this it was plain that Israel was no longer the people of God, but a rejected nation. It is no longer worth while to fix upon it the attention of history."[75] Fahey, by his own admission, was influenced by Kurth. He sang his praises to every class. He did not, however, follow Kurth's advice in regard to history and the Jews. Fahey fixed a major part of his attention upon them.

Nicholas Deschamps, S.J.

The second "guiding line" mentioned by Fahey, *Les Sociétés Secrètes et la Société* by Nicholas Deschamps, S.J., was described by the Irish priest in his *Apologia* as follows—quoting in part from Leo XIII:

> The latter [volume] showed that the revolutions of the modern world "were but one phase in the development of a pre-arranged plan, which is being carried out over an ever-widening area to multiply the ruins of which We have previously spoken." (Pope Leo XIII, Review of Our Pontificate, March

19, 1902). I understood that all the revolutions were bringing about the elimination of the rule of Christ the King in view of ultimately eliminating the Mass and the Supernatural Life of Christ, the Supreme High Priest.[76]

Nicholas Deschamps, S.J. (1797-1872) was born in Villefranche, France, and entered the Society of Jesus in 1826. He taught literature and rhetoric and wrote, apart from a few didactic and devotional books, polemical works on the crucial questions of the day such as state faculties of theology, the Organic Articles, liberty of association, paganism in education, and communism. His most famous work, mentioned above, was not published until after his death.[77] Edward Cahill, S.J., Fahey's friend and author of *Freemasonry and the Anti-Christian Movement*, described Deschamps' work as: "Incomparably the best general survey of the anti-Christian and revolutionary activities of Freemasonry and kindred secret societies in all countries during the past two centuries."[78]

Deschamps traced European Freemasonry back to Manichaeism. He saw in the phenomenon a sinister force disguised as philanthropy, working against religion and also against the social order, patriotism, and morality.[79] In *The Mystical Body of Christ and the Reorganization of Society*, Fahey referred to *Les Sociétés Secrètes et la Société* as a monumental work. Although he admitted not quoting Deschamps directly in his chapter, he stated that the work was "continually utilized." Fahey imbibed Deschamps' view of a world permeated with plots and conspiracies against the Kingship of Christ. Although the content focused on Freemasonry and other secret societies, Fahey's perception of the relationship between Jews and Freemasons allowed for Deschamps' ideas to spill over to Fahey's attitude toward the Jews. This was not without foundation in Deschamps. One section of Deschamps' work on "Le Rôle des Juifs dans la Maçonnerie," discussed Judaism and Masonry as "parallel institutions."[80] Both groups, he claimed, were corrupting the world by their naturalistic ideas.

Jacques Maritain

Fahey used the writings of the French philosopher Jacques Maritain (1882-1973) selectively. Maritain's small volume, *Three Reformers* (1928), a type of intellectual history, provided Fahey with three figures on whom to focus when tracing the history of ideas in the modern world: Luther, Descartes, and Rousseau—a reformer of religion, a reformer of philosophy, and a reformer of morality. Maritain believed them to be "the begetters of what M. Gabriel Seailles called the modern conscience."[81] Maritain's approach, while different, was not unlike Kurth's in looking for "the turning points" in history, but for Maritain it was the history of ideas.

A substantial portion of Maritain's first chapter on Luther was devoted to "The Individual and the Person." He discussed Luther's "egocentrism," and how the reformer's theology of grace as "extrinsic" contributed to the disintegration of the Thomistic ideal. Fahey acknowledged his indebtedness to Maritain in *The Mystical Body of Christ in the Modern World* and added: "M. Maritain shows that Luther's career is a triumph of Individuality as opposed to Personality."[82] This is only one example of Fahey's reliance on an early work of Maritain.[83] *Three Reformers* is one of the few volumes of the French scholar that some would consider polemical.

Maritain's *The Things That Are Not Caesar's*, a translation of *Primauté du Spirituel* (1927), was first published in English in 1930. Fahey quoted frequently from this volume and it is specifically mentioned by John Charles McQuaid,C.S.Sp. in his preface to *The Kingship of Christ According to the Principles of St. Thomas Aquinas* as a work complementary to Fahey's. Maritain in his discussion of the temporal and spiritual powers of the church stated directly: "It is in the 'indirect power' of the Church of Christ over the temporal domain that the primacy of the spiritual finds its most concrete realisation in the most apparent, vivid, and significant manner."[84] His first chapter focused on "The Two Powers," while in the second he discussed the relationship of the "indirect power" to "the crisis lately traversed by a number of Catholics in France"—namely the condemnation of the *Action Française*.[85] Maritain had for a time been involved with the *Action Française*, and felt deeply about the papal statements condemning certain works of the leader, Charles Maurras, and the newspaper *L'Action Française*. This event caused him to delve into political philosophy, and to examine the question of the "indirect power" of the church in temporal affairs. He wrote in his diary many years later:

> Today more than ever, I bless the liberating intervention of the Church which, in 1926, exposed the error of the Action Française, following which I finally examined Maurras'doctrines and saw what they were worth. There began for me then a period of reflection devoted to moral and political philosophy in which I tried to work out the character of authentically Christian politics and to establish, in the light of a philosophy of history and of culture, the true significance of democratic inspiration and the nature of the new humanism for which we are waiting.[86]

Fahey, too, was affected by the papal condemnation of the *Action Française*. While there is no evidence that he was involved directly with the movement, two persons whom Fahey ardently admired—Louis Cardinal Billot, S.J. and Henri L'Floch,C.S.Sp.— were removed from powerful positions of authority by Pius XI, allegedly because of connections to the right-wing group.[87] Both Fahey and Maritain were challenged to examine their ideas of authority as a result of the papal action. The Irish priest responded with his staunch sense of obedience and loyalty to the papacy, by adhering to "the letter of the law." Maritain—while no less obedient—moved in the direction of an "integral humanism."

As Maritain's thought grew and developed, expressed first in *Humanisme Intégral* (1936), he became more accepting of a democratic system, and religious liberty. His anti-Franco stand during the Spanish Civil War was particularly painful to Fahey. A Spanish article criticizing the French philosopher, "La Nueva Christiandad de Jacques Maritain," by E. Guerrero, S.J. in the Fahey Papers, was used as documentation by the Irish priest on the Spanish situation. Guerrero concluded: "It is evident, then, that the new Christian society of Maritain is not Christian but a manifest denial of Catholic principles, and a scandalous translation in vague Christian-sounding phrases of a Masonic type of society."[88] Fahey connected this "Masonic type of society" to the Jews. In *The Mystical Body of Christ and the Reorganization of Society* he stated:

> In the Spanish crisis, M. Maritain seemed to lose sight of the fact that the horrible designs of the Jewish Rulers of Russia were a consequence of Israel's refusal to conform its will to the will of God. It is also a sign of the deplorable decay of the doctrine of the Mystical Body of Christ in the world that a man of M. Maritain's knowledge and ability should set out to direct the world, with regard to the interests of Our Divine Lord in Spain, in concrete opposition to the Spanish hierarchy.[89]

Although *Les Juifs parmi les Nations* (English translation, *Anti-Semitism*) by Maritain does not seem liberal by today's standards, Fahey thought the French philosopher was soft on the Jews. Maritain stated: "To be hated by the world is the glory of the Jews as it is the glory of Christians who live by faith."[90] Fahey attempted to refute Maritain:

> Now, the world of which Our Lord speaks in the Gospel is the entire collection of forces marshalled by Satan against the Supernatural Life of Grace. It

is, therefore, the naturalistic camp, of which Satan is the leader. The Jews, under their rulers, entered that camp, and led the others in the attack on the Supernatural Life in Person, Our Lord Jesus Christ.[91]

More than one person who knew Fahey stated that the Irish priest explained Maritain's attitude toward the Jews by reminding them that his wife, Raissa, was a convert from Judaism. How could the French philosopher be objective about the question?[92]

Maritain and Fahey corresponded in their earlier years. The letters of Maritain to Fahey were warm and friendly. When writing on November 30, 1923, Maritain commended the Irish priest for preparing an article on the influence of Nominalism on Luther's theology, and offered a few suggestions. He requested a copy of Fahey's article on "The Introduction of Scholastic Philosophy into Irish Secondary Education" recently published in *The Irish Ecclesiastical Record*.[93] The French philosopher's letter of May 1926 was largely on art and Scholasticism. He expressed his belief that "romantic art" suffered from two defects: (1) the "disequilibrium of intimacy," and (2) "intellectual indigence." A shorter note of August 3, 1930 thanked Fahey for some articles and suggested some of his own that would be published soon.[94] It is noteworthy that the majority of references to Maritain in any of Fahey's writings are from this early period during which they were communicating, and when Fahey was in agreement with Maritain's thought.

In the early 1950s, Fahey carried on correspondence with two young Frenchmen—a Holy Ghost Father, Hevre Le Lay (who later left the Congregation, but not the priesthood), and his friend, Paul Poitevin. They sent Fahey typed articles in French, many of which were anti-Maritain. Some of the titles include: "Un immense danger: LE MARITAINISME," "Jacques Maritain n'est plus un philosophe catholique et Thomiste," and "JACQUES MARITAIN ET LA MAIN TENDUE AU MARXISME." In a letter of November 12, 1951, Poitevin thanked Fahey for sending him a copy of "Mythe le Maritain," which he passed on to Père Le Lay.[95]

The letters from Le Lay and Poitevin indicate that they were in sympathy with rightist elements in both the church and state. They supplied Fahey with French material, keeping him current with articles on objections to Maritain, on the Masons, and on the occult—one article entitled: "Jésuites et Occultisme."[96] Poitevin also sold copies of Fahey's books in France. Other French anti-Maritain material was sent to Fahey by Philippe Levagne d'Ortigue from Paris, December 3, 1950.[97]

Fahey continued to quote at length from Maritain's earlier works, particularly *Three Reformers* and *The Things That Are Not Caesar's*. Maritain's effort to reflect on philosophical questions as related to historical personages and events was also a goal of Fahey's. The Irish priest was unwilling, however, to explore new philosophical vistas, even within a Thomistic terrain such as Maritain's. Fahey was influenced by the early work of the prolific French writer, but felt the need to refute Maritain's later writings. Certainly he would not succumb to the "naturalistic separation of the historian and the believer."[98]

Nesta Webster

Fahey's admiration for Nesta Webster, an English writer, was well known by his students and colleagues. Exactly when he discovered her writings is uncertain, but in the preface to Fahey's *The Kingship of Christ according to the Principles of St. Thomas Aquinas* (1931), John Charles McQuaid singled her out as an enlightened Protestant who perceived the true problems of the world overlooked by some Catholic writers. The future archbishop wrote "of the non-Catholic, Mrs. Nesta Webster, who, though she has always been gravely hampered by the want of the True Faith, has yet proved one of the most able historians."[99] Her influence on Fahey's work was noted as positive. It should, of course, be recalled that McQuaid was a student of Fahey's in his seminary days.

One of Webster's earlier volumes, *World Revolution: The Plot against Civilization* (1921), was frequently quoted in Fahey's writings. Webster believed that twentieth century revolutionary movements were born in the middle of the eighteenth century, and found their first expression in France in 1789. What the world was experiencing in the 1920s was a continuation: "The revolution through which we are now passing is not local but universal, it is not political but social, and its causes must be sought not in popular discontent, but in deep-laid conspiracy that uses people to their own undoing."[100]

Some historians have written about socialism, anarchism, and communism as outward revolutionary movements. Others have written about hidden powers and secret groups which have attempted to manipulate world events. Webster's effort was "to trace the connection between the two in the form of a continuous narrative." She stated clearly:

> The object of this book is, therefore, to describe not only the evolution of Socialist and Anarchist ideas and their effects in succeeding revolutionary outbreaks, but at the same time to follow the workings of that occult force, terrible, unchanging, relentless, and wholly destructive, which constitutes the greatest menace that has ever confronted the human race.[101]

Webster herself relied on Deschamps' work, as well as A. Cowan, *The X-Rays of Freemasonry*, and Werner Sombart's *The Jews and Capitalism*—all volumes from which Fahey quoted liberally. She emphasized the involvement of the Jews in secret societies and in the Bolshevik Revolution, and used parallel columns to compare sections from *The Protocols of the Elders of Zion* with documents of Illuminism, Bolshevism, and other revolutionary groups.[102]

Secret Societies and Subversive Movements (1924) was a sequel to *World Revolution*. In the preface Webster responded to criticisms that she received in the first volume. She stated: "...we are accused of raising a false alarm, of creating a bogey, or of being the victims of an obsession. Up to a point this is comprehensible."[103] The problem was that the English were oblivious to the machinations of secret societies so commonplace on the continent. She claimed that she would "not base assertions on merely 'anti-Semite' works, but principally on the writings of the Jews themselves."[104] Substantial sections of the book were devoted to the Essenes, Gnosticism, and the Kabbala as Jewish sources for the origins of Freemasonry.

The Protocols of the Elders of Zion was the subject of Appendix II of this later volume. Webster's opening declaration claimed: "Contrary to the assertions of certain writers, I have never affirmed my belief in the authenticity of the Protocols, but have always treated it as an entirely open question." Webster's thesis was that the Protocols are not a forgery copied largely from Maurice Joly's Dialogues aux Enfers entre Machiavel et Montesquieu (1864) as many believed. The resemblance existed because they were both copied from a common source.[105]

Nesta Webster, in a letter to Fahey in 1939, replying to a request of the Irish priest for notes she might have on this subject, admitted that she did not have a script as such. Rather, she had purchased a copy of the Dialogues and compared it to the Protocols paragraph by paragraph. She then marked a copy of the Protocols "showing which passages were identical with the 'Dialogues,' which were added and which were missing." From this process she concluded that both books drew on a common source.[106]

With apologies, she told Fahey that she "dare not send it by post to Ireland because it is of great value to me." She would be happy to have him see the copy if he were to come to England, "Or if you have some friend in London perhaps you could send him your own copy and he could transfer the marks from mine into it."[107] Marie G. Endean, a young woman of college years whose family knew and admired Fahey, and with whom he corresponded, accomplished that task for him.[108] In a letter of March 3, 1939,

Webster confirmed the fact that Miss Endean would be undertaking that project.[109]

Fahey's acceptance of Webster's view was by no means total. Attached to the flyleaf of his copy of *World Revolution* are two long typed sheets entitled "Some Notes on Mrs. Webster's Philosophy of Life," almost certainly by Fahey. He stated: "On account of the great value of Mrs. Webster's contributions to Modern History, it may be useful to give some guidance to Catholic readers concerning Mrs. Webster's philosophy of life as revealed in *Secret Societies and Subversive Movements.*" He then added: "... the esteemed historian is not clear about the infinite distance which separates natural life, even though spiritual, from Supernatural life." Fahey's critique focused largely on theological questions involving possible salvation for those who have never heard of Christ. He feared that Webster's thesis was too broad, and if brought to conclusion "Mahomet is put on the same level as Our Lord."[110]

Fahey's appreciation of Webster was well known at the seminary at Kimmage. Although others often questioned her credentials as a historian, he spoke of her glowingly. Her work was particularly useful to him in regard to the *Protocols*. Fahey followed the same line as Henry Ford, Charles Coughlin, and Nesta Webster, all of whom admitted that they could not prove the authenticity of the document—but stated vehemently that what was described in the *Protocols* was what was going on in the world at that time. Fahey's increased tendency to use the *Protocols* as if they were authentic was encouraged by the information which Webster provided. She was, for him, "a twentieth century Deschamps," contributing material on secret societies, Jews and Freemasons.

Kurth, Deschamps, Maritain, and Webster—four influences on Fahey's historical orientation. Kurth and the early Maritain saw history in terms of "turning points;" Deschamps and Webster were consumed with fear of conspiracy and secret societies, and convinced that world revolution was being achieved by Jews and Freemasons. Reliance on these authors furthered Fahey's project of focusing on the Jews as the cause of "anti-supernaturalism" in the world.

Principal themes for Fahey were always "the Mystical Body of Christ," and "the Kingship of Christ." His three small volumes which begin with the title "Kingship of Christ" were more theologically oriented. The two major tomes which begin with the title "Mystical Body of Christ" emphasized the historical dimension, and attempted to portray how the Divine Plan for Order was accepted or rejected through the centuries.[1] The two themes are by no means mutually exclusive; his approaches—historical and theological—are interwoven, but the distinction is helpful in analyzing Fahey's work.

"The Mystical Body of Christ" for Fahey was coextensive with the Roman Catholic Church. This required a consideration of the church's involvement in history as part of the Divine Plan. Fahey believed that he understood that plan, and expanded it in his more historical volumes to include a variety of subjects such as economics, education, and ecology. As he integrated all of these elements into his theology of "Organized Naturalism," Fahey committed himself to alerting humankind to possible diabolical effects from the programs of those who had "rejected" Christ. His "theology of history" did not admit of any who had not accepted "Real Life." For Fahey, the Jews were foremost in that category.

[1]Interview with Enda Watters,C.S.Sp., HGP, March 12, 1979. Confirmed in interviews with Bernard Kelly,C.S.Sp., and John Chisholm, C.S.Sp.

[2]KCCJN, p. 184. Fahey accepted the thesis of Fr. Augustine Lémann in his book *L'Antéchrist* (Paris: Librairie Catholique Emmanuel Vitte, 1905), as will be discussed later.

[3]See below regarding pressure exerted by Fahey over John Chisholm,C.S.Sp. for a favorable review of KCCJN in the IER.

[4]*The Mystical Body of Christ in the Modern World* (Dublin: Browne and Nolan, Ltd., 1938), 2nd ed. rev. and enl., p. 1. Hereafter MBCMW.

[5]Ibid.

[6]"Our Real Life," IER 27 (1926): 490-502; 27 (1926): 611-629; 29 (1927): 600-616; 30 (1927): 41-53.

[7]IER 21 (1923):261.

[8]Ibid., pp. 261-262.

[9]*Mystical Body of Christ and the Reorganization of Society* (Cork: The Forum Press, 1945), p. 3. Hereafter MBCRS.

[10]Ibid., p. 6.

[11]Ibid., p. 7.

[12]*The Kingship of Christ and Organized Naturalism* (Cork: The Forum Press, 1943). Hereafter KCON.

[13]KCPSTA, p. 13. See also *Mental Prayer According to the Principles of St. Thomas Aquinas* (Dublin: M.H. Gill and Son, Ltd., 1927), p. 14, hereafter MPPSTA; and IER, Vol. 30 (1927).

[14]"Latin and the Supernatural," IER 23 (1924):196.

[15]MBCRS, p. 1.

[16]"Latin and the Supernatural," IER 23 (1924): 196.

[17]"The Introduction of Scholastic Philosophy into Irish Secondary Education," IER 22 (1923):181.

[18]"Nationality and the Supernatural," IER 21 (1923):262. Fahey had a particular reverence for Louis Cardinal Billot's second volume of *De Ecclesia Christi*.

[19]Ibid.

[20]"Human Personality and Individuality," IER 59 (1942):339-348. Reprinted in MBCRS, pp. 12-20 with exception of concluding paragraph.

[21]Ibid., p. 340.

[22]Ibid., p. 341.

[23]"Latin and the Supernatural," IER 23 (1924): 196.

[24]"Human Personality and Individuality," IER 59 (1942): 339-348.

[25]Ibid., p. 347.

[26]Ibid., p. 348.

[27]KCPSTA, p. 20.

[28]Ibid., p. 21.

[29]Ibid., pp. 21-22.

[30]Ibid., pp. 24-25. See also MBCRS, pp. 40-41.

[31]Ibid., pp. 26-27.

[32]Ibid., pp. 27-28.

[33]Ibid., pp. 31-32. Fahey acknowledged that he based his work on a series of articles by Ch. V. Heris,O.P., a Professor at the Dominican House of Studies at Le Saulchoir, Belgium, which was in *The Catholic Mind* (Dublin) "since April 1931"—"with the author's kind permission."

[34]Ibid., pp. 34-35. Emphasis added.

[35]Ibid., pp. 36-37. Emphasis added.

[36]MBCMW, pp. 141-142.

[37]MBCMW, p. 14. Emphasis added.

[38]KCPSTA, pp. 38-39.

[39]APVM, p. 3 of ms.; p. 2 of typed copy.

[40]Ibid. All of the quotations of Cardinal Pie in Fahey's writings are from *La Royauté de N.S. Jésus-Christ d'après le Cardinal Pie* by P. Théotime de Saint-Just (Paris: Société et Librairie S. François d'Assise, 1925). None are from the several volumes of Pie's writings. When Fahey acknowledged his indebtedness to this volume in the introduction to MBCRS, he cited it in French with the English title in parenthesis. Thereafter, and in other volumes with no indication to the contrary, he cited the title in English. There is, however, no English translation, as far as this writer can determine.

[41]KCON, p. 124. Fahey indicated that this quotation was cited from pp. 24-25 of Théotime de Saint-Just's volume. It is not to be found there, or anywhere in that source, although the second edition is the only one available. See also pp. 182-183 on the union of Church and State as the first condition for Christian government according to Cardinal Pie.

[42]MBCMW, pp. 158-159. Emphasis added. See also Godefroid Kurth, *The Workingmen's Guild of the Middle Ages* (Cork: The Forum Press, 1943), trans. Denis Fahey, C.S.Sp., and Stephen Rigby, p. 3. The citations in both Fahey volumes state that the quotation is on p. 59 of T. de Saint-Just's work referred to above. It is not there, but is substantively included in that volume in n. 5, pp. 93-94 as a quotation in *Pages Choisis de Cardinal Pie*, Introduction, LXI.

[43]KCPSTA, pp. 48-49.

[44]Letter of Pius VII to Msgr. de Boulogne, Bishop of Troyes, April 29, 1814, as cited in KCPSTA, pp. 48-49.

[45]MBCMW, pp. 251-252. Article 44 of the Irish Constitution continued to be an issue around which Fahey and the *Maria Duce* crusaded even into the 1950s.

[46]Ibid., p. 253.

[47] KCPSTA, p. 109.

[48]Ibid., p. 71. Emphasis added.

[49]KCON, p. 36. Emphasis added.

[50]Ibid., pp. 54-80.

[51]KCPSTA, pp. 110-111. The quotation is repeated on p. 146.

108

[52]APVM, p. 2 of copy; p. 3 of ms. Fahey said in discussing this volume: "I went over it twice during my stay in Rome, and at least twice more since then. That does not mean I simply read it. No, I have gone over it between four and five times in mental prayer, asking Our Lord to help me to *understand* it and *teach* it and *live* it."

[53]Louis Billot,S.J., *De Ecclesia Christi* (Rome: S.C. de Propaganda Fide, 1903), II, 38, quoted in KCPSTA, p. 71.

[54]Ibid., p. 42, quoted in KCPSTA, pp. 72-73. Emphasis added.

[55]KCPSTA, pp. 117-118.

[56]Ibid., p. 119.

[57]Ibid. Cf. *Summa Theologica* (New York: Benziger Brothers, 1947), II, 2080-2081.

[58]KCPSTA, pp. 117-118.

[59]Ibid., p. 129.

[60]Ibid.

[61]MBCRS, p. 231.

[62]Ibid., xix-xx. See also KCON, p. 5.

[63] Ibid., p. 210. Fahey stated: "Satan pleaded, too, for an oath of secrecy, knowing its appeal to the curious and the adventurous. Thus was brought into existence *a naturalistic caricature* of the Mystical Body of Christ, in which men reject the Supernatural Life of Grace and, in addition, go against their natural reason by an oath of blind obedience." Emphasis added.

[64]Ibid.

[65]Interview with Michael O'Carroll,C.S.Sp., March 13, 1979.

[66]APVM, p. 3 of copy; p. 4 of ms.

[67]Ibid., p. 1 of copy; p. 1 of ms.

[68]See Godefroid Kurth, *The Church at the Turning Points of History*, trans. Victor Day (Helena, Montana: Naegle Printing Co., 1918), p. 13.

[69]APVM, p. 1 of copy; p. 1 of ms.

[70]Kurth, *The Church at the Turning Points of History*. See foreword by Bishop John P. Carroll of Helena, Montana, pp. 3-11. Former students of Fahey's (Enda Watters, Michael McCarthy, Desmond Byrne and Leo Layden), remember this volume as one which Fahey recommended most highly.

[71]Kurth, pp. 15-17.

[72]Godefroid Kurth, *Les Origines de la Civilisation Moderne* (Paris: Victor Retaux, Libraire-Editeur, 1898), quoted in "Latin and the Supernatural," IER 23 (1924): 194-195. I could not locate the passage in Vol. I, Chapter 4, pp. 156 ff. as Fahey indicated.

[73]Kurth, *The Church at the Turning Points of History*, pp. 22-23.

[74]Ibid., pp. 25-26.

[75]Ibid., p. 40.

[76]APVM, p. 1 of copy, p. 1 of ms.

[77]J.F. Sollier, "Nicholas Deschamps," *Catholic Encyclopedia* (New York: Encyclopedia Press, Inc., 1908), IV, p. 748.

[78]Edward Cahill,S.J., *Freemasonry and the Anti-Christian Movement* (Dublin: M.H. Gill and Son, Ltd., 1949). In the preface to the first edition (1929), Cahill states: "The writer wishes to acknowledge with gratitude his indebtedness to the Rev. Dr. Fahey,C.S.Sp., of Blackrock College, for his generous and effective assistance which he has given him. Dr. Fahey placed at the writer's disposal some of his own papers; and was always ready to assist him with the deep and comprehensive knowledge of the subject which he himself possesses." (xiii-xiv)

[79]Sollier, p. 748.

[80]Nicholas Deschamps, *Les Sociétés Secrètes et la Société* (Paris: Oudin Frères, 1882), III, p. 24.

110

[81]Jacques Maritain, *Three Reformers: Luther—Descartes—Rousseau* (London: Sheed and Ward, 1947), p. 4. First published 1928.

[82]MBCMW, p. 11.

[83]See KCPSTA, and articles in the IER.

[84]Jacques Maritain, *The Things That Are Not Caesar's* (London: Sheed and Ward, 1930), xxvi.

[85]Ibid.

[86]Jacques Maritain, *Integral Humanism* (Notre Dame, Indiana: University of Notre Dame Press, 1973), v-vi. First published 1936.

[87]Interview with John Daley,C.S.Sp., March 5, 1979. It should be noted that the circumstances surrounding the removal of Billot and L'Floch are unclear even today.

[88]Fahey Papers, HGP. Fahey passed this material on to Brian O'Ruairc to help him "clarify" his ideas about Maritain. See eight letters of O'Ruairc to Fahey.

[89]MBCRS, pp. 183-184.

[90]Ibid., p. 182.

[91]Ibid.

[92]Interviews with Bernard Kelly,C.S.Sp., Enda Watters,C.S.Sp., and Desmond Byrne,C.S.Sp.

[93]Jacques Maritain to Denis Fahey, November 30, 1923, FP-HGP.

[94]Jacques Maritain to Denis Fahey, May 10, 1926 and August 3, 1930, FP-HGP.

[95]Ten letters from Paul Poitevin to Fahey beginning in October 1951, some of them quite lengthy. There are also articles, translations and excerpts of articles which were forwarded to Fahey by Poitevin. Thirteen letters from Hevre Le Lay to Fahey beginning January 1951, all of them lengthy. There is one postcard from Citeaux dated "le 14 juillet 1953" written by Le Lay, but also signed by Poitevin. FP-HGP.

[96]Poitevin to Fahey, FP-HGP.

[97]Philippe Lavagne d'Ortigue to Fahey, December 3, 1950, FP-HGP.

[98]APVM, p. 3 of copy; p. 4 of ms.

[99]KCPSTA, p. 11.

[100]Nesta Webster, *World Revolution: The Plot Against Civilization* (Boston: Small, Maynard and Company, 1921), viii.

[101]Ibid.

[102]Ibid., pp. 298-305.

[103]Nesta Webster, *Secret Societies and Subversive Movements* (n.p.: Christian Book Club of America, n.d.), x. First published 1924.

[104]Ibid.

[105]Ibid., pp. 408-414.

[106]Nesta Webster to Denis Fahey, February 20, 1939, FP-HGP.

[107]Ibid.

[108]Seven letters from Marie G. Endean to Fahey between November 23, 1939 and April 25, 1953, with a long interruption during World War II, FP-HGP.

[109]Nesta Webster to Denis Fahey, March 3, 1939, FP-HGP.

[110]See Fahey's copy of *World Revolution*, Holy Ghost Missionary College Library, Kimmage, Dublin. Although Fahey does not state that he wrote the article, the language and style (e.g. "our Real Life"—capitalized as he always did in articles in the IER 1926-1927), strongly suggest that he is the author.

[111]KCPSTA, KCON, and KCCJN; MBCMW, and MBCRS.

CHAPTER IV

FAHEY AND "THE JEWISH QUESTION"

> The hillock of Calvary is really and truly (if metaphor may be allowed) the watershed of the world's history. The human race moves on down to Calvary and from Calvary onwards, dividing at the foot of the Cross, according as men accept or reject the Divinity of Him who died there on the first Good Friday. But this view of Calvary requires, for its completion, to be supplemented by a full perspective of the doctrine of the Mystical Body of Our Lord.[1]

The Jews, by their rejection of Jesus—according to Fahey—became the major antagonists in the Christian drama. They not only refused to accept Jesus as the Supernatural Messias, they continued to await their own Natural Messias. Their role in history was that of actively combatting the Divine Plan for Order. This constant theme in Fahey's writings was described most graphically in the title of the last chapter of *The Mystical Body of Christ in the Modern World* (2nd edition, 1938), "The Struggle of the Jewish Nation against the True Messias."[2]

Fahey's History and "the Jews"

Jesus Christ was, for Fahey, the center and culminating point in history because "through Him humanity is linked to God."[3] The study of history hinged on the struggle of those for or against the True Messias. In recounting major periods since the coming of

Jesus, Fahey acknowledged that the Jews were without power in a Christian world after their political demise with the fall of Jerusalem, and with the recognition of Christianity as the religion of the Roman Empire. Throughout the Middle Ages, they were kept in a subordinate role by not being allowed citizenship.

It was "the Lutheran revolt"—Fahey's description of the Protestant Reformation—that shattered Christendom. Luther's emphasis on individualism, and his concepts of grace as "extrinsic," of private interpretation of scripture, and an immediate relationship to God, all militated against the sense of community and integrated living that many believed had characterized medieval times.[4] Fahey saw the influence of Ockham and his Nominalism on Luther as primarily responsible for the rejection of the Divine Plan for Order as outlined by the Angelic Doctor and approved by the Popes throughout the ages.[5] The result was a radical erosion of the Mystical Body of Christ. Fahey stated:

> Protestantism, therefore, substituted for the corporate organization of society, imbued with the spirit of the Mystical Body and reconciling the claims of personality and individuality in man, a merely isolated relation with our Divine Lord. This revolt of the human individual against order on the supernatural level, this uprise of individualism, with its inevitable chaotic self-seeking, had dire consequences both in regard to politics and economics.[6]

Of the political results of the Reformation, the most obvious was the increase in the power of temporal rulers. Authority over spiritual affairs passed to some monarchs, a few of whom—such as James I of England—claimed "Divine Right."

The economic consequences of the Protestant Reformation were clearly linked by Fahey to what he labelled "Judaeo-Protestant Capitalism." Economic life in the Middle Ages had found an expression of solidarity in the guild system. The growth of individualism in the Reformation led to "unbridled self-seeking."

Fahey claimed: "The Lutheran separation of the Christian from the Ruler or the Citizen shows the decay in the true idea of membership in our Lord's Mystical Body." Even more contributive were the Calvinistic doctrines of predestination and election, which favored unlimited competition in society. Fahey quoted Troeltsch's *Protestantism and Progress* to support his claim that Calvinism was "the real nursing-Father of the civic industrial capitalism of the middle class."[7]

Werner Sombart was invoked by Fahey to support his stand on the Jewish responsibility for the Protestant Reformation. At that point, the Irish priest believed that Sombart was a Jew, which supposedly added to the strength of his statement: "The Jew it was, according to Sombart, who broke down the mentality of the Middle Ages and commercialized all the relations of men."[8] Fahey saw Calvin's justification of usury, which drew heavily on the Hebrew Scriptures, as the link between Judaism and Protestantism; hence—"Judaeo-Protestant Capitalism" which, Fahey believed, reached a high point in the twentieth century with the control of the international bankers.

Ockham's Nominalism divided into two currents with further deleterious effects on modern thought, the first being the philosophy of Descartes emphasizing innate ideas and "sacrificing" the sense faculty. The second current was Lockean thought, which "gradually got rid of the intelligence, finally reducing it to the rank and function of an internal sense." Since the Fall, sense life had tended to dominate human beings, so it was no wonder that Locke's approach became the more influential. It was particularly welcomed by the *philosophes* of the eighteenth century.[9] Fahey stated: "...individualism in religion prepared the way for individualism and separation in political and economic activity. Naturalism grew apace."[10]

Locke's influence was particularly strong during the Glorious Revolution of 1688 in England, when he was instrumental in the founding of the Bank of England—"an event of outstanding importance in economic history." It created, according to Fahey, a financial revolution which kept the Catholic Stuarts from ever regaining the throne. The Irish writer added:

> What has not been so frequently noticed is that with the English Revolution of 1688 there began the transference of the Jewish financial centre from Amsterdam to London. The Jewish Nation, in pursuit of its naturalistic Messianic ideal, has always aimed at control of trade and commerce and also of bullion. That means, as we say today, control of raw materials, of imports and exports, of price-fixing and of gold. When the arrogance of the Jews and their double-dealing with regard to religion had led to the establishment of the Inquisition and their expulsion from Spain and Portugal, they transferred their centre of financial action to Amsterdam and the Netherlands.[11]

At one point, Locke manifested an interest in joining the Free-masons. Whether he did or not is unknown. For Fahey, however, it was one more example of a Liberal, involved with Jews and Freemasons, attempting to destroy the Mystical Body of Christ. Freemasonry, operating as a secret society, was a major challenge to the Mystical Body. Fahey believed:

> In this wise, Freemasonry, *a naturalistic caricature of the Mystical Body of Christ*, was brought into existence. The so-called Reformation had not attempted to set up a supra-national organization in the place of the Catholic Church. The French Revolution of 1789 witnessed the first appearance in public of the new ideal of a purely naturalistic society striving for the universality of the Catholic Church.[12]

Fahey was convinced that modern history since 1789 was an account of the domination of state after state "by the naturalistic supranationalism of Freemasonry, behind which has been steadily emerging the still more strongly organized naturalistic supranationalism of the Jewish Nation."[13] Largely through the work of Freemasons, Jews were admitted to citizenship in France in 1790. Thus, two forces working for the defeat of the Mystical Body of Christ joined together, and the Divine Plan for Order was being radically imperilled in Europe.

The opposition between the Catholic Church and the French Revolution was not casual or accidental, Fahey claimed, but essential. "It is opposition between Naturalism and the Supernatural Life of Grace."[14] The tenets of the Revolution found in the Declaration of the Rights of Man had been duly condemned by the Catholic Church, particularly in the *Syllabus of Errors* (1864). Those who would traffic with revolutionaries were enemies of the Church.

Fahey distinguished two currents emanating from the Declaration of the Rights of Man: (1) Rousseauist-Masonic Liberalism (sometimes referred to as Rousseauist-Masonic "Democracy"), and (2) Socialism, Collectivism, and Communism. Both groups were in league with the Jews. Fahey concluded: "For behind the naturalistic Masonic Society which prepared the French Revolution, the better organized and more cohesive naturalistic organization of the Jewish Nation has been steadily preparing for the advent of the new Messianic era."[15] The Socialist and Communist currents which issued from the Declaration emerged with greater strength in the Russian Revolution of 1917.

Interpreting the Role of the Jews in the Bolshevik Revolution

Jewish control of the Bolshevik Revolution was the outstanding example of the machinations of evil attempting to destroy the Church in the twentieth century, according to Fahey. This was the subject of the center chapter of *The Mystical Body of Christ in the Modern World*, entitled "The Agents of Revolution."

This controversial core is an example of Fahey's methodology as well as his willingness to identify the Jews as the source of all the problems in history. Because substantial portions of this chapter were quoted by Father Coughlin in America, and a portion of it was published under the title *The Rulers of Russia* and widely disseminated in the United States, it warrants substantial consideration.[16]

Fahey began by identifying the objective of Freemasonry and its vassal societies as "the complete overthrow of the order of the world founded upon the Supernatural Life of the Mystical Body of our Lord, Redeemer of the fallen race." Institutions targeted for destruction were (1) the Catholic Church; (2) the states and nations which acknowledged "the indirect power" of the Catholic Church; (3) the family founded upon the unity and indissolubility of marriage contracts; and (4) Catholic education which allowed for the development of every human personality.[17]

Both invisible and visible forms were working to overthrow the Catholic Church. Fahey categorized them: (1) Satan; (2) the Jews; (3) subordinate agencies of revolution. This latter group was sub-divided into (a) revolutionary societies which were strictly Masonic and secret; (b) revolutionary societies which have only the hierarchy of government and which were directed toward a special object, i.e. The Internationale of the Jews, and the Irish Republican Brotherhood; and (c) non-secret societies which were imbued with the Masonic naturalistic spirit such as the Rotary International.[18]

On the role of Satan, Fahey summarized all his conclusions from previous writings, and emphasized: "St. Thomas contrasts the headship of Satan over all evil men with our Lord's Headship of the Mystical Body of Christ in III P.Q.8,a.7." Thomas was quoted directly to support the thesis that—even if it is only in regard to exterior guidance—"the devil is the head of all evil men."[19]

Fahey's material on the Jews in the first part of this chapter was largely a repetition of his earlier statements. He distinguished between the "Personality" and the "Individuality" of Jesus as a Jew, and explained how the Jews had ceased to be the chosen people and were now "the Jewish Nation." Fahey expanded on the Jewish expectation of the natural Messianic era, and the influence this exercised in every area of human life. They were "dragging the world down to a state inferior to that in which Jesus found it. The whole struggle in the world ultimately centers round the acceptance or rejection of His Divinity."[20]

Opposition of the Jewish Nation to the Mystical Body of Christ was codified, according to Fahey, in the Talmud and the Kabbala. He commented:

> The Talmud contains, chiefly, but not exclusively, the deviations from the order of the world in regard to the organization of society. The terrible pride of the Jewish race, due to their having lowered and corrupted the idea of the mission to which God had called them, is very visible therein. While the Talmud represents the codification of Jewish opposition to the Kingship of Christ, the Kabbala reflects rather the opposition to the priesthood of Christ.[21]

Fahey emphasized the "pantheism" of the Kabbala.

Of the subordinate agencies of revolution, the short section on Masonic societies was largely a recapitulation from prior writings, including an extended quotation from *Humanum Genus*—the papal encyclical "On Freemasonry." A disproportionate number of pages focused on the Communist Internationale. Fahey's goal was to prove that it was controlled by the Jews—both Bolsheviks and financiers—whose objective was the overthrow of the Mystical Body of Christ in the modern world:

> For a full answer, however, it would be necessary to study the careers of the Jewish founders of this society, Karl Marx and Frederich Engels. A few words must suffice here, but they will be enough to show that many of the Gentile instruments, who

figure as leaders, are really dupes of Jewish capitalism. Let us examine Marx's formation and his outlook on life.[22]

Marx was described as the grandson of a Jewish rabbi of Cologne whose real name was Mordechai. Jewish influence on Marx by Leopold Zunz, and Moses Moser, Fahey believed, led to the neo-Messianic thesis that "the Jewish nation and not a member of that nation was to be the Messias who should conquer the world and subject all nations to itself."[23] Marx, according to Fahey, combined this idea with the pantheistic philosophy of Hegel:

This awful pantheism swept away any traces of Jewish Deism which Marx still retained and left him only his pride in his race and the certitude that the sovereign thought, which was destined to rule the world and enable it to progress indefinitely, was, indeed, that of his race.[24]

Influenced also by the materialism of Feuerbach—"the proletariat class, which produces the material goods on which human society lives, is a Messianic class destined by its rule to bring about a new era for the world." The Messianic expectations of the Russian people in this period provided fertile ground for this concept of Messianic vocation of the proletariat. Fahey added:

But both the proletariat in general and the Russian people in particular are only means for the realization of the Messianic dreams of Marx's own people. Masters of production through finance, they will shape the destinies of the world-God or collectivity-God.[25]

After a discussion of Hegelian dialectics, and the influence of Feuerbach, Fahey concluded that Marx's dialetical materialism was ultimately faulty because "the distinction of matter and spirit is denied."[26]

When Marx launched the First Internationale in London in 1864, Fahey claimed that it was not a spontaneous movement, but had been in the process of preparation for years by a contingent of Jews. Beginning with Lasalle, he listed Jewish members of socialist groups in Germany, Austria, France, and the United States who were involved. This was one of the many listings of Jews in suspect movements which Fahey included in his writings.

The Irish priest admitted that it would be too lengthy to discuss the development of the whole Communist movement in Europe, but suggested that the plan of revolution was always the same. France in 1789 was only the beginning. Fahey speculated that had Marx's agents in the Paris Commune succeeded in 1871, France would have gone the route of Russia in 1917.[27] Fahey then moved to the identification of Marxian Socialism and Jewish Neo-Messianism:

> Russian Communism is, then, the triumph of the Marxian deification of man. But is Jewish thought the directing and controlling *sovereign thought*, which is striving to mould the destinies of Russia, and, through Russia, of the world? We must here quote a certain number of documents to show how the Marxian neo-Messianic programme was inaugurated in Russia and continues to be applied therein.[28]

Here began Fahey's citations from controversial documents. The first was reprinted as an extract from *The Patriot* (December 5, 1929), a conservative and inflammatory organ published in London. Later quoted by Coughlin in one of his most volatile radio speeches, this document described a complicated and unsubstantiated claim that an original British White Paper "Russia No. I (1919)—A Collection of Reports on Bolshevism in Russia" was suppressed, and an edited version made available to the public at a later date because of politically sensitive material in it that indicated that the Jews were in control of the Bolshevik Revolution. The report was originally written by a representative from the Netherlands, a M. Oudendyke, who sent the communiqué from St. Petersburg, a copy of which was eventually forwarded to Arthur Balfour in Britain, who had it published as a White Paper. The controversial passage follows:

> The danger is now so great that I feel it is my duty to call the attention of the British and all other Governments to the fact that, if an end is not put to Bolshevism at once, the civilization of the whole world will be threatened.   This is not an exaggeration, but a sober matter of fact.... I consider that the immediate suppression of Bolshevism is the greatest issue now before the world, not even excluding the war which is still raging, and unless, as above stated, Bolshevism is nipped in the bud immediately, it is bound to spread in one form or another over Europe and the whole world, as *it is organized and worked by Jews who have no nationality and whose one object is to destroy for their own ends the existing order of things*. The only manner in which this danger can be averted would be collective action on the part of all the Powers.   I would beg that this report be telegraphed as soon as possible in cipher in full to the British Foreign Office in view of its importance.[29]

The Patriot claimed that the original British White Paper became unprocurable in a short time, and an abridged version was made available to the public with the above paragraph and other sections deleted. This example was cited by Fahey as an illustration of how the British Foreign Office, controlled and manipulated by Jews, attempted to hide the danger of the Bolshevik Revolution from the public.   The original British White Paper continues to be available in the library of Trinity College, Dublin, as Fahey himself admitted.

It was not uncommon, however, to publish abridged versions of government documents so that they could be more easily read by the ordinary citizen. The abridged version sold for six pence, and the original for nine pence; the abridgement, therefore, was substantially shorter, and not just the absence of a paragraph or two. Fahey, Coughlin, and *The Patriot* all preferred to identify the situation as a subterfuge. It is, however, clearly a case of interpretation.[30]

The second document which Fahey cited as evidence for the financing and control of the Russian Revolution by the Jews is attributed to the "American Secret Service," and "transmitted by the French High Commissioner to his Government." Published in *Documentation Catholique* (Paris: March 6, 1920), an introductory paragraph reads: "The authenticity of this document is guaranteed to us. With regard to the exactness of the information which it contains, the American Secret Service takes responsibility."[31] It was pointed out by those who refuted the authenticity of this document that the U.S. Secret Service was never officially referred to as the "American Secret Service."[32]

The sections quoted in Fahey's volume were also cited and later published as part of Coughlin's controversial broadcasts of November-December 1938 in regard to the Jews. One part included the names of Jewish bankers who supposedly supplied funds for Trotsky and others in 1917. Another section listed "the following individuals who make themselves remarkable" in the Soviets. Lined in three columns under "Assumed Name," "Real Name," and "Nationality," are twenty-five persons beginning with Lenin—the only one identified as a Russian; the others were all specified as Jews who had changed their names. Even this was qualified, because a footnote stated: "The present writer wishes to add that some authors are convinced that Lenin's mother was a Jewess."[33] The above was provided as "proof" that the Bolshevik Revolution was a master plot of the Jewish world.

Although Msgr. John A. Ryan and others in the United

States ably refuted Coughlin's use of the material from Fahey's book,[34] for those who wished to identify Jews with Communism, Fahey's presentation of such documents and his additional comments provided "evidence." For Fahey it was enough to state: "From information furnished by French sources, Mr. Jacob Schiff appears to have given 12,000,000 dollars for the Russian Revolution of 1917...." He did not name his "French sources." In a footnote Fahey commented that there was "some proof" that Kerensky may have been a Jew.[35] Vague allegations of this nature seemed to have been sufficient for him to conclude that the Jews were in control in Russia.

Fahey warned his readers that the Communist Internationale had made efforts to subject other countries to its world plan, particularly Spain. Ireland, too, should be alert. The Irish Republican Army (I.R.A.) Manifesto of January 8, 1933 affirmed public ownership of the means of production and other Communist doctrines. Fahey concluded: "Thus, if ever a Communist Republic is set up in Ireland, we shall be trampled under foot in another world-empire ruled from Moscow—or Jerusalem."[36]

"Agents of the Revolution" was Fahey's most provocative statement on the Jews in the 1930s. Prior to that, he discussed the Jews within a more general historical and theological framework. He had charged—in a less specific way—that they were responsible for the corruption of society due to their control of media and finance. This effort to provide "documentary evidence" to prove their involvement in the Bolshevik Revolution (which Fahey saw as a direct attack on the Mystical Body of Christ), was indicative of his own shift from a theoretical to a more practical stance. Although his leadership in the development of *Maria Duce*, and his other quasi-political activities did not emerge until somewhat later, his targeting of the alleged Jewish relationship to contemporary political issues began in this chapter.

In *The Rulers of Russia*, the pamphlet in which the political portions of this chapter are reprinted, Fahey very clearly stated his case:

The pamphlet proves that Bolshevism is an instrument in the hands of the Jews. The book shows Bolshevism in its proper perspective, namely, as the most recent development in the age-long struggle waged by the Jewish Nation against the Supernatural Messias, our Lord Jesus Christ, and His Mystical Body, the Catholic Church. Our Lord Jesus Christ is at one and the same time the Second Person of the Blessed Trinity and a Jew of the House of David. He spoke to the Jews of a higher life to be obtained by incorporation into His Mystical Body. The Jews set up racial descent from Abraham, in opposition to spiritual descent from Abraham by faith in the Supernatural Messias and refused to subject their national life to the Mystical Body of Christ.[37]

Here Fahey accused the Jews of deifying their own race:

They thus put their race and nation in the place of God, deified them in fact. They then rejected the Supernatural Messias, and elaborated a programme of preparation for the Natural Messias to come. The Natural Messias can have but one object, the imposition of Jewish national supremacy. There is no alternative.[38]

Readers on both sides of the Atlantic were hungry for interpretations of the world scene which would allow them to understand their own frustrations. For Fahey, it was the Jewish international financiers, and the "Judaeo-Masonic Communists" whose activities explained the dark days between the wars. Copies of *The Rulers of Russia* were disseminated in America in substantial numbers. Coughlin, Gerald L. K. Smith and other influential figures recommended it to their audiences. Some thought that Fahey had the answer.

Fahey, the Holocaust, and the State of Israel

One might think that after World War II and the destruction of European Jewry as a result of the Holocaust, Fahey would have questioned whether the Jews were as powerful as he had claimed. In the Foreword to his final volume, *The Kingship of Christ and the Conversion of the Jewish Nation* (1953), he tried to clarify what he saw as the confusion over the term "Anti-Semitism":

> The Hitlerite naturalistic or anti-supernaturalistic regime in Germany gave to the world the odious spectacle of a display of Anti-Semitism, that is, of hatred of the Jewish Nation. Yet all the propaganda about that display of Anti-Semitism should not have made Catholics forget the existence of the age-long Jewish Naturalism or Anti-Supernaturalism. Forgetfulness of the disorder of Jewish Naturalistic opposition to Christ the King is keeping Catholics blind to the danger that is arising from the clever extension of the term "Anti-Semitism," with all its war connotation in the mind of the unthinking, to include any form of opposition to the Jewish Nation's naturalistic aims.[39]

Throughout the work Fahey indicated that he believed the number of Jews killed under Hitler was inflated and that the Jewish press was using "the six million" figure to further the cause of Zionism, which ultimately hoped to take over the world.[40] In reading the paragraph below, one would never know that the Holocaust had occurred:

> In order to understand the different currents in the German reaction against Judaeo-Masonic influence, we must bear well in mind that the Jewish Nation and Freemasonry are working in the camp of Satan

for the reign of Naturalism, that is, for the disruption
of the Divine Plan for the order and the elimination
of the Supernatural Life from the world. They will
hotly deny this or scoff at it, but the objective order
of the world is a fact. Further, the leaders of the
Jewish Nation aim at the inauguration of the reign
of the Natural Messias and the rejection of Our
Divine Lord, in view of their own domination, and
they use their undeniable influence in Freemasonry
for that purpose.[41]

"Contemporary Jewish Aims" was the title of Chapter VIII
of Fahey's culminating work, and was an effort to "document"
Jewish conspiracy not dissimilar to his treatment of the Bolshevik
Revolution. He attempted to prove that the Jews were continuing
in their machinations to control the world and dethrone the real
Supernatural Messias.[42] He began, as usual, with the Divine Plan
for Order, but moved quickly to the rejection of the True Messias
and the responsibility of the Jews for deicide. Not only had the
Jews publicly rejected Jesus at the crucifixion, but they determined
"to work against God for the enthronement of another Messias."
Fahey continued:

Since the True Supernatural Messias came to found
the Supranational Kingdom of His Mystical Body,
into which He asked the Jewish nation to lead all
other nations, the future Messias must be a purely
Jewish National Messias, and his mission can have
no other object than to impose the rule of the Jewish
nation on the other nations.[43]

Fahey believed that the Jewish nation had "turned
downwards to the slavery of self-centred ambition dictated by
national pride."[44] He reminded his readers that not every individual
member of the Jewish Nation was working consciously against a
Christian society, but he claimed:

It does mean, however, that all Jews, in proportion
as they are one with the leaders and rulers of their
race, will oppose the influence of the Supernatural
Life of the Mystical Body in society and will be an
active ferment of Naturalism by their striving for the
Messianic domination of their race.[45]

It was from this point of view that Fahey related his earlier
statements on the anti-supernatural stance of the Jews who were
preparing the world for a Natural Messias, to the state of Israel
recently established in 1948. He announced clearly: "The situation
since the Second World War is being cleverly exploited to prevent
anyone from opposing Jewish aims, through fear of being dubbed
as 'anti-Semite'!"[46] Fahey viewed violations of the Jews as
regrettable, but stated that the Catholic Church was also persecuted
in Germany. He believed that Jewish control of the media was
responsible for exaggerated accounts regarding the extermination
of the Jews, and quoted Arnold Leese from "Leese's Bureau of
Anti-Jewish Information" in Surrey, England, which published
Gothic Ripples to "disprove" the figure of the six million Jews
supposedly destroyed by Hitler.[47]
   The footnotes in this chapter give the reader a flavor of the
sources which Fahey was relying on at this stage in his career. In
addition to *Gothic Ripples*, there is material from *Christ Losing His
World*, a pamphlet by Lon Francis; *We Must Abolish the United
States: the Hidden Facts behind the Crusade for World Government*,
and *It Isn't Safe to Be an American* by Joseph P. Kamp; *Somewhere
South of Suez* by Douglas Reed; *The Palestine Mystery* by Arthur
Rogers; *The "Palestine" Plot*, and *The UNRRA Infiltra(i)tors* by
B. Jensen. Rogers and Jensen are quoted copiously. Robert H.
Williams' writings, *Know Your Enemy, The Anti-Defamation League
and Its Use in the World Communist Offensive*, and the *Williams'
Intelligence Summary* provided Fahey with sources especially useful
for his purposes.[48]

Zionism and the state of Israel continued to be the focus of this chapter. Fahey underscored the "theological" dimension: the Jewish claim to Palestine was a denial that the Jews had disobeyed God by rejecting the Supernatural Messias. In stating that the promised Messias had not yet come they were anticipating their national domination over the world. To allow the Jews to return to Israel was to admit that the Messias had not come.[49]

Fahey then probed "the real, as distinct from the alleged, motives behind the conquest of Palestine and the erection of the Jewish State...." He found his answer in *The "Palestine" Plot* by B. Jensen, who quoted an article from *The New York Herald Tribune*, January 14, 1947:

> Since 1916, Zionists have proceded (sic) on the theory that their plan for creating an independent Jewish State in Palestine was the only certain method by which Zionists could acquire complete control and outright ownership of the proven Five Trillion Dollar ($5,000,000,000,000), chemical and mineral wealth of the Dead Sea. A Jewish State possessing this fabulous wealth would, by virtue of its financial power, soon become a nation with greater international importance than any nation in the history of the world.[50]

Arthur Rogers' *The Palestine Mystery* was used for further documentation that the chemical wealth in the Holy Land would allow the Jews to control the world if they set up their independent state.[51]

The "Outline of the Conquest" began with Theodore Herzl and the First Zionist Congress (1897). Intrigue regarding the assassination of the Archduke Francis Ferdinand in 1914 by Gabriel Princip (a Bosnian Serb who was alleged to be a Jew) was linked to the fact that the Archduke had been "condemned to death" by Freemasonry two years before, according to the *Revue Internationale des Sociétés Secrètes*. This event which triggered

World War I—the war that was responsible for the Balfour Declaration and the Bolshevik Revolution—was seen as part of the great Jewish master plan.[52]

World War II provided additional "opportunitites" according to authors whom Fahey cited. A sample from Robert H. Williams follows:

> Readers of the Intelligence Summary and the booklet *Know Your Enemy* doubtless will recall that, just after the war, General Mark Clark was moved from Italy to command the U.S. Occupation Zone in Austria, and immediately there came a great flood of Jews from Marxist indoctrinated Eastern Europe, pouring through the Clark Command into our Displaced Persons camps, throwing themselves on the American government and taxpayer. The Jews were running from no danger: the Nazis were crushed; they were protected by the (Jew-dominated) Red Army east of the iron curtain and by the (Jew-commanded) U.S. Army in Austria.[53]

The flood of literature of this quality found in the Fahey Papers allowed the Irish priest to believe that such interpretations were authentic.[54]

The murder of Count Bernadotte of Sweden, the United Nations Mediator in Palestine, and the plight of the Arab refugees, was seen as the final stage. For Fahey, and others of his orientation, the United Nations was the epitome of international control by the Jews. Especially dangerous was UNESCO which was making efforts to control the minds of the young and lead them away from the Kingship of Christ. An international as opposed to a national perspective was the first insidious step. Sex education would be next. When piety and Patriotism were diminished, the Mystical Body of Christ would become radically endangered.[55]

Challengers might ask—how could high finance favor Bolshevism which was against private ownership of property?

Fahey gave the following explanation as he described a lecture of a Jewish banker from Budapest:

>...the Jewish banker began by explaining that those who are astonished at the alliance between Israel and the Soviets forget that the Jewish Nation is the most intensely national of all peoples and that Marxism is simply one of the weapons of Jewish Nationalism. Capitalism, he added, is equally sacred to Israel which makes use of both Bolshevism and Capitalism to remould the world for its own ends. The process of renovation of the world is thus carried on from above by the Jewish control of the riches of the world and from below by the Jewish guidance of the revolution. Israel has a divine mission, in fact, Israel, become its own Messias, is God.[56]

Fahey never doubted that Judaeo-Protestant Capitalism and Judaeo-Masonic Communism could be at home with one another.

One writer who attempted to broaden Fahey's view regarding the Jewish situation in Russia was Vladimir Lezar-Borin, a Czech Protestant who moved to London shortly before World War II. He believed that there was a gigantic struggle between the Jewish nationalistic bourgeoisie (political Zionists) and Russian Bolsheviks for world domination. Lezar-Borin concluded that the latter were more clever than the Jews. The result was that "the Jews are simply tools in the hands of the Bolsheviks." Fahey disagreed with him, and devoted considerable space to reinforcing ideas that Jewish money and manpower were responsible for the Bolshevik Revolution, and Jews continued to be in control in Russia at that time.[57]

Lezar-Borin tried to alert Fahey in 1946 to some of his errors in statements about the Central Committee of the Communist Party which were published in *The Rulers of Russia*. He attempted to convince Fahey that he was misinterpreting the relationship of the Central Committee and the Politburo. Fahey liked Lezar-

Borin, and even invited him to stay at Blackrock when he was in Dublin in 1952. He recommended articles of the Czech author to a Dublin newspaper, the *Sunday Independent*. He refused, however, to accept Lezar-Borin's conviction that Jewish Nationalism in Russia was being suppressed, and that Jews were being purged in the trials of 1952.[58]

Fahey, instead, agreed with the interpretation of the *Williams Intelligence Summary* which stated that the only reason the Jews were being persecuted in Russia was for Communist propaganda purposes. If Zionists were persecuted by Communists—the conclusion would be that "the Zionists in America must be considered anti-Communists and therefore trustworthy!" Fahey quoted Williams further:

> Above all, the purge trials and the new propaganda line are making the kindly, gullible American think that "Communism is persecuting the Jews just as Hitler persecuted them," and thus we are once more being ribbed up to fight a world war to "rescue" the Jews from "persecution"—and if this war comes, God help America. The Zionists (or Communists hiding behind the front of Zionism) already have set up the machinery inside the U.S. Department of Defense for seizing absolute power, if they can hold their now dominant position over the White House.[59]

Fahey's scheme had categorized the Jews as the enemy. No other interpretation was admissible.

The Appendix to this chapter lists "Members of the Jewish Nation in the United Nations Organization."[60] This method of enumerating Jews who held important offices hearkens back to the lists of Jews involved in the Bolshevik Revolution from *The Mystical Body of Christ in the Modern World* and *The Rulers of Russia*. Before his inventory of U.N. personnel who were Jewish he included an extract from *The Canadian Intelligence Service*, May 1952:

> It has been estimated that one tiny group, constituting less than one per cent. of the world's population, hold no less than sixty per cent. of the permanent posts in the U.N. Organization. As of last year (1951) this tiny but powerful group of Zionist nationalists had the following key posts:...[61]

Thereafter are listed the names. That Jews should be allowed to be citizens of any other nation than their own was abhorrent to Fahey. By indicating that they represented a variety of countries, he believed that he had proved that they were able to control the world. Fahey's methodology never changed, but his use of sources degenerated steadily over the years.

"The Jews" in Fahey's Theology

If anyone doubted whether the Jewish question had been a preoccupation for Fahey for the majority of his writing career, one need only look to the second footnote on the first page of his first volume, *Mental Prayer according to the Principles of St. Thomas Aquinas* (1927). It is a clue to understanding Fahey's later work:

> As the Press of the world is in great part in the power of the descendants of those who passed Mount Calvary blaspheming Him, "wagging their heads, and saying yah, thou that destroyest the temple of God, and in three days buildest it up again: save thyself, coming down from the Cross" (Mark xv. 29), we may expect to find in it an educational programme in complete opposition to that of the Vicars of Him who died on Calvary.[62]

It is difficult to comprehend how such a note could be considered appropriate anywhere, much less on the first page of a book on mental prayer.

Fahey's major tenets about the Jews have already been examined. As stated earlier, however, the three books which begin with the title "Kingship of Christ" emphasize the more theological dimensions in his writings. One key idea from each of these volumes will be discussed to illustrate Fahey's theological effort to establish the Jews as the enemies of Christ and of the true order of the world: (1) the responsibility of the Jews for the death of Jesus, the Supernatural Messias, and the effects of that on the world from *The Kingship of Christ according to the Principles of St. Thomas Aquinas*; (2) the results of "Organized Naturalism" with the consequent contrasting programs of the Mystical Body of Christ—the Catholic Church—and the Jewish Nation, from *The Kingship of Christ and Organized Naturalism*; and (3) "The Coming of Antichrist" from *The Kingship of Christ and the Conversion of the Jewish Nation*.

The Responsibility of the Jews for the Death of Jesus

Fahey's first systematic attempt to reflect on the theological position of the Jews in history was in "The World Struggle around the Divinity of Our Lord"—Chapter VIII of *The Kingship of Christ according to the Principles of St. Thomas Aquinas* (1931). As noted earlier, Fahey discussed "the agents of Christ's Passion and Death" in their order of guilt and malevolence according to Aquinas: Satan; the leaders of the Jewish nation; the rank and file of Jews; the Gentiles, Pilate, and the soldiers who acted as executioners. The Jews, therefore, had the major responsibility for this most heinous act.[63]

Fahey continued with the Thomistic development which distinguished between the leaders of the Jewish race (Maiores Judaei), and the rank and file of Jews (Minores Judaei). Thomas emphasized that the elders of the Jews (Maiores Judaei) were those whose "ignorance did not excuse them from the crime because it was affected ignorance." Thomas added: "But those of lesser degree—namely the common folk—who had not grasped the mysteries of the Scriptures, did not fully comprehend that He was the Christ or the Son of God."[64] (See above, p. 118.) Fahey's confused language when describing these distinctions, however, could easily lead the reader to believe that the rank and file Jews also participated in "affected ignorance" and were, therefore, substantially guilty. Such lack of clarity contributed to the anti-Jewish tone of the presentation.

Over the centuries, Fahey contended, the supernatural character of the Catholic Church had become more evident. There was no excuse, therefore, for the Jews to continue to reject Jesus as Messias. Fahey incorporated one of his relatively rare quotations from Scripture into the discussion—a long passage from John (8:24-25, 28, 39-44), which concluded: "If God were your Father you would indeed love Me.... You are of your father the Devil, and the desires of your father you will do." This statement was primary for Fahey in establishing Satan as the head of all evil men and women: "Here Our Lord proclaims that fact that all those who reject the supernatural, by refusing to submit to God's order, come under the leadership of Satan, who was the first to reject the supernatural."[65] Satan was indeed the first Naturalist.

Fahey immediately applied his conclusion to the contemporary scene:

If only the Jewish nation had freely corresponded with the incomparable graces it received through Jesus, it would have been the herald of the Divine Life to a regenerated world, but it obstinately refused. Today, by its vast financial power over the world's processes of exchange and its wide spread influence on the Press and cinema, it is placing terrible obstacles in the way of those who are striving to live that Life.[66]

From the press and the cinema, Fahey launched into one of his earliest discussions on money: "...the manipulation of money or token wealth can become a terrible instrument in the hands of the adversaries of the Supernatural Messias and of the supernatural life He confers, by hampering instead of facilitating exchange."[67] He pleaded, "Efforts must be made to bring about an organization of society in which the life of the people will not be subordinate to and at the mercy of the Stock Exchange operations and financial coups by the few."[68]

Fahey's later book, *Money Manipulation and the Social Order* (1944), expanded on this theme.[69] Although Fahey frequently digressed to discuss Masonry, money, and movies, his basic thesis was: "The Jews as a nation rejected Our Lord Jesus Christ, the True Supernatural Messias, and have never ceased to look forward to another Messias, who must of necessity be purely natural."[70] It was because the Jews were unwilling to recognize Jesus as the True Messiah that He was put to death. They were, therefore, responsible.

"Organized Naturalism": The Jewish Nation versus the Mystical Body of Christ

Twelve years later Fahey published *The Kingship of Christ and Organized Naturalism*, dedicated to the Immaculate Heart of Mary, "to St. Michael the Archangel, Prince of the Supernatural Host in combat against Satan, the first Naturalist," and three other favorites of the Irish priest—St. Joseph, St. Joan of Arc, and St. Thérèse of the Child Jesus.[71] This 143-page paperback, made available for only one shilling six pence, was welcomed by a war-weary public in 1943. Included on the dedication page is a statement Fahey frequently quoted from Cardinal Pie of Poitiers:

Naturalism is more than a heresy: it is pure undiluted anti-christianism. Heresy denies one or more dogmas; Naturalism denies that there are any dogmas or that there can be any. Heresy alters more or less

what God has revealed; Naturalism denies the very
existence of revelation. It follows that the inevitable
law and obstinate passion of Naturalism is to
dethrone Our Lord Jesus Christ and to drive Him
from the world. This will be the task of Antichrist
and it is Satan's supreme ambition....[72]

Heeding the injunction of Cardinal Pie to warn the world of the
evils of Naturalism, Fahey composed this booklet largely of
excerpts from *The Mystical Body of Christ in the Modern World*
and *The Mystical Body of Christ and the Reorganization of Society*.
Even subtitles in many of the chapters are the same.

For Fahey, however, the emphasis was not just Naturalism,
but "Jewish Naturalism," which did not accept the Kingship of
Christ. In this volume, Fahey expanded on Jewish pride which he
saw as the root of the crime of deicide:

Their pride or lack of humility or docility caused
them to set their faces against God. When they
refused to enter into His designs, God permitted the
crime of deicide and, by the supreme act of humble
submission of Our Lord on Calvary, the Life of
Grace was restored to the world. Calvary, however,
was a consequent of the refusal of the Jews to submit
humbly to God the Father and accept His Son.[73]

Fahey did not allow Jewish rejection of Jesus to remain an
event of the past. In *The Kingship of Christ and Organized
Naturalism* he provided another juxtaposition of "contrasting
programmes" aimed directly at the Jews. This six-point schema was
also included in *The Mystical Body of Christ and the Reorganization of Society* and *The Kingship of Christ and the Conversion of the Jewish Nation*. It became an integral part of Fahey's
thought, and was repeated by him and his disciples for many years.

CONTRASTING PROGRAMMES

Programme of Christ the King through His Mystical Body, the Catholic Church.	*Programme of the Jewish Nation since the rejection of Christ before Pilate and on Calvary.*
FIRSTLY	**FIRSTLY**
(I) *The Catholic Church, Supernatural* and *Supranational,* is the *One Way* established by God for the ordered return of human beings to Him. All States and Nations are bound to acknowledge it as such and all men of all nations are called upon to enter it as Members of Christ.	(I) *The Jewish Nation* under the *Natural Messias* will establish union among the nations. That necessarily involves aiming at the elimination of every vestige of the Supernatural Life that comes from Christ.
SECONDLY	**SECONDLY**
(II) *The Catholic Church* is the *sole divinely-appointed Guardian* of the whole moral law, natural and revealed.	(II) *The Jewish Nation* under the *Natural Messias* will decide what is moral and what is immoral.
THIRDLY	**THIRDLY**
(III) *Christian Marriage,* the foundation of the Christian Family, as the Symbol of the union of Christ and His Mystical Body, is *One* and *Indissoluble.*	(III) *Divorce* and *Polygamy* according to Jewish law will take the place of Christian Marriage.

FOURTHLY

(IV) *Children* must be educated as *Members of Christ's Mystical Body,* so that they may be able to look at everything, nationality included, from that standpoint.

FOURTHLY

(IV) As the doctrine of membership of Christ is a corruption of the true Jewish message to the world, *all trace of membership of Christ and of the Supernatural Life of Grace must be eliminated from education.* Non-Jews must be trained to accept submission to the Jewish Nation, and non-Jewish nationality must not conflict with Jewish world-wide supremacy.

FIFTHLY

(V) *Ownership of property* should be *widely diffused,* in order to facilitate families in procuring a sufficiency of material goods for their members. Unions of owners and workers in Guilds will reflect the solidarity of the Mystical Body of Christ.

FIFTHLY

(V) Complete *Socialization* of *property,* either in the form of ownership of everything by the State or by the relatively few financiers who control the State, must be aimed at. *Ownership of property,* especially in land, makes for independence, so *it must be eliminated.*

SIXTHLY

(VI) *The Monetary System* of a country is meant to be *at the service of production* in view of the virtuous life of Members of Christ in contented families.

SIXTHLY

(VI) Money is the instrument by which State-control or State-socialization is brought about. Instead of the correct order of finance for production and production for Members of Christ, *men must be subservient to production and production to finance.* State-control can be maintained by means of financial control.[74]

The Kingship of Christ and Organized Naturalism, a "handbook" of Faheyism, became the pocket manual for members of the *Maria Duce* and others who became involved in Fahey's quasi-political activities in the post-World War II era.[75]

The Jews and the Coming of Antichrist

The last chapter of *The Kingship of Christ and the Conversion of the Jewish Nation*—"The Coming of Antichrist"—was Fahey's finale.[76] The two preceding chapters, which discussed "the apostasy of the nations" and the grandiose plans of the Jewish nation for an anti-supernatural organization of the world were preludes to this dissertation on the apocalyptic. He acknowledged his reliance on *L'Antéchrist* by the Jewish convert priest, Father Augustine Lémann, professor of Hebrew and Sacred Scripture in the Catholic University of Lyons, and author of *Histoire Complète de l'Idée Messianique*.[77] Fahey's chapter, totally dependent on Lémann, was largely a summary of the first three sections of *L'Antéchrist*, with which the Irish priest was in obvious agreement. St. Paul in II Thessalonians had assured the early Christians that two events were to take place before the end of the world: (1) the apostasy of the nations; and (2) the appearance of Antichrist. Fahey saw this in conjunction with the tradition that the Jews would be converted to Jesus as the Messias at the end times. He quoted portions of Origen, Jerome, and John Chrysostom who suggested that just as the failure of the Jews to accept Jesus was the occasion for the Gentiles to receive salvation, subsequently "the apostasy of the nations" would be the cause for God to recall the Jews a second time.[78]

Fahey looked first to authoritative statements of the sovereign pontiffs for warnings about the advent of apostasy, and accepted Lémann's five citations of Leo XIII, and additional admonitions of Pius X—particularly from his encyclical *E Supremi Apostolatus Cathedra* (October 4, 1903). They supported Lémann's thesis, which was: "In our day, it is man in general, the human race in revolt against God, which ranges itself along with the Antichrists of old, preparing the way for the outstanding Antichrist, Antichrist properly so called. This Antichrist properly so called is clearly foretold...."[79]

Continuing his reliance on the Jewish convert-priest, Fahey examined three biblical portraits of Antichrist: (1) the "little horn that grows" in Daniel 7; (2) the Beast in the Apocalypse; and (3) the man of sin in II Thessalonians. In each of these images, certain Fathers of the Church discovered the Antichrist. Father Lémann claimed that from these portraits "it is possible to deduce a number of conclusions with regard to the person, the reign, and the end of Antichrist."[80] He then classified his conclusions under four headings: things that are (a) certain; (b) probable; (c) undecided; and (d) without a solid foundation.[81]

Fahey dealt only with the first three categories, and presented the conclusions of Lémann in summary form: Antichrist will be a human person, not Satan in human form; he will have great powers of seduction; and his rule will be world-wide.[82] Fahey specifically quoted Lémann: "With the help which will be furnished him by anti-Christian societies, this enemy of Our Lord Jesus Christ will be able to form a gigantic empire in a short time."[83]

Fahey continued with his summary of other conclusions from Lémann about the Antichrist that are "certain": Antichrist will wage a terrible war against God and the Church; Antichrist will claim to be God and will demand exclusive adoration; by means of diabolical prodigies, Antichrist will seek to prove that he is God; the domination and persecution of Antichrist will be merely temporary. The man of sin will be destroyed (Dan.7:26; Apoc. 19:20, I Thess. 2:8).[84]

In the next category, only two "probabilities" are presented —the first being the most important for Fahey's thesis: *"The Jews will acclaim Antichrist as the Messias and will help to set up his kingdom."*[85] The scriptural foundation for this is an interpretation of John 5:43: "I am come in the name of my Father, and you receive me not: if another shall come in his own name, him you will receive." Lémann then developed this possibility, and Fahey quoted the following portion from *L'Antéchrist*:

> It is upon this reproach addressed by Our Lord Jesus Christ to the Jews, his contemporaries and adversaries, that this belief is based, and it can be

said that it is the common opinion of the Fathers of the Church, for example, St. Jerome, St. Ambrose, St. Gregory the Great, St. Ephraim, St. John Chrysostom, etc., etc.,.... When we see the enormous financial power of the Jews increasing daily, when we consider their intrigues, their successful occupancy of the chief places in the principal States, their mutual understanding from one end of the world to the other, then in presence of such a preponderance, we have no difficulty in realizing that they will be able to contribute to the estabishment of the formidable empire of Antichrist. *The joyous welcome the Jews will give to Antichrist and the aid they will furnish him are therefore probable.*[86]

Lémann then mentions that most of the texts of the Fathers refer to John 5:43. In this regard, according to the French priest, Thomas Aquinas remarks that "after the true Christ, a great number of false messiahs had appeared and had been welcomed by the Jews." Therefore, the text might refer not to the Antichrist but to the false messiahs. On the other hand, it could "be held to refer to the Antichrist with probability, because of the authority of the holy Fathers who have so understood it."[87] The second probability—that the persecution of Antichrist will last three and one-half years—was based on Daniel 7:25 and Apocalypse 13:5. While it was probable, it was not certain.

In the third category, four "undecided points" were discussed: (a) the nationality of the Antichrist; (b) the name of Antichrist; (c) the seat of Antichrist's empire; and (d) the temple in which the Antichrist would present himself for adoration.[88]

Finally, the date of the coming of Antichrist was "God's secret." In Matthew 24-25, the end of the world and accompanying signs were outlined, but no specific time was given. According to Lémann and Fahey, however, it would be preceded by the apostasy of the nations referred to in II Thessalonians. In keeping with

Fahey's orientation, he concluded this volume with a papal statement: Leo X to the Fifth Lateran Council (1516) forbidding anyone, particularly preachers, to fix a date for future evils, whether for the coming of Antichrist or for the Day of Judgment, under pain of excommunication.[89] Clearly, Fahey would not allow himself to fall into that category.

Fahey considered "The Coming of Antichrist" an essential part of his summary statement on the Jews. He adopted Lémann's work as his own, and was able to present this controversial thesis to the English-speaking world under the unlikely title *The Kingship of Christ and the Conversion of the Jewish Nation*. If the Irish priest's basic orientation had changed at all over the years, it was to assign even greater responsibility for evil to the Jews.

Controversy and Conclusions

The controversy over this book was not only in regard to the imprimatur (see above, p. 34). When the *Irish Ecclesiastical Record* did not choose to review it, Fahey asked if he could get someone to do so, would they publish it? They agreed. He called upon his former student, John Chisholm C.S.Sp., then the youngest member of the faculty at the Holy Ghost Missionary College, Kimmage and requested that he undertake the task. Chisholm felt obliged and agreed, but admitted that the chapter on "The Coming of Antichrist" caused him great concern, so he decided not to make any reference to it. When completed, Chisholm showed the review to Fahey, who was wounded by the omission. Fahey came to the room of his younger colleague, stood over him at his desk, and asked him to write in that it was an excellent chapter. Chisholm stated that Fahey exerted a "strong moral ascendency" over him in those years, so he complied with the request, painful as it was at the time.[90]

The peculiar preoccupation of the Irish priest with "the Jewish Question" evolved because he began with the wrong conclusion: that because the Jews did not accept Jesus as the Supernatural Messias, they had vowed themselves to a Natural

Messias. He then drew all of his other conclusions regarding historical events in the world from this major premise.[91] Looking back on history with that perspective, he felt it imperative to warn Christians of the dangers of the war that was going on against the supernatural.

Fahey's indiscriminate use of source material, which deteriorated with the years, contributed to the undergirding of his method. Sensationalist literature and scab sheets provided "proof" of alleged conspiracies. Once convinced that the enemy of Christ the King was the Jewish Nation, any scrap of paper that contributed to that notion became valid for a footnote; any writer—with the most meager (or no) credentials—became an "authority."[92] Even the more substantial authors whom Fahey admired—Pie, Billot, and the early Maritain—were quoted very selectively. Certain preferential sections were referred to frequently. One wonders if the volumes were ever read in their totality.[93]

Fahey was not a creative philosopher or theologian, but rather a writer and teacher who tried to indicate how various philosophical and theological currents had affected history. Yet, he was not really a historian either, because he was incapable of realizing, as many of his confreres observed, that "life is larger than logic."[94] His desire to place the whole world in a system based on Christian theological presuppositions of a particularistic kind left no openness to the real world.

Fahey's "fundamentalist" interpretations of Scholastic thought, Scripture, and papal encyclicals allowed him to support his hypothesis of "Organized Naturalism" dominated by the Jews. There are sections in those documents which can be used for that purpose, and elements in the tradition which he could use to support his view. His major problem was his inability to understand history contextually. It left him with diagrams on the blackboard which were unrelated to the twentieth century.

In the 1930s, Fahey produced his writings largely in a scholar's cell. At that time he was not politically active. There were those across the Atlantic, however, who found in the Irish priest's writings a theological rationale for their political and social anti-Semitism. They would use Fahey for their own purposes.

[1]KCPSTA, p. 107.

[2]MBCMW, Chapter XI.

[3]KCPSTA, p. 107.

[4]MBCMW, Chapter III.

[5]MBCRS, Part III is entitled "Ockhamism or Nominalism and Political and Economic Decay." A statement contrasting the epistemology of Aquinas and Ockham introduces the section.

[6]MBCMW, p. 11.

[7]Ibid., pp. 15-16. The quotations from Troeltsch are as cited in G. O'Brien, *The Economic Effects of the Reformation*, not from the original.

[8]Ibid. Werner Sombart (1863-1941) was not a Jew, as Fahey learned in a letter from Léon de Poncins from France in December 1938 (FP-HGP). Sombart is best known for *Die Juden und das Wirtschaftsleben* (1911), English translation *The Jews and Modern Capitalism* (1913, 1951). He viewed the Jews as principally responsible for the disruption of the medieval economic system, and its replacement by capitalism. His study aroused considerable controversy. See *Encyclopedia Judaica* (New York: Macmillan, 1971), XV, pp. 134-135. In the MBCRS Fahey rectified his error, and refers to "the non-Jewish writer, Werner Sombart...." (p. 393). Poncins, author of *La Mystérieuse Internationale Juive*, was leader of a French organization entitled *Contre Révolution*. There are eighteen letters from Poncins to Fahey, FP-HGP.

[9]MBCRS, pp. 249-250.

[10]Ibid., p. 278.

[11]Ibid., pp. 390-391.

[12]Ibid., p. 279. Emphasis added.

[13]Ibid., p. 280.

[14]Ibid., p. 288.

[15]Ibid., p. 295.

[16]MBCMW, Chapter VI.

[17]Ibid., p. 69.

[18]Ibid., pp. 70-113.

[19]Ibid., p. 71.

[20]Ibid., pp. 72-75.

[21]Ibid., pp. 75-76.

[22]Ibid., p. 82.

[23]Ibid. Fahey referred readers to *World Revolution* by Nesta Webster.

[24]Ibid., p. 84.

[25]Ibid., p. 84.

[26]Ibid., p. 85.

[27]Ibid., p. 86.

[28]Ibid., p. 87. Emphasis added.

[29]Ibid., p. 88. Emphasis added.

[30]Government Documents Division, Library. Trinity College, Dublin. Discussion with Mr. Goodwille, member of the library staff, March 27, 1979. The abridged version was not available there.

[31]MBCMW, pp. 88-89.

[32]John A. Ryan, "Anti-Semitism in the Air," *Commonweal* (December 30, 1938): 260-262; George Shuster, "The Jew and the Two Revolutions," *Commonweal* (December 30, 1938): 262-264.

[33]Ibid., pp.89-92.

[34]See Ryan and Shuster, *Commonweal* (December 30, 1938), pp. 260-264.

[35]MBCMW, p. 92; note on Kerensky, p. 89.

[36]Ibid., p. 97.

[37]*Rulers of Russia* (Dublin: Holy Ghost Missionary College, 1938), p. 48. Third ed. rev. and enlarged, 1939. It continued to be reprinted in that form in Ireland until 1954, shortly after Fahey's death. It was available in the United States until at least 1976 as indicated by advertisements in Gerald L.K. Smith's periodical *The Cross and the Flag*.

[38]Ibid.

[39]KCCJN, pp. 5-6.

[40]Ibid., p. 125.

[41]Ibid., p. 42.

[42]Ibid., pp. 120-168. The earlier chapters of this book are sections lifted *in toto* from previous works of Fahey. Chapters VIII-IX contain the only new material.

[43]Ibid., p. 121.

[44]Ibid.

[45]Ibid., p. 124.

[46]Ibid., p. 205.

[47]Ibid. See extended footnote on Leese's interpretation of the impossibility of six million Jews dying in the Holocaust. In the Fahey Papers there is a leaflet advertising "Leese's Bureau of Anti-Jewish Information," and a copy of *Gothic Ripples* (February 21, 1949). There are eight letters from Leese to Fahey from 1949-1953, FP-HGP. They shared information mostly regarding the identification of various persons as Jews. Tracing the "pedigree" of suspect persons to ascertain if they had Jewish blood was more than a pastime for the bureau. In a letter of April 6, 1950 Leese confirmed Fahey's questions regarding the speculation that the Crown Prince Charles was circumcised by a Jew, Dr.

Jacob Snowman, and encloses a copy of *Gothic Ripples* with an "account" of the event.

[48]Lon Francis, *Christ Losing His World* (Indiana: Our Sunday Visitor Press, 1946); Joseph P. Kamp, *We Must Abolish the United States: the Hidden Facts behind the Crusade for World Government* (New York: Constitutional Educational League, n.d.), and *It Isn't Safe to Be an American* (New York: Constitutional Educational League, n.d.); Doughlas Reed, *Somewhere South of Suez* (New York: Devon-Adair Company, n.d.); Arthur Rogers, *The Palestine Mystery* (London: Sterling Press, n.d.); B. Jensen, *The "Palestine" Plot* (Scotland: Aberfeldy, n.d.), and *The UNRRA Infiltra(i)tors* (Scotland: Abernathy, n.d.). For Robert H. Williams see below, pp. 128, 130, 224.

[49]Ibid., p. 132.

[50]Ibid., p. 133.

[51]Ibid., pp. 134-135. Captain Arthur Rogers, Founder and Honorary Secretary of the Liberty Restoration League, asked Fahey for assistance with Russian émigrés in London. Rogers to Fahey, July 18, 1950, FP-HGP.

[52]Ibid., pp. 135-140.

[53]Ibid., p. 140. There are eight letters from Robert H. Williams to Fahey (1946-1949), FP-HGP, which provide an important link between Fahey and the U.S.A. as will be discussed later.

[54]There are four boxes of excess material in the FP-HGP—booklets, articles, leaflets, newspaper clippings, and early drafts of some of Fahey's manuscripts—which have been divided into four categories: "Freemasons," "Communism," "Money," and "Jews." The books in Fahey's library fall into the same categories, with the one exception of his resources on agriculture which were sent to Rockwell College, Cashel, County Tipperary.

[55]Ibid., pp. 141-144; 152-154.

[56]Ibid., pp. 144-145.

[57]Ibid., pp. 154-158.

[58]Vladimir Lezar-Borin to Fahey, December 17, 1945, FP-HGP.

[59]KCCJN, pp. 161-162.

[60]Ibid., pp, 169-173.

[61]Ibid., p. 169.

[62]MPPSTA, n. 2, pp. 1-2.

[63]KCPSTA, Chapter VIII. See pp. 117-118.

[64]Ibid., p. 126.

[65]Ibid., pp. 128-129.

[66]Ibid., p. 134.

[67]Ibid., p. 135.

[68]Ibid., pp. 135-136.

[69]*Money Manipulation and the Social Order* (Dublin: Browne and Nolan Ltd., 1944). This monograph was largely Part V of MBCRS. Hereafter MMSO.

[70]KCPSTA, p. 120.

[71]KCON, p. 3.

[72]Ibid. See T. de St. Just, *La Royauté Sociale de N.-S. Jésus Christ d'après le Cardinal Pie*. The quotation on Naturalism is not on pp. 57-58 as is indicated, but is in a note on p. 92 of the second edition.

[73]Ibid., p. 45; MBCRS, p. 152.

[74]KCON, pp. 52-53; see also MBCRS, pp. 193-194, and KCCJN, pp. 191-192.

[75]Interviews with two former members of the *Maria Duce*: Frank Murtagh, Dublin, March 20, 1979, and another member who prefers to remain unidentified.

[76]KCCJN, pp. 175-192.

[77]Ibid., p.175. See Augustine Lémann, *L'Antéchrist* (Paris: Librairie Catholique Emmanuel Vitte, 1905). Augustine Lemann and his brother Joseph, also a convert to Catholicism and a priest, petitioned the Bishops at Vatican I for a *Postulatum pro Hebraeis* which received 510 signatures before the Council was abruptly terminated because of war. The two brothers collaborated on other works including *La Question du Messie et la Concile du Vatican*, and *La Cause des Restes d'Israël*. See pp. 92-96 for comments on Father Lémann.

[78]Ibid., p. 175, 101, and 109-110.

[79]Ibid., pp. 177-178.

[80]Ibid., pp. 179-180.

[81]Ibid., p. 181.

[82]Ibid., p. 182.

[83]Ibid.

[84]Ibid., pp. 183-184.

[85]Ibid., p. 184. Emphasis added.

[86]Ibid. Emphasis added. Because Lémann's volume was not available to me, there was no way for me to determine what material was omitted between his discussion of the Fathers of the Church, and the modern financial power of the Jews.

[87]Ibid., p. 185.

[88]Ibid., pp. 186-189.

[89]Ibid., p. 190.

[90]Interview with John Chisholm,C.S.Sp., March 11, 1979. The exact statement in the IER (1954) 81:79, is: "The book concludes with an excellent chapter on the coming of Anti-Christ." Chisholm added that he received some very unpleasant letters as a result of the review, including one from England. He seems to regret having been intimidated at the time.

[91]Interview with Michael O'Carroll, C.S.Sp., March 13, 1979.

[92]FP-HGP. The anti-Semitic leaflets and other material from Arnold Leese and others illustrate this point.

[93]Bernard Kelly, C.S.Sp., Enda Watters, C.S.Sp., and others point out that Fahey's books were often underlined through the first or second chapter, but other parts remained untouched, which led some to question whether he ever read the books *in toto*.

[94]Interviews with Enda Watters, C.S.Sp., William Jenkinson, C.S.Sp., and Michael O'Carroll,C.S.Sp. The latter suggested that Fahey's philosophical training injured his approach to history. In fact, O'Carroll did not think Fahey was a historian, although his historical education did manifest itself in his affection for the thirteenth century.

CHAPTER V

THE COUGHLIN-FAHEY CONNECTION

In describing the period of the 1930s in the United States, Sydney E. Ahlstrom comments: "Americans of every type sought and found scapegoats and panaceas; racist attitudes and ethnic animosities sharpened. Political and religious views gravitated to the extremes; and demagogues, often with the Cross of Christ on their banners, began to gather followers."[1] One of these "demagogues on the Right" whom Ahlstrom includes on his list along with Gerald Winrod, Gerald L.K Smith, and William Dudley Pelley is Father Charles E. Coughlin, famous "radio priest" of the pre-World War II period. In the past, writers have reflected on Coughlin chiefly from a political and socio-cultural point of view.[2] Little had been done, however, in exploring the theological framework out of which Coughlin operated, and the intellectual underpinnings of his thought. Key questions which will be explored are: (1) Within what kind of theological orientation did Coughlin function which allowed him to make some of the rabidly anti-Semitic pronouncements which he articulated in the years 1938-1942? (2) Did Coughlin's relationship to Fahey provide him with a theological rationale for his anti-Jewish stance? (3) How did that relationship affect Fahey—his writings, and his potential for influence in America?

Although the number of those who remember hearing the voice of Father Coughlin on the radio on Sunday afternoon is dwindling, those who do recall generally respond with adulation or disdain. Even the children of that generation recall passionate arguments surrounding "the radio priest," both extolling and denouncing him. Coughlin, like his contemporary Franklin D. Roosevelt, was either loved and admired or held in a kind of contempt. One can read copies of Coughlin's weekly newspaper, *Social Justice*, published from March 1936 to April 1942, in many libraries.[3] From 1930 on, his radio addresses were usually available in book form. As a controversial figure in the New Deal years, in both his appreciation of and anger against Franklin D. Roosevelt, he warranted coverage by the secular and religious press. One had to *hear* him, however, to understand the influence he had on a whole generation of Americans.

Coughlin: Priest, Politician, Social Reformer, Foe of Communism

Charles Edward Coughlin was the only child of parents of Irish ancestry. His great-grandfather helped to build the Erie Canal. His father, Thomas Coughlin, became a sailor on a Great Lakes steamer and later settled in Ontario, Canada, where he met and married Amelia Mahoney. Charles was born on October 25, 1891.

Both of his parents were devout Catholics and he was close to the church from his childhood. In June 1903, at age thirteen, Charles entered the preparatory seminary at St. Michael's College, Toronto, to begin studies for the priesthood. In 1911, he was president of the first graduating class to receive a degree from the University of Toronto and the newly federated St. Michael's College. He then proceeded to a more intense preparation for the priesthood at St. Basil's Seminary. During part of that time he studied in a college run by the Basilian Order in Waco, Texas. He was ordained on June 29, 1916, in St. Basil's Church in Toronto.[4]

From 1916-1918, Coughlin taught psychology, English, and logic at Assumption College in Ontario on the Canadian border near Detroit. He directed the dramatic society as well. On weekends he assisted at St. Agnes Church in Detroit. When changes developed in the Basilian Order in Canada in 1918 requiring that the men take a vow of poverty, the priests of the order were given three alternatives. One of the options was to leave and join the diocesan clergy. This was Coughlin's choice, and on February 6, 1923, he was incardinated into the diocese of Detroit.

Bishop Michael J. Gallagher of Detroit was to become Coughlin's close friend and defender. After three brief and successful assignments, Gallagher asked Coughlin, early in 1926, to build a new parish in an obscure suburban area of Detroit called Royal Oak, at the intersection of Woodward Avenue and Twelve Mile Road. It was to be named in honor of the recently canonized St. Thérèse of Lisieux, "the Little Flower," as she was affectionately known. In an effort to raise funds for the endeavor, Father Coughlin negotiated his first radio program which aired on October 17, 1926, over WJR in Detroit.[5]

At first the program was primarily sermonizing. With the advent of the depression, Coughlin changed his format, and spoke more of the frustration of people. He attacked Bolshevism, and became an "authority" on Communism and monetary issues. By 1930, CBS picked up his program nationally, and he had an estimated forty million listeners. Short-wave from Philadelphia carried his voice all over the world on "The Golden Hour of the Little Flower."

By 1933 Coughlin had four personal secretaries and 106 clerks employed to answer the mail which he received. The Royal Oak Post Office revealed that in 1935 the Radio League of the Little Flower had cashed four million dollars in money orders in a twenty month period. Considering the financial condition of the country at the time, that was remarkable. Most of the contributions were in small sums. The cost of his radio program at this period was about $14,000-$15,000 weekly. He was no longer just the pastor of a small church in Royal Oak.

Coughlin was an ardent supporter of Franklin D. Roosevelt in the early 1930s and hoped to have a place of influence in the new administration. He met the presidential candidate for the first time in the spring of 1932. In the course of the conversation, according to Coughlin, Roosevelt promised the priest that he would be a close confidante on economic and social issues, and Coughlin in turn promised to use his influence on the air waves to support Roosevelt's campaign for the presidency. Coughlin coined the expression "Roosevelt or ruin!" as well as "the New Deal is Christ's Deal."

After his inauguration, President Roosevelt did not look to Detroit for advice. Coughlin felt rejected and his antagonism toward Roosevelt and the "New Deal" grew into enmity. In 1936 he founded his weekly newspaper *Social Justice*. In the same year Coughlin joined the heir apparent of Huey Long's program, the Reverend Gerald L. K. Smith, and Dr. Francis Townsend of California who was promoting a program for the elderly known as the Townsend Plan, to form the Union Party to oppose Roosevelt in his bid for reelection. The colorless Congressman William Lemke of North Dakota was nominated for president, and Thomas O'Brien, District Attorney of Boston, as the vice-presidential candidate. Both Smith and Coughlin dominated the campaign, however, with their efforts to be center-stage. At a concluding speech of the Townsend Convention, Coughlin—hoping to top Smith's earlier performance—over-extended his theatrical tactics. He ripped off his Roman collar, called FDR "Franklin Double-Crossing Roosevelt," a liar, and a betrayer. This language shocked Catholics and non-Catholics alike and exceeded the limits of respectability.[6]

The Vatican was disturbed by his activities, but technically it was Coughlin's bishop who should take action, and Gallagher was supportive of Coughlin to the end. The Apostolic Delegate to the U.S., Ameleto Cicognani, was told to convey the message that an apology to the President was in order. Coughlin himself realized that he had overstepped his bounds, and was sorry that he used such intemperate language. While on a trip to Rome, Gallagher was told to restrain Coughlin, but upon returning to the U.S. the Bishop of Detroit was quoted in *Newsweek* as saying: "It's the voice of God that comes to you from the great orator in Royal Oak. Rally round it."[7] Pope Pius XI was reportedly angry that nothing more was done. Shortly after that, the Vatican

Secretary of State Eugenio Pacelli (later Pope Pius XII), on a trip to the United States, instructed Gallagher that he should exercise more control over Coughlin, and that after the 1936 election the "radio priest" was not to participate in future political campaigning. According to Gerald L. K. Smith, Coughlin interpreted this action as a Roosevelt political maneuver to get Rome to silence him.[8]

The Detroit priest was not quieted by this activity. On one occasion when a reporter took exception to Coughlin's calling David Dubinsky and Felix Frankfurter Communists, Coughlin lunged at the reporter, ripped off his glasses, and punched him in the face. On another occasion he called Roosevelt a "scab President." His dramatization of the names of the international bankers—mostly Jewish—was commonplace. By the end of the campaign he was suffering from physical and emotional exhaustion.[9]

Coughlin had promised that if he did not deliver nine million votes for the Union Party, he would retire from the radio and from political life. Lemke received fewer than a million out of more than forty-five million votes cast. For a brief time, Coughlin did quit the air-waves (November 1936-January 1937). After Bishop Gallagher's death on January 20, 1937, Coughlin returned to the radio stating that it was his bishop's deathbed wish.[10]

Detroit was then upgraded to an archdiocese, and Edward Mooney became the first archbishop. Coughlin was shocked to discover that his new Ordinary was less than enthusiastic about his endeavors. When Coughlin made a statement that the CIO was incompatible with Catholicism, believing that Communists had infiltrated important offices in that organization, Mooney announced that Coughlin's views did not express those of the archdiocese. A series of incidents occurred wherein it seemed clear to Coughlin that Mooney wanted to censor his speeches. Rather than submit, he cancelled his 1937-38 radio series.[11]

For a short time again, Coughlin was off the air. Through the efforts of his friends and those nominally in charge of *Social Justice*, the Vatican was deluged with mail begging that Father

Coughlin be reinstated. Part of a form letter which people were encouraged to send to Rome read:

> Holy Father, we plead for our Father Coughlin —Have him continue his Radio Broadcasts in the same heartfelt way, not in censored platitudes which defeat the dignity God bestowed on man, but as an "Alter Christus," fearless and outspoken, going about doing his Father's business, spreading the doctrine of the Mystical Body—a brotherhood of man with a fatherhood in God—to confute the Atheistic Communism and other Godless isms—to continue to espouse the cause of the poor, for the rich have ample means. Holy Father, many of us were tricked by artful propaganda, but now we humbly ask Your Holiness to give us back our Father Coughlin, as he should be—free and unrestrained in preaching the doctrine of Christ to the poor and to all who will listen.[12]

The crusade had the desired effect. Coughlin met with the Apostolic Delegate in December 1937. The result was a statement that he would resume broadcasting on January 9, 1938. Archbishop Mooney accepted the decision gracefully. Coughlin believed that he was successful because he had friends in the Vatican.[13] Neither Mooney nor any other Catholic ecclesiastic would be quick to confront Coughlin after that incident. As will be discussed later, the "radio priest" became more radical and more anti-Semitic in 1938 and thereafter.

Coughlin saw himself, especially in the years 1929-1936, as a social reformer. He prided himself upon the fact that he was popularizing the papal social encyclicals, particularly *Rerum Novarum* ("On the Condition of the Working Classes"), promulgated by Pope Leo XIII in 1891, and *Quadragesimo Anno* ("On Reconstructing the Social Order"), issued by Pius XI in 1931, both basically concerned with the needs of the working classes.

Coughlin's "Sixteen Points for Social Justice" which he announced in a radio broadcast on November 11, 1934 when he was preparing to found his National Union for Social Justice, comprised a liberal platform for that day. Although he spoke loudly for the right of private ownership of "all other property," his third point stated: "I believe in nationalizing the public resources which by their very nature are too important to be held in the control of private individuals." He wanted to abolish the privately owned Federal Reserve Bank, and establish a government owned Central Bank. He spoke out for a living family wage, demanded a fair profit for the farmer, and believed that the right of the laboring man to organize in unions included "the duty of the Government, which that laboring man supports, to protect these organizations against the vested interests of wealth and intellect.[14]

The "radio priest's" theories on money fluctuated. He was often inconsistent and took a simplistic view, but he came to be considered an "expert" and was called to testify before the Banking Subcommittee in the U.S. House of Representatives in March 1934. His break with FDR seems to have been largely over Roosevelt's unwillingness to back the monetization of silver. Marcus quotes from an interview with Coughlin in April 1970: "The President promised me that the country would go on the silver standard. It turned out that he was lying to me. But he was so damn charming that you couldn't help but like him."[15] In those early days, Coughlin continued to give the President advice, and alluded in his broadcasts to having an inside view. He became angry, however, when FDR did not take him seriously, and by 1934 had begun to criticize him openly.

In late April 1934, in an effort to discredit Coughlin and others who were pushing for silver monetization, Secretary of the Treasury Henry Morgenthau, Jr. released a list of the names of individuals and organizations who had substantial holdings in silver. Father Coughlin's secretary, Amy Collins, who was the secretary and treasurer of the Radio League of the Little Flower, was highest on the list of all those possessing silver in the state of Michigan. She claimed that she had made an investment of $20,

000 of League money in silver on her own. It was known to all, however, that Coughlin had complete control over all the activities of the corporation.[16]

As a result of this disclosure, many persons became disillusioned with the "radio priest." Coughlin retorted that he was a victim of the gold advocates. He sincerely believed that the people around the President were out to get him. It became clear, however, that while Coughlin condemned speculators, he himself was involved. He was always crying out against Wall Street brokers who controlled the government, yet it was the firm of Harris and Vose which had handled the purchase of the 500,000 ounces of silver with Radio League money—the same corporation that was active in lobbying with Senator Elmer Thomas of Oklahoma for the passage of the silver legislation.[17]

Coughlin was apparently attempting to maneuver events to his own advantage. Be that as it may, his pleas for silver and cheap money, plus his concern for the farmer (as in the Frazier-Lemke Bill), do identify him with the descendants of the Populist platform. During an appearance before the House Committee on Coinage, Weights and Measures in 1934, he concluded dramatically with a statement reminiscent of Bryan's "cross of gold" speech: "Silver is just as good as gold. Christ was betrayed for thirty pieces of silver."[18]

The "radio priest" continued to receive basic political support from the urban areas, where the Catholic population, only recently emerging from its immigrant status, was largely entrenched. Concern for the working person placed him in the American Catholic tradition of James Cardinal Gibbons and Archbishop John Ireland. In Coughlin's earlier years he was lauded by Msgr. John A. Ryan, author of *A Living Wage*, and the "Bishop's Program for Social Reconstruction," because of his vehement advocacy of the rights of workers and of a living family wage.

Coughlin, as well as Fahey, found their authorities in Thomas Aquinas, the statements of the popes (especially Leo XIII), and scattered references to Scripture. Coughlin's addresses and essays, however, are largely pious and emotional religious tracts, or political polemic, and sometimes both. The discouraged unemployed person of the Depression era found the "radio priest" an articulate disputant who challenged the government to help the distressed, and provide for justice in society. Coughlin's references to philosophical and theological issues, however, are largely superficial, as can be noted in a brief discussion of "naturalism" and "supernaturalism" in his 1930-1931 radio series.[19] When his subject was "Where Money Is King," "Gold and Silver and the Child Welfare Bureau," or "Christ or Chaos?"—he told people what they wanted to hear.[20]

Both Fahey and Coughlin were concerned with social reform, but the "radio priest" was primarily a politician, a pragmatist, and a popularizer. Fahey became involved in politics only in his later years, and then as a priest and a professor who approached social reform from his specifically Irish Catholic position. In comparing and contrasting Coughlin's "Sixteen Points of Social Justice"—reprinted in every issue of *Social Justice* from 1936 until its demise in 1942, and Fahey's "Six Points of the Catholic Plan for Social Order"—reprinted in each issue of *FIAT*, it is clear that although the Irish priest would agree with much of Coughlin's economic platform, he could not accept the pluralistic American approach, and the lack of emphasis on a Catholic stance.[21]

Both priests claimed to have found the mid-point between extreme capitalism and atheistic communism. Fahey's program is clearly more comprehensive in terms of the Christian life. Coughlin's is specific and pragmatic, focusing on eliminating economic injustices in society. Both committed themselves with their particular talents—Coughlin as a radio "evangelist," and Fahey as a prolific writer—to promulgating that message to the English-speaking world.

The fear of Catholics regarding "godless Communism" was alive and well in post-World War I America. Communism was not only anti-religious, but also anti-American. Although a Canadian by birth, Coughlin was an "Americanist" of the first order. He saw Communism as an international conspiracy which was luring the working class into its fold by denying the right of private property, and promising the benefits of prosperity to all. With the disillusionment which followed "The Great War," persons in every country were susceptible to this cry. Coughlin expounded:

> Patriotism, my friends, holds the same relation between a citizen and his country as fidelity does between a man and his wife; as piety does between a child and its parent; as religion does between a creature and his Creator...Patriotism and internationalism! The one born of Godliness and Christliness; the other, the offspring of atheism and greed![22]

Communism, he believed, primarily wanted to destroy the Church and the nation and spread its own materialistic international gospel. He felt compelled to warn the people of America against the beguilements of Soviet Russia and its subversive activities in many nations, including his adopted home.

Coughlin's sympathetic attitude toward Hitler must be understood in this framework. The radio priest believed that Nazism was "a political defense mechanism against Communism."[23] It was Hitler who would "save" the West from Communism. If his methods were occasionally undesirable, Coughlin claimed in the 1930s, the German leader was at least rescuing the world from a far worse evil. The friendships of the "radio priest" with Henry Ford who had been decorated by Hitler in the summer of 1938 with the Grand Cross of the German Eagle, and with Fritz Kuhn, leader of the German-American Bund, no doubt enhanced Coughlin's admiration of the Fuhrer.[24]

Fahey's response to Hitler was not dissimilar to that of Coughlin. Although Ireland's neutrality in World War II was based largely on her unwillingness to fight on the same side as Great Britain rather than on her affection for Germany—Fahey's later efforts to disprove the Holocaust, and his omission of major references to Hitler even after the war, while blaming the Jews for the continued evil in the world—suggest that his sympathies were not unlike Coughlin's.[25]

Both Coughlin and Fahey viewed the civil war in Spain as a microcosm of the real battle of the world: the Communists against the Catholic governments of Europe. If autocratic rulers such as Hitler, Mussolini, and Franco arose, while they were not to be condoned, they were preferred to the atheistic Communists who were subverting the Kingship of Christ. It was on the subject of Communism and the Jews that Coughlin and Fahey first communicated. The "radio priest" found a kindred spirit in an Irish professor in Dublin.

Coughlin, Fahey and the Jews

The evolution of Coughlin's position on the Jews is evident when reflecting upon events of 1934, 1936, and 1938. When founding the National Union for Social Justice in 1934, Coughlin had a relatively all-encompassing vision for his program of social reform. His stated purpose in his November 11 broadcast was "to organize for action, if you will: to organize for social united action which will be founded on God-given social truths which belong to Catholic and Protestant, to Jew and Gentile, to black and white, to rich and poor, industrialist and laborer."[26]

After his political defeat in 1936, however, Coughlin became convinced that the ultra-capitalists (the international bankers) and the ultra-Communists (the Bolsheviks) were in league to destroy the world.[27] How could two groups which seemed to be mutually exclusive form an alliance? Similar to Fahey, Coughlin believed it was because they were both controlled by Jews who had an ulterior motive: Zionist domination of the world. Dominating the press, Jews were in a pivotal position to espouse their cause. Who else aroused the sympathies of Americans regarding the treatment of Jews in Nazi Germany, and neglected the sufferings of Catholics in Spain, Mexico, and Russia?[28]

Shortly after Coughlin's return to the air following Bishop Gallagher's death, a headline in *Social Justice* issued a summons: "Father Coughlin Calls on NUSJ to Awake."[29] Although the major themes in the weekly issues and in his radio broadcasts continued to be Communism, labor, and the money question—the "radio priest" definitely moved to a more pro-Christian emphasis. The June 21, 1937 newspaper carried the following statement:

> The Divine Master said: "You are either with Me or against Me. If you are luke warm, I will begin to spew you out of my mouth." He meant that if you are a compromiser and a fence-straddler belonging to the genus of "pussy-footer," you are even worse than an honest Communist or any other honest enemy. Hence, we are pro-Christ 1,000 per cent. We are for his principles and for his teachings 1,000 per cent. If the doctrines or the practices of the Brahman, the Mohammedan or the Jews are not in harmony with Christ's doctrines, 1,000 per cent we are anti, even though the enemies wish to call it so. Really, we are pro-Christ![30]

August of that year, however, brought about Coughlin's great confrontation with Archbishop Mooney over Catholic participation in the CIO and censorship. This subject preoccupied *Social Justice* for the succeeding months of 1937.

In 1938, a "new" *Social Justice* appeared. The February 2 issue had a slick new format, rather like *Life* magazine, with color added and Coughlin on the cover. New columnists were enlisted, including Hilaire Belloc, who was Visiting Professor at Fordham University in the 1937-1938 academic year. It was announced that the British author would contribute fifty-two articles "of original observation" written especially for *Social Justice*. By May 9, 1938, however, expense proved too much, and the format was cut back—less slick, but still with color.

The first article by "Ben Marcin" appeared March 21, 1938. Coughlin claimed that this writer, who contributed articles to *Social Justice* defending *The Protocols* and defaming the Jews, was himself a Jew. In an interview with Sheldon Marcus in April 1970, however, Coughlin admitted that the articles were ghost-written, possibly by the editor, E. Perrin Schwartz, or Leo Reardon. He stated, "...to my knowledge there never was such a person."[31] Yet this was the "Jewish authority" who wrote for *Social Justice* during this crucial period.

The build-up of anti-Jewish material continued through the spring. Coughlin's exclusion of non-Christians became more intense. The June 20, 1938 issue entitled "The Christian Front," pictured Pius XI on the cover, and the following statement below:

At the mere mention of the Christian Front there is gnashing of teeth on the part of non-Christians. The words "Christian Front" are an abomination to those whose objective is to de-christianize America. Is it not time for the Christians in our country to realize that if this is not a Christian country in its politics, its education, its industry, and its finance, then it will be a non-Christian country in all these and other branches? "You are either with Me or against Me," are the words of Christ. *Too long have we adopted the poisonous philosophy of tolerance in the sense that we have compromised our principles in order not to offend the principles of those who love paganism or non-Christianity.*[32]

In the summer of 1938, a concerted effort against the Jews was in progress in *Social Justice*. Sections of *The Protocols of the Elders of Zion* were printed weekly, beginning July 19, with commentaries and one response, through November of the same year. Coughlin used the same dodge as Henry Ford and Fahey by stating that the question wasn't whether *The Protocols* were authentic, but whether they described what was going on in the world. He added:

> The book of *The Protocols of the Meetings of the Learned Elders of Zion* is preeminently a communistic program to destroy Christian civilization. The best rebuttal which the modern leaders of Zion can offer to the authenticity of the Protocols is to institute a vigorous campaign against Communism.[33]

Each week Coughlin's commentary on *The Protocols* was longer, more repetitious, more intense. On August 1, 1938, he wrote: "a correspondence between the prophecy contained in this book and its fulfillment is too glaring to be set aside or obscured." In conclusion he stated: "The authors of *The Protocols of the Wise Men of Zion* actually did outline a plot and the plot has, in part, been carried out in our day—a plot against Christian civilization."[34] The following week Coughlin remarked:

> Be it also emphasized that we entertain no animosity whatever against the individual Jew: He is more to be pitied than to be blamed, for he has carried the badge of suffering from nation to nation with such persistency that, from a historical viewpoint, it is not illogical to presume that he *will not* escape persecution even in nations which hitherto have shown friendliness to him.[35]

One wonders if the "radio priest" is suggesting the United States in this latter statement. After sowing seeds of suspicion, mistrust, and fear of plots for weeks, Coughlin stated in the ninth installment: "If and when anti-Semitism shows its ugly head here, I shall be the first, without hope of receiving reward, to condemn it both by voice and deed."[36]

"The Jewish Answer: The Truth about the Protocols" was presented by Philip Slomovitz, editor of *The Detroit Jewish Chronicle*, in *Social Justice*, September 26, 1938. He began:

"The Protocols have been condemned by Catholics and Protestants alike as a vicious libel upon a people who have been peace-loving and law-abiding wherever they have lived." He then discussed the facts and errors at length.[37] The response to Slomovitz was "The Truth about the Protocols" by the fictitious "Ben Marcin." This was a repetition of the allegations which were a part of the commentaries over the weeks.[38] One would think that the whole agonizing episode might be over, but in *Social Justice*, November 21, 1938, the day after Father Coughlin's famous speech "Persecution— Jewish and Christian," Protocol No. 16 was published, and the series began again for a short time.[39]

Why did Coughlin become so radically anti-Semitic in the fall of 1938? A combination of forces seems to have influenced his move to the "radical right." His anger at Roosevelt and his humiliation over the defeat of 1936 led him to the identification of the Jewish bankers as the primary enemy. He was alienated from the two-party system and consumed with a fear of plots and conspiracy. The success of his altercation with Archbishop Mooney gave him fresh incentive to speak out. Few members of the American Catholic hierarchy would challenge him when "Rome" was on his side.

Yet none of these reasons satisfactorily explains why the "radio priest" became fixed on attacking the Jews in the second half of that year. One name emerged, however, in the summer of 1938, whom Coughlin quoted as an authority in his controversial writings and speeches: Denis Fahey,C.S.Sp.

Coughlin first introduced the Irish priest to the readers of *Social Justice* in the August 8, 1938 issue. In his weekly column, "From the Tower," which was one of his many articles devoted to *The Protocols of the Elders of Zion*, Coughlin stated:

At the present moment, according to Rev. Dennis [sic] Fahey, in his "Rulers of Russia," (a book which has received the imprimatur of the Archbishop of Dublin),—at the present moment,

many Jews occupy the chief positions in the Russian
political scheme. Father Fahey says:....[40]

Several columns of quotations from *The Mystical Body of Christ
in the Modern World* and the *Rulers of Russia* follow, including
the material on the "British White Paper," and the statements from
Documentation Catholique. The lists of "Jewish names" are cited
at length. Coughlin had read Fahey's books well.

When did Coughlin discover Denis Fahey? Very likely it
was in early or middle 1938. The first correspondence in the
Fahey Papers linking the Irish priest to Coughlin, however, is a
letter from E. Perrin Schwartz, editor of *Social Justice*, to Fahey
on November 8, 1938, just as Coughlin's anti-Jewish campaign was
approaching its height. Schwartz stated clearly that Fahey's
valuable material was "co-relative to the editorial policies" of
Social Justice, and asked Fahey if he would consider contributing
to their publication. Father Coughlin's editor then stated that the
social encyclicals of Leo XIII and Pius XI were foundational to
their philosophy, and added that no true social reform could be
achieved without commitment to the Kingship of Christ and His
Mystical Body—Fahey's two favorite subjects. Because of that,
"...*it behooves us at present to deliver an understanding of this
spiritual structure to our readers.*"[41] Implied is that Fahey's more
theological framework could serve Coughlin's program well.

It was not only the spiritual dimension, however, which
attracted Coughlin and Perrin Schwartz to Fahey. They were particularly interested in his discussion of the disputed authorship of
The Protocols of the Elders of Zion and an analysis of the factuality
of the documents.[42] It should be noted here that although E. Perrin
Schwartz was editor of *Social Justice* from 1936-1942, it was very
clear who was in charge. He admitted in 1939: "I just carry out
instructions.... I have nothing to do with policy. Father Coughlin's
the man to ask. I'm just a newspaper man. I just carry out
instructions...."[43] A request to Fahey to write for *Social Justice*
would never have been made without Coughlin's express approval,
and was very likely at his instigation.

Coughlin lost no time in taking advantage of Fahey's fund of knowledge. D. O. Kelly of Browne and Nolan Limited of Dublin informed Fahey on November 17, 1938:

You will no doubt be very pleased to hear that the celebrated Fr. Coughlan [sic] of Radio fame has ordered a special edition of 2000 copies of "The Kingship of Christ" at 1/8d. a copy. On looking up your agreement, I see that we made no provision for the American Market, but presume you will be willing to accept the usual terms of 10% of the actual price received by us.[44]

Exactly how Coughlin discovered Fahey's books is unknown, although it may have been through their mutual friend, Arnold Lunn. Father Coughlin was also friendly with members of the Holy Ghost Congregation in Detroit. One of them may have recommended Fahey's books to him.[45]

The "radio priest" quoted Fahey in extended fashion in the November 14, 1938 issue of *Social Justice* regarding the incomprehension from which many Catholics suffer regarding the struggle surrounding the Mystical Body of Christ, and the accurate grasp of the situation which many of her enemies enjoy. The column concluded with Fahey's statement:

Let us hope that the integral truth will come home to all Catholics that the world is divided into two camps, the camp of those who stand for Christ the King and His rule in all its integrity, and the camp of Satan with its motto, *Non serviam*—"I will not serve" (Jeremias ii.20).[46]

Coughlin's Dependency on Fahey

Coughlin's greatest reliance on Fahey was during his fall radio series (November 6, 1938-January 1, 1939), published under the title *"Am I an Anti-Semite?"*. It contrasts vividly with the spring broadcasts (January 9-April 17, 1938), which had focused on the New Deal, labor problems, money, war and peace. Although there were the usual indictments of international bankers, and condemnation of Communists in the earlier months, the emphasis had been largely on the domestic scene.

The murder of a German official in Paris by a young Polish Jew whose parents had been expelled from Germany became the occasion for Coughlin's tirade. When the Nazi government imposed a fine of $400 million on the 600,000 German Jews resident in Germany, leaders from around the world expressed dismay at such vengeance.[47] It is noteworthy that Coughlin does not refer to the horrifying experience of the *Krystallnacht* on November 7, 1938, when synagogues and Jewish businesses in Germany were destroyed in what became known as "The Night of Broken Glass"—an event which made more than explicit the anti-Semitism of the Nazi regime. Coughlin's November 20, 1938 radio speech focused on "Persecution—Jewish and Christian." He admitted that "...cruel persecution to German-born Jews had been notorious since 1933—particularly since the loss of their citizenship—nevertheless, until last week the Nazi purge was concerned, chiefly, with foreign-born Jews."[48] What disturbed Coughlin most was that the sufferings of Christians had received no publicity:

> While it is true that foreign citizen Jews resident in Germany were disparaged and expelled, it is likewise true that many social impediments were placed in the pathway of Catholics and Protestants by the Nazi government—impediments which are revolting to our American concepts of liberty. But despite all this, official Germany has not yet resorted to the guillotine, to the machine gun, to the kerosene-drenched pit as instruments of reprisal against Jew or gentile.[49]

Why had this event received so much news coverage? Coughlin was convinced that it was because of (1) Jewish control of the press, and (2) Jewish financial strength which supported the Bolshevik Revolution.

Of the fifteen million Jews in the world (Coughlin quoted *The World Almanac*), only four million were resident in North America. He described them as:

> ...a closely woven minority in their racial tendencies; a powerful minority in their influence; a minority endowed with an aggressiveness, an initiative which, despite all obstacles, has carried their sons to the pinnacle of success in journalism, in radio, in finance, and in all the sciences and arts.

Coughlin then stated that no story of persecution had ever been half so well told as the $400 million fine of the German Jews, because of Jewish control of the media.[50]

The "radio priest" asked why Nazism had been so hostile to Jewry, and responded:

> It is the belief, be it well or ill founded, of the present German government, not mine, that Jews—not as religionists but as nationals only—were responsible for the economic and social ills suffered by the Fatherland since the signing of the Treaty of Versailles.[51]

Coughlin believed that during the early 1920s when Communism had begun to make substantial advances in Germany, Hitler and his followers organized for two purposes: "First, to overthrow the existing German government under whose jurisdiction Communism was waxing strong, and second, to rid the Fatherland of Communists whose leaders, unfortunately, they identified with the Jewish race." Then followed Coughlin's frequently repeated statement: "Thus, *Nazism was conceived as a political defense mechanism against Communism*, and was ushered into existence as a result of Communism." According to the "radio priest," Communism was seen by the Germans not as Russian, but as the product "of a group of Jews who dominated the destinies of Russia."[52]

Were the Nazis acting only on a surmise, or did they have "facts"? It is here that Coughlin draws on Fahey's "evidence," although he does not refer to the Irish priest by name at this point: "Uncontradictable evidence gleaned from the writings and policies of Lenin, proved indisputably that the government of the Soviet Republics was predominantly anti-Christian and definitely anti-national."[53] Coughlin then stated that he had before him a list of "25 quasi-cabinet members, 24 of them atheistic Jews." In addition there is the enumeration of the fifty-nine members of the central committee of the Communist Party, fifty-six who were supposedly Jews and the other three married to Jews. All of this material is directly from Fahey's writings.[54]

Although it had been clear from the pages of *Social Justice* that Coughlin accepted Fahey's thesis of the suppressed British White Paper, and the "American Intelligence Report" published in *Documentation Catholique*, his emotional presentation of the material to a ready and accepting radio audience gave it additional credence. In the published version of this address he stated that because his sources had been questioned, he was providing "proof:" "I am also supplying photostatic copies—pp. 88, 89, 90, 91, 291, 292, 293 of Father Fahey's book, 'The Mystical Body of Christ' ...."[55] One wonders if—in not acknowledging Fahey in his November 20 broadcast—Coughlin hoped to communicate that he had uncovered the material himself.

Response to Coughlin's allegations from Jews and most Christians was outrage.[56] WMCA of New York City refused the "radio priest" further access to their station unless he submitted his speeches forty-eight hours in advance. Coughlin hoped to refute those who questioned his sources in his broadcast the following week entitled "Let Us Consider the Record." He reiterated his key points, played a transcript of the previous Sunday's speech, and concluded with a strong statement as to why his defamers had been disproved.[57]

The primary witness whom Coughlin called forth in his radio address was Fahey. Following the transcription of the earlier broadcast, he stated:

> It is regrettable that I am forced to read into the record a part of a closely guarded, certified document. I trusted that I should be spared doing this in order to avoid personalities.
>
> However, since I am forced to defend myself, not for myself, but for the cause I uphold, let me introduce into court as my witness the scholarly Professor Denis Fahey.
>
> Professor Denis Fahey—one of the most outstanding scholars in Ireland—an honor graduate in arts, philosophy, divinity, economics and sociology is a professor of philosophy at Blackrock Seminary, Dublin, Ireland. He says on p. 88 in "The Mystical Body of Christ in the Modern World:"....[58]

Coughlin then quoted Fahey regarding "the suppressed British White Paper," and the "American Secret Service Report" and commended the Irish priest for making it available. Coughlin accepted Fahey's conclusion that an international Jewish conspiracy existed whereby bankers and Bolsheviks were taking over the world. To allow oneself sympathy for the persecution of the Jews in Germany was to miss the larger picture. Unless Jews committed themselves to being anti-Communist, then they were probably in league with their fellow nationals in favor of Communism, and deserved neither sympathy nor trust. Once Coughlin had "proved" that the Jewish international bankers had financed the Bolshevik Revolution, he pleaded with non-Communist Jews to see the light:

There is no Jewish question in America.
Please God, may there never be one. However,
there is a question of Communism in America.
Please God, we will solve it. If Jews persist
in supporting Communism directly or indirectly,
that will be regrettable. By their failure to use the
press, the radio and the banking house, where they
stand so prominently, to fight Communism as
vigorously as they fight Naziism [sic], the Jews
invite the charge of being supporters of
Communism.

For as Christ said, "you are either with Me
or against Me."[59]

"Not Anti-Semitism but Anti-Communism" is the title of
Coughlin's radio speech of December 4, 1938. Once again he
defended himself against those who questioned his facts. Once
again Father Fahey was brought forward. With his usual flair for
the dramatic, the "radio priest" announced:

Last week I telephoned to Dr. Denis Fahey at
Blackrock Seminary, Dublin, Ireland, asking him to
reinspect an original British "White Paper" from
which I quoted. He assures me that an original
copy is still available, safely guarded and at my
disposal; . . .[60]

The famous phone call from Coughlin to Fahey caused much
excitement at Blackrock, according to Brother Benignus, C.S.Sp.,
who was at the switchboard that day. It was the first transatlantic
call to be received at the seminary from the United States, and was
even the subject of an article in the Blackrock annual. Fahey was,
no doubt, delighted. Some who were then seminarians recall that
he spoke of Father Coughlin carrying out "his work" in America.[61]

With Christmas approaching, Coughlin delivered a speech
entitled "A Chapter on Intolerance." The General Jewish Council

had invited Mr. Frank Hogan, President of the American Bar Association, to respond to the Detroit priest's emotion-laden rhetoric which was deeply dividing Americans, and causing extreme pain to Jews. Coughlin anticipated Hogan's remarks in his broadcast of December 11, 1938. After reiterating his earlier claims, he stated:

> Tolerance, then, becomes a heinous vice when it tolerates the theology of atheism, the patriotism of internationalists and the justice of religious persecution. No matter, then, what ties of blood and common parentage bind the God-fearing Jews in New York with the atheistic Jews in Moscow, those ties must be severed for God, and for country and for the preservation of the teeming masses of Jews in America who have been victimized by the silence of their leaders and the propaganda of the press.[62]

Coughlin could not have been unaware of the fact that the Christmas season in America was a time for Jews and others who are non-Christian to feel disincluded from society. Yet it was this very subject of "Easter and Christmas practices" which became a major topic for his discussion.

The radio priest reminded his listeners that the teaching of religion was no longer possible in the schools. Many states had even excluded Bible reading. There were those who wanted to eliminate the celebration of Christmas and Easter. The Jews, he said, are to be "congratulated" for this. They succeeded in getting their policies enacted, even as a minority. He alerted his audience:

> But, remembering that godlessness is the poisoned spring whence Communism originates; remembering that this United States was founded by Christians, pioneered by Christians and developed, in great part, by Christians with no more than 4-million Jews

claiming residence amongst our 130-million population, why do the local Jewish Community Councils cooperate with others in imposing their policies, their constitutional policies, of opposition to "Christmas and Easter practices"? Why do they propagate that policy through the agency of a law that is on their side? Why do they boast in their publications that they have sown seeds—what shall I call them—seeds of godlessness?[63]

Jews were within their rights to subscribe to such a policy—that was the letter of the law—but, Coughlin stated, "the letter killeth." While intolerance was reprehensible, it was provoked by "injudicious and erroneous policies." Coughlin's words stirred up emotions against the Jews:

Therefore, I appeal to the General Jewish Council and to the local Councils. I ask you: Even though you are within your constitutional rights; even though we dare not protest legally—why have you closed the minds of our children to the beautiful story of Bethlehem and the Messias? Was not that an act of poor judgment?

Why have you blotted out the cycle of the Easter story with its Pilate's hall, its crucifixion and its glorious resurrection of the Victim of mob violence and hate?

We Christians—we have no constitutional redress. We should not even complain because you are within your rights. But, I repeat, it appears that you are injudicious.

Even if you Jews and gentiles in great number consider that these practices are idle dreams and poetry--why not leave us with our dreams, our poetry--dreams and poetry that we learned at our mother's knee; dreams and poetry which were

carried here by Columbus in his Santa Maria; ...
Oh, my fellow citizens, it was the dreams and
poetry born in the crib of Bethlehem and spoken
from the pulpit of the Cross that made this country
the land of the free and the home of the brave.

In an attempt to diffuse the response of the Irish Catholic lawyer
Frank Hogan, Coughlin continued:

> Oh, how can the General Jewish Council and
> the Jewish Community Councils who are about to
> answer me today through the lips of a fellow
> religionist, and with the voice of a fellow
> descendent of that same Irish race which suffered
> death and persecution—how can they be so unkind
> to us with their admitted preeminence in banking, in
> press, in cinema and in radio, and with the law on
> their side—to protest against the innocent practices
> of Christmas and Eastertide?
>
> The banking institutions can rob our
> Christian citizenry through the practice of usury.
>
> A controlled press can veil the eyes of a
> nation against the Christian blood which has run
> ankle-deep in Barcelona.
>
> Members of your race can devise reasons to
> exclude a voice from the airways which seeks to tell
> America the truth.
>
> And pitiless propaganda can exhibit itself upon
> the silver screens of our nation to deceive us....[64]

Why this emotional outburst against the Jews at this time?
The very day following Coughlin's radio sermon on "Tolerance,"
the picture on the front page of *Social Justice* was the cover of
Denis Fahey's volume, *The Mystical Body of Christ in the Modern
World—New and Enlarged Edition.* Against the background of a
Gothic cathedral the caption reads:

> SOCIAL JUSTICE departs from custom in giving its
> front page, not to the man or news event of
> importance this week, but to the most significant
> contribution to Christian civilization in this year, if
> not this decade. Quotations from "The Mystical
> Body of Christ in the Modern World," have been
> frequent in these columns and the radio addresses of
> Father Coughlin. Its wider acquaintance is almost
> indispensable.[65]

The reader is told that in this book the "real struggle going on in
the world to dethrone Christ and His philosophy" is described.
The study deals "from a theological, philosophical and historical
standpoint, with this modern revolt against the divine plan for the
organization of Christian society." Those who receive the
newspaper are reminded that this book "from which SOCIAL
JUSTICE will continue frequently to quote, is available at your
bookshop."[66] No other published work except those of Coughlin
himself received such prominence. When Coughlin introduced
Fahey to America, he did it with flourish.

Instead of Coughlin's regular column that week, his special
page, "From the Tower," was given over to a "Guest article by
Rev. Denis Fahey, C.S.Sp., B.A., D.Ph., D.D." with the headline
"The International Bankers." A preliminary note stated: "Hoping
to publicize 'The Mystical Body of Christ in the Modern World,'
I am inviting you to read this excerpt—C.E.C." The extended
sections which follow are Coughlin's summary of Fahey's key
points on the bankers with quotes from Fahey interspersed. A final
paragraph concludes: "All those who desire a copy of this
364-page book, may obtain same by writing direct to the SOCIAL
JUSTICE PUBLISHING COMPANY, INC. Limited number of
copies available at $2.50."[67] Coughlin was clearly convinced that
Fahey should be read in the United States.

Preceding this article was one entitled "The Talmud as a
Cause of Persecution" by none other than "Ben Marcin." This

author quoted seven paragraphs from the same volume of Fahey, including the Irish priest's reference to Aquinas' explanation that "Father forgive them..." was spoken on behalf of the common people, "but NOT on behalf of the princes of the Jews."[68] This essay also quoted from Hilaire Belloc's *The Jews*, although the largest part was from Fahey and his sources.

The following week (December 19, 1938), Coughlin took advantage of the disclaimer of George Cardinal Mundelein of Chicago regarding the "radio priest's" sermons by utilizing it to his own advantage. The Chicago ecclesiastic had stated: "As an American citizen Father Coughlin has the right to express his personal views on current events, but he is not authorized to speak for the Catholic Church, nor does he represent the doctrine or sentiments of the Church." Coughlin added: "Neither is any other priest, bishop or cardinal.... Pius XI alone is authorized to speak for the Catholic Church."[69]

Coughlin also used the opportunity to discredit the press. The Detroit clergyman invoked his Irish counterpart who had written at great length about the control of the press by monied interests:

> Speaking about news correspondents and news commentators and the press in general, the Rev. Denis Fahey in his book, "The Mystical Body of Christ in the Modern World"—a book which has received not only the imprimatur of his Bishop but his superior's warm approval says: "Nowadays, the vast majority of human beings in all countries are at the mercy of the newspapers for information about the world. And the newspapers mislead them atrociously."[70]

Fahey is quoted extensively not only in regard to the control of the press by financiers via ownership and advertising, but also in reference to the lax approach of many Catholic papers in terms of supporting Catholic ideals. Coughlin quoted Fahey whenever possible during this period.[71]

Although *The Mystical Body of Christ in the Modern World* was Fahey's most popular book at that time, and the one most frequently cited by Coughlin, *Social Justice* did not want its readers to forget the Irish priest's earlier volume, which was available at the Shrine of the Little Flower. In the February 6, 1939 issue of *Social Justice*, the following notice is included:

THERE ARE TWO FAHEY BOOKS

In giving publicity to "The Mystical Body of Christ" by Dr. Denis Fahey, SOCIAL JUSTICE has, perhaps neglected to say enough about Father Fahey's earlier book, "The Kingship of Christ." "The Kingship of Christ" by Father Fahey is also for sale by Social Justice Publishing Co. and can be obtained, while they last, for $1.25. The price of "The Mystical Body" is $2.50. Write enclosing money order to Social Justice Publishing Co., Royal Oak, Michigan.[72]

Very few books other than Coughlin's were ever made available directly through Social Justice Publishing Company.[73] As a result of Coughlin's admiration for Fahey's work, a variety of Americans began corresponding with the Irish priest, and some became distributors of his books in the United States.

Coughlin claimed that Fahey's presentation of theological, philosophical, and historical material was key to understanding the modern revolt against Christian society. The ideas of the Irish theologian, permeated as they were with the writings of Thomas Aquinas and the papal encyclicals, were more than amenable to Coughlin. In addition, because they were presented in a scholarly fashion, they provided the "radio priest" with an intellectual framework to support his own approach. The actual quotations which Coughlin cited from Fahey were largely about bankers,

Communists and Jews, but Coughlin clearly approved of Fahey's theological orientation.

In early 1940 Coughlin conceived the idea of Social Justice Publishing Company reprinting Fahey's booklet *The Rulers of Russia* in Royal Oak. A cablegram was sent to Dublin:

> REV DENNIS [sic] FAHEY HOLY GHOST
> MISSIONARY COLLEGE
> KIMMAGE DIBLIN [sic]
> RULSER [sic] RUSSIA RECEIVED CABLE
> PERMISSION REPRINT HERE PROFITS FOR
> YOU - REV CHAS COUGHLIN[74]

Unfortunately, the date on the cable is unclear.

On March 29, 1940, Coughlin wrote to Fahey on his own personal stationery, thanking him for "sending the corrections"—possibly the galley sheets? He then announced: "I know you will be interested to learn that we have distributed 350,000 copies of your book "Rulers of Russia." I am sending a bound copy to you under separate cover so that you may know how we presented it."[75] This sizable edition, made available in the United States, certainly enhanced Fahey's popularity among some segments of the population in America particularly in the pre-World War II period.

Profits from the 350,000 copies, however, were not forthcoming and Fahey wrote to inquire. His response from Cora Quinlan, Secretary-Treasurer of Social Justice Publishing Company, is puzzling: "Unfortunately, we were not permitted to sell the book, but were forced to distribute copies freely." She sent along $100 to help defray expenses on Fahey's new work.[76] Coughlin wrote a long letter to Fahey the same day. He expressed his pleasure that the Irish theologian was preparing a new volume on the Mystical Body of Christ, and concluded with the comment that Miss Quinlan would be sending the check for $100.

Coughlin's lengthy letter will be discussed below. The question raised by the above statements is—why were the copies of

The Rulers of Russia given away freely instead of sold? There is no explanation in Coughlin's correspondence with Fahey, but when the "radio priest" wrote to Hilaire Belloc in January 1938 he explained that copyrights purchased by Social Justice Publishing Corporation were handed over to the Radio League of the Little Flower. Because the latter was a charitable and non-profit organization, books were not sold, but were distributed gratis to members who supported the Shrine of the Little Flower.[77] One can presume that the reprint of *The Rulers of Russia* was treated similarly. Coughlin's statement "Profits for you" in his cable to Fahey, however, was misleading.

In Coughlin's letter of March 5, 1941 to Fahey, he stated: "As you know, I am no longer broadcasting. This is thanks, chiefly, to my own Archbishop who saw fit to impose such restrictions upon me that they rendered broadcasting, writing and public preaching an impracticality. It is his right to order. It is my duty to obey." The paragraph immediately following added to Coughlin's interpretation of the action:

> The good Archbishop has been busied with bankers
> this last year or so endeavoring to refinance the debt
> of his diocese. He succeeded in doing so recently.
> In the meantime, he has not uttered one word
> against America's entrance into war; not one word
> against the Lend-Lease Bill which bestows
> dictatorial powers upon Mr. Roosevelt to support
> Great Britain's economic system of international
> gold-banking and bondage.

Further on in the same letter Coughlin reflected: "These are only a few rambling thoughts which occur to me as I behold the almost universal ecclesiastical subservience to Franklin D. Roosevelt who is surrounded by high Masons and dominated by crafty Jews."[78]

Social Justice continued to quote Fahey at length in succeeding issues. A photostat of the "British White Paper" was on the cover of the January 23, 1939 issue, and a lengthy article

therein.[79]   A series of articles entitled "An Answer to Father
Coughlin's Critics" by "Ben Marcin" used extensive material from
The Mystical Body of Christ in the Modern World. This was later
republished under the same title, but the authorship was attributed
to "Father Coughlin's Friends." In it Coughlin admitted that he
misunderstood Fahey's answer to his "misunderstood question"
regarding the relationship between the "British White Paper" and
the "American Secret Service Report."[80] Fahey was referred to
frequently as a scholar whose credentials were impeccable.
Another advertisement for his books appeared in July:

> "Who is the Lord of the World—Christ or
> the Politician?" Definitely, Christ. Definitely, No
> Politician. The Neutrality Bill Will Disenthrone
> Christ. Read *"The Kingship of Christ"* and *"The
> Mystical Body of Christ in the Modern World."*
> You may send your order directly to Rev. Chas. E.
> Coughlin Royal Oak, Michigan. *"The Kingship of
> Christ"*—$1.25; *"The Mystical Body of Christ in the
> Modern World"*—$2.50.[81]

Other than the Popes and Thomas Aquinas, no other author with a
theological orientation was quoted as frequently as Fahey to support
Coughlin's ideas.

Coughlin, Fahey, and the "Mystical Body of Satan"

During the same period in 1938 when Coughlin became
acquainted with Fahey's works, there emerged in *Social Justice* an
emphasis on "the mystical body of Satan." In his broadcast of
November 6, 1938, Coughlin had the proclaimers of Naturalism
state: "God has no place in business or in government or in
economy, if His principles are detrimental to *the activities of the
mystical body of Satan"*.[82] Coughlin's November 13 radio address
included a key statement: *"Communism is only one manifestation*

of the power of the mystical body of Satan. "[83] In the November 14 issue of *Social Justice*, he further described this phenomenon:

> Let us be realistic enough to recognize that if there is a Mystical Body of Christ with which every one of us must be identified in order to obtain salvation hereafter and prosperity now, *there is also a mystical body of Satan which is well-organized, well-officered and well-disciplined under the leadership of Lucifer* who goes about the world seeking whom he may devour. It is a preview of the most important piece of history ever written not yet enacted upon the stage of life. I refer to the "Apocalypse" which one day will cease to be a prophecy and will remain to be sad history.[84]

Later in the same article, Coughlin quotes six paragraphs from *The Mystical Body of Christ in the Modern World* as mentioned above, concluding with Fahey's statement regarding the camp of Christ and the camp of Satan.

"Ladies and Gentlemen—Meet Satan" was the cover title for *Social Justice* February 6, 1939, introducing a two-part article entitled "The Mystical Body of Satan" by Reverend W. J. Randall, C.M.S. This author, described as an "able English writer, long popular with the readers of this National Weekly," wrote articles for *Social Justice* on *Divini Redemptoris*, the papal encyclical "On Atheistic Communism," and on the "Possibility of a Corporative State in England."[85] The sensationalist cover of the issue which introduced the article on Satan pictured a man in high hat with devilish features and the statement:

> *Has he horns?* He has not!
> *Has he hoofs?* Most certainly not!
> But he has an intellect a thousand times bigger than yours or mine. He was the light-bearer in heaven and the fire-tender in hell.

The devil, politely referred to as Lucifer, was the most brilliant angelic intellect God ever created. He has forgotten more—if forgetting is possible with him—than all other creatures combined (save the mother of God) ever knew or probably ever will know.

He is God's enemy—and yours.

Meet him face to face in the "Mystical Body of Satan."

Meet his Satanic Majesty in this issue.[86]

"The mystical body of Satan is a terrible reality," warns Randall. "It is an existing corporation which is actively opposed to the divine corporation which is the Mystical Body of Christ, the Church." He then cites Coughlin's statement describing it as "well-organized, well-officered, and well-disciplined under the leadership of Lucifer."[87]

Drawing on St. Augustine's images of the "two cities," the author contends that such a situation exists at the present time: "the two cities are there as ever, fighting respectively beneath the sooty flag of Satan and the Standard of the Cross." Since the time when Satan was expelled from heaven as described by St. John in the Apocalypse, the devil has come to earth and is seducing the world.[88]

Randall was more explicit regarding his designated topic the second week:

It is clear what is meant by the Mystical Body of Christ. This will help us to understand the nature of the "mystical body of Satan." It is that corporate body (or society) which exists in the world under the leadership of the devil. It consists of those men and women who in all ages are united by some evil principle (or a number of evil principles), against the Church and its teaching.[89]

The "mystical body of Satan"—"embraces the enemies of Christ and His Church through the ages." The English priest examined the topic chronologically, beginning with the primitive Church "when the majority of first-century Jews took the side of Satan against Christ." After reviewing the historical panorama, he concluded:

> Though Satan has not been permitted to appear in the world in person and to found one visibly united society as an exact replica of the Christian Church, he has nevertheless led groups of men whose thought and action may be summed up in one phrase—anti-Christianity. These groups, viewed as a whole in the course of history CONSTITUTE THE MYSTICAL BODY OF SATAN.[90]

Rationalism, Liberalism, and Freemasonry were designated as modern forms of "Satanic machinations." The atheistic Communism of Soviet Russia, Randall wrote, was the greatest evil in the world:

> There are several well-defined characteristics in Soviet Communism which make it peculiarly qualified to represent the society of Satan in the world today.... (a) militantly atheistic; (b) highly organized; (c) definitely located; (d) world-wide in activity.[91]

Although the author concluded his article abruptly, it was clear that his approach to a "theology of history" was not dissimilar to Fahey's; yet, as will be described, he was closer to Coughlin, and possibly influenced Coughlin in his understanding of "the mystical body of Satan." Randall's presence in *Social Justice*, however, was brief.

Coughlin's shift from *Social Justice* articles dealing largely with politics, labor and financial issues, to cover stories on "The

Mystical Body of Christ" (December 12, 1939), and "The Mystical Body of Satan" (February 6, 1940) was conspicuous. His extraordinary reliance on Fahey during this period indicated an effort to understand the concrete "diabolical" events of the world within a theological framework evolving out of Thomistic thought and papal encyclicals.

It is in Coughlin's letters to Fahey, however, that references to "the mystical body of Satan" become connected to the Jews. Coughlin always claimed that he was not anti-Semitic—as did Fahey. Both stated that they respected the religious God-fearing Jews, but their words and actions on too many occasions belied those statements. Coughlin often preached his anti-Semitic message through innuendo. The style and speech patterns which he used in delivering his broadcasts contributed to the total impression—such as the affected pronunciation of Jewish names.

In a letter to the Irish priest on March 5, 1941, Coughlin shared his thoughts on the issue of anti-Semitism and anti-Judaism, introduced by a comment on "the mystical body of Satan." As mentioned above, after telling Fahey that he was happy to hear that another volume on the Mystical Body of Christ was in preparation, Coughlin suggested, "*Perhaps you could find room for a chapter or two relative to the mystical body of Satan.*"[92] The "radio priest" continued:

> Speaking colloquially, Satan endeavors to imitate Christ in many ways despite the fact that he constantly works for disorder instead of order, for falsehood instead of truth, for negatives instead of positives. Nevertheless, he endeavors to bring these evils under the guise of good.

Coughlin further asserted:

> Definitely there is a mystical body of Satan operating in the world. Just as there are concrete

members belonging to the Mystical Body of Christ, so there are concrete members—working in unison—belonging to the mystical body of Satan. To my mind, all those who are not with Christ are against Him—even the lukewarm; all those who are rejectors of Christ are the chief factors in the mystical body of Satan.[93]

He then moved directly from his discussion of the "mystical body of Satan" to his understanding of anti-Semitism and anti-Judaism: "While anti-Semitism is to be abhorred in so far as it is related to hatred for the Jews as individuals and racials, nevertheless, *anti-Judaism, which means opposition to the Judaic concept of life, is not to be so condemned.*"[94]

It was because of "purchased propaganda," the Detroit priest believed, that the word "Jew" had become identified with religion in America. "Ninety per cent of our people believe that a Jew is a religionist." He noted that meetings of Catholics, Protestants and Jews were well advertised. Appreciating the fact that he and Fahey shared certain understandings, Coughlin added:

You and I recognize that a Jew is a racialist as well as a religionist. Moreover, we understand that the vast majority of Jews are not religionists. The majority of them do not attend church regularly and do not observe the precepts of the Jewish Orthodox religion. And among the Jewish religionists, as well as among those who are non-religionists, there is a common dogma concerning the rejection of Christ.[95]

It was this rejection of Christ which precluded the possibility of the Jew reaching God. Coughlin theologized:

In my concept of theology it is impossible for individuals or nations to adhere to God under the conditions of fallen nature except through the acceptance of Christ. In other words, through the proclivity of debased human nature, men and mankind will become practical atheists. Without Christ we can do nothing. Judaism, which rejects Christ entirely as the Mediator and the Messias, will devolve according to the teaching above expressed, into practical atheism.[96]

Once again, Coughlin "advocated tolerance" toward individual Jews, but with qualifications. "...I cannot understand how so many amongst our hierarchy and clergy are demonstrating tolerance toward Judaism. It is a leaning-backwards so far that eventually it will pull us into the ditch."[97] Coughlin lamented the fact that "those who support Judaism" had gained control of many governments, including the United States. He had harsh words for the American bishops: "...I observe how many members of our American hierarchy have adopted the policy of supporting the de facto government in the United States *with all its works and pomps.*" Although many of them may have been internally opposed to government policies, externally "they appear to be indulging in criminal prudence."[98]

The above letter, written privately to Fahey, sums up much of Coughlin's thought. The "radio priest" began with a suggestion that the Irish professor write some chapters on "the mystical body of Satan." He immediately discussed the rejectors of Christ—the Jews—distinguishing between (1) anti-Semitism and anti-Judaism, and (2) the Jew as racialist and as religionist. He concluded that the only alternative to the acceptance of Christ was practical atheism; therefore it was inappropriate for the American Catholic hierarchy to show tolerance for Judaism. This letter was not written for public consumption. It was not doctored with platitudes and pious protestations. It stated clearly, however, what Coughlin believed: "While anti-Semitism is to be abhorred in so far as it is related to hatred for the Jews as individuals and racials, nevertheless, anti-Judaism is not to be so condemned." Such assertions leave few doubts as to the basic stance of the "radio priest" in 1941.

Fahey: Satan as "the Head of All Evil Men"

The Irish theologian never used the expression "the mystical body of Satan." Drawing on St. Thomas, however, he emphasized Satan as "the head of all evil men" (cf. IIIa., P.Q. VIII. a.7). He also described the body of "Organized Naturalism" as a kind of network of all the evil forces in the world—all those who had rejected the True Messias and were working militantly to dethrone Christ the King. As earlier explored, this body was looking forward to a Natural Messias who was the enemy of the Supernatural Messias—Jesus Christ. Fahey categorized the enemies of Jesus as (1) Satan; (2) Jews; and (3) Gentiles—largely Freemasons who were controlled by Jews. In *The Mystical Body of Christ in the Modern World*, even in the chapter added in the 1938 edition, "The Struggle of the Jewish Nation against the True Messias," he did not unduly emphasize Satan, although there are references to the machinations of the demonic in the world. Radical as was Fahey's last statement in *The Kingship of Christ and the Conversion of the Jewish Nation*—that it was probable that "The Jews will acclaim Antichrist as the Messias and will help to set up his kingdom"—former students have no recollection that he ever used the expression "the mystical body of Satan."[99]

An entire section of *The Mystical Body of Christ and the Reorganization of Society*, however, is devoted to the organized opposition to the Mystical Body of Christ, and it is here that Fahey returns to his three-fold division of the enemies of Christ. The first category, "Satan and His Fellow Demons," is expanded—particularly the section on the headship of Satan. The Irish writer is careful to rely on St. Augustine, St. Thomas, and the encyclicals, with a few minor exceptions.[100] Fahey found ample material in the writings of the Popes about Satan, and never tired of quoting Leo XIII's *Humanum Genus* ("On Freemasonry), and Pius XI's *Caritate Christi Corsi* ("On the Troubles of Our Times").

He found periodic warnings against the satanic, but he never found the expression "the mystical body of Satan."[101]

What is distinctive in Fahey's post-1938 writings is the stark contrast he achieved by the use of parallel columns to juxtapose "The Programme of Christ" and "The Plans of Satan." This schema acquired additional refinement in *The Kingship of Christ and Organized Naturalism*. The popular "Fahey pocket manual" also included the contrasting programs of the Catholic Church and the Jewish Nation, and the Catholic Church and Freemasonry.[102] In these pages, the imagery of Satan takes on new importance. As the head of the body of "Organized Naturalism" who is confronting Christ, Satan leads all those who have opposed Christ through the centuries. In substance, Fahey's doctrine is not radically different from Coughlin's.

Did Coughlin's letter in 1941 encouraging Fahey to write a few chapters on "the mystical body of Satan" become a kind of seed from which grew some of the poisonous weeds of the Irish priest's writings in the 1940s and 1950s? Coughlin's advice certainly would have been taken seriously by Fahey, and could well have enhanced the emphasis on Satan in his later works. Without more specific phraseology from the popes and St. Thomas, however, Coughlin's suggestion was not enough to convince the professor from Kimmage to include the phrase "the mystical body of Satan" in his writings.

In the Foreword to *The Kingship of Christ and the Conversion of the Jewish Nation*, Fahey stated: "As I was not able to bring out this book when it was originally written, it has been laid aside for years."[103] Confusion over the word "Anti-Semitism," particularly as a result of World War II, he believed, made the book even more necessary:

> The Hitlerite naturalistic or anti-supernatural regime
> in Germany gave to the world the odious spectacle
> of a display of Anti-Semitism, that is, of hatred of
> the Jewish Nation. Yet all the propaganda about
> that display of Anti-Semitism should not have made

> Catholics forget the existence of age-long Jewish Naturalism or Anti-Supernaturalism. Forgetfulness of the disorder of Jewish Naturalistic opposition to Christ the King is keeping Catholics blind to the danger that is arising from the clever extension of the term "Anti-Semitism," to include any form of opposition to the Jewish Nation's naturalistic aims.[104]

It was for an autographed copy of this book and the accompanying letter that Coughlin wrote an acknowledgement on May 27, 1953. He told Fahey, "I appreciate them deeply and congratulate you upon the wonderful work you are doing."[105]

Coughlin, who by this time had been "silenced" for more than ten years, once again offered Fahey a suggestion:

> It is my opinion that we need a book on the Mystical Body of Satan. Parallel it with the Mystical Body of Christ. The Mystical Body of Satan has an unholy spirit, an Anti-Christ and members, just the same as the Mystical Body of Christ has the Holy Spirit and the Christ and members.[106]

Other than the two-part article by Randall in *Social Justice* in February 1939, no one else in Coughlin's circle seems to have written on this topic, so he volunteered a free-floating outline:

> Of course, the Mystical Body of Christ, the mystical corporation—the Holy Ghost, as it were—is Chairman of the Board, the Board being the Cardinals; and each unit of the corporation has its own president, namely, the Bishops. The parallel holds good for the Mystical Body of Satan. Moreover, in the Mystical Body of Christ we have a multiplicity of religious organizations such as the Benedictines, the Franciscans, the Holy Ghost

Fathers, etc., etc. In Satan's organization, there is
a parallel such as the Nazis, the Fascists, the
Communists, the Masons etc., etc.[107]

The question of membership in the Mystical Body of Christ
and the mystical body of Satan is raised again by Coughlin. His
conclusion is that it is settled with Jesus' assertion: "No one can
come to the Father except through Me." The "radio priest" expli-
cated this in one of the most telling paragraphs of his missive to
Fahey:

> I suppose, by the use of dogmatic logic, we could
> conclude that all who reject Christ must end up by
> being cut off from the Father. Definitely, those
> who have rejected Christ beyond all doubt are
> those advocating the heresy of Judaism, which
> rejects Him in person; and the second heresy,
> which rejects Him in word. Possibly, the Hindus,
> Mohammedans [here the word "Protestantism" is
> handwritten in the margin of this typed letter, with
> an arrow pointing to this section] etc., have not
> formally rejected Him, either in person or in word,
> to the extent the others just mentioned have done.[108]

From the progression of the letter, it was clear that the Jews fell
into a special category vis à vis the mystical body of Satan.
Coughlin's less severe interpretation regarding Hindus and
Mohammedans was—apparently in an afterthought—extended to
the Protestants. For the reasons explained, they were "rescued"
from membership in the diabolical corporation.

Coughlin offered to help Fahey develop these ideas. It is
significant that he did this in terms of the Third Person of the
Blessed Trinity, considering that the Irish professor was a member
of the Holy Ghost Congregation. In addition, there was special
reference to the Antichrist, about which Fahey had just written.
Coughlin continued:

Had I time, I would be glad to work this thing out
specifically and conclude the latter part of the book
with the Holy Ghost in the economy of the battle
between Christ and Anti-Christ. I mean we would
regard the Holy Ghost in this battle particularly as
the Advocatus, or the Paraclitus, which words can
be translated into American English as "prosecuting
attorney." In other words, the Holy Ghost is here
to convict the world of sin, justice, and judgment.
To be efficacious in His conviction, He, like any
other prosecuting attorney, requires witnesses. We
are the witnesses to the Gospel of charity and
peace, as predicated by Christ.[109]

The word "witness," he added, comes from the Greek word
"marturios"—martyr. Here Coughlin described the fate of one
who would be a witness and who ends up a martyr. Although in
veiled terms, there is a distinct allusion to himself.

The Pastor of the Shrine of the Little Flower then
suggested a middle chapter of the book on how "all our good
turns to ill" (from the Sequence of Pentecost), if we fail to be
united to the Mystical Body of Christ. Lastly, Coughlin
emphasized devotion to the Holy Ghost as more necessary at that
time than at any other in history. He exhorted: "All progress is
retrogression; all victory is defeat, unless governments and
peoples and institutions turn to Christ and to the Holy Spirit."[110]

Coughlin concluded: "This is the theology which I have
been preaching constantly and the thesis which to my mind
requires development."[111] Had the priest of Royal Oak been free
to speak and write at this time, it seems reasonable to presume
that these would have been his areas of concentration. In view of
Coughlin's having been "silenced"—it appears that he was hoping
to convince Fahey to put into print what he could not. Had Fahey
wanted a collaborator, Coughlin would have been more than
willing.

The above letter was received by the Irish priest probably in June or July 1953, about six months before his death. If he responded to Coughlin, he kept no copy. Although it is impossible to know the answer, one wonders—had Fahey lived longer, would he have written a book on "the mystical body of Satan"? Considering all the difficulties he had with the imprimatur for *The Kingship of Christ and the Conversion of the Jewish Nation*, it seems doubtful. The suggestion in Coughlin's letter twelve years earlier may have encouraged the Irish priest's emphasis on Satan, and his chapter on the Antichrist. Fahey did not, however, accept the first challenge to write about "the mystical body of Satan" in 1941; it is unlikely that he would have accepted the second in 1953.

A Transatlantic Relationship and the Growth of Anti-Semitism

When asking within what kind of theological orientation Coughlin functioned which allowed him to make some of the anti-Semitic pronouncements which he articulated in the years 1938-1942, one is reminded of the comment of the English author Arnold Lunn to Father Fahey, after returning from America and a visit with "the radio priest." He stated emphatically: "Father Coughlin is a man of one book—*your* book!"[112] Certainly there were important influences in Coughlin's life before Fahey, especially in his seminary training. Preparing for the priesthood in the Roman Catholic Church in the first half of the twentieth century meant being steeped in Thomistic thought and papal encyclicals. As has been indicated, portions of these documents contributed to establishing a base for the repudiation of the Jews, especially when these were interpreted in a fundamentalistic way.[113] The study of Scripture and the Fathers of the Church, while not emphasized in that period, would also have been accepted literally, and would have been used to bolster an anti-Judaic stance.[114]

Coughlin was ordained in 1916, and his formal studies in theology ended then. He never pursued any advanced degrees. Diocesan clergy in those days were expected to update themselves, and that would have been dependent on the particular motivation of each priest. Coughlin, always a good student, was an avid reader, as is obvious in his speeches. He was selective, however, according to his needs, and read what was most helpful for his sermons and articles. His background as an English and speech teacher, as well as his experience as director of the dramatic society at Assumption College, prepared him for life as an orator.

It was believed in that era that once a priest had completed his studies, he was equipped with "the answers" which he then communicated to the people. Because the clergy were generally better educated than the majority of their congregants, there was little need to probe new theological questions. In addition, the mystique enjoyed by many Roman Catholic priests in an immigrant culture—that the ordained had a direct line to God and to Rome—removed any demand for additional study in theological areas.

Fahey, on the other hand, spent an extended time in studies. As a member of a religious congregation which staffed secondary schools, colleges, and seminaries, he enjoyed an excellent education, doing doctorates at both the Gregorian and the Angelicum in Rome, and studying later at Fribourg. His command of other languages opened up new vistas to him, and his years at the *Séminaire Française* certainly gave him a larger picture of the world. As a member of the Holy Ghost Congregation, although he never served in "the third world," he was in contact with those working in the missions—particularly in Africa.

Although the Irish priest experienced a breadth of education and travel, on one level, studying and being ordained in the Rome of Pius X certainly circumscribed his view. His exposure to French and Roman conservative Catholic thought in an anti-Modernist milieu certainly did not encourage creativity, or allow him to understand concepts such as religious freedom in America.

What kind of relationship did these two priests enjoy—many miles distant and with very different backgrounds? In both cases, it was probably one of need. Coughlin's experiments in politics had not gone well. In promoting "The Christian Front" in 1938, it was as if he wanted to inject a more religious dimension into his program. With his conviction that the Jews, as bankers and controllers of the media, were in good part responsible for his political defeat, and with conditions worsening in foreign policy in which he believed Jews had major influence, what other tome could have brought together Coughlin's major concerns and placed them in a theological framework more clearly than *The Mystical Body of Christ in the Modern World?*

Fahey provided the rationale which Coughlin could use in an effort to make his vendetta "respectable." The Irish professor had done his homework, and produced a volume which "convicted" the Jews of both money manipulation and financing the Bolshevik Revolution—all within the setting of "The Divine Plan for Order," and "The Modern Struggle around the Kingship of Christ." Pragmatist that he was, Coughlin knew "a good theologian" to use when he saw one, and Fahey genuinely satisfied his needs. In addition, it gave Coughlin a sense of adding "theological depth" to his journal and his program. As indicated by his last letters, however, Coughlin did not think Fahey was willing to go far enough on the concept of "the mystical body of Satan."

Fahey was complimented by Coughlin's use of his material. The vast correspondence of the Irish priest with Americans was a result of the publicity he received in *Social Justice.* What emerges from a study of the two men, however, is that although Fahey may not have been a creative philosopher/theologian, or a balanced historian, the major thrust of his life had been in the intellectual and spiritual spheres. He required a certain amount of evidence and internal consistency before he was willing to advance a thesis. He insisted upon fitting everything and everybody into a tight system; he allowed no space for growth or development; no place for those who had not accepted Jesus as Messias; he came to frightening conclusions. Interpreting the writings of the Popes and Thomas, and selected passages from Scripture, he could defend "his system" of a body of "Organized Naturalism." He could not advocate a "mystical body of Satan." Compared to Coughlin, he was cautious in his theologizing.

When Coughlin was convinced of a proposition, he was willing to promote it, speculating in his own way, oftentimes irrespective of Scripture or the writings of Popes and theologians. Both priests jumped quickly to practical conclusions from their earlier premises, but Coughlin exceeded Fahey in this—and because of his powerful oratorical ability to sway an audience, he was indeed rightly labelled a "demagogue of the depression" by more than one author.[115]

Both men were sensitive to the question of authority in the church. Coughlin eventually bowed to Archbishop Mooney, but he used every effort short of direct defiance of his religious superiors, to manipulate both audiences and authority figures in his life. Fahey, too, committed himself with special reverence to the Supreme Pontiff and other superiors, but was not above attempting to influence the bishops of Ireland. The unclear picture regarding the imprimatur for his last book raises a question as to his role in its publication before final approbation. Once "Rome had spoken," however, both priests exhibited soldier-like obedience to the commander of the regiment. One might ask if—after Coughlin was "silenced"—Fahey might have been more cautious regarding the ideas of the priest of Royal Oak. Perhaps—but the alternate possibility is that he would have agreed with Coughlin that Jewish pressure was responsible for the restriction.

It is noteworthy that before Fahey's correspondence with Coughlin, he was not involved in political issues in an active way. In the post-World War II period, however, as a guiding force in the formation of *Maria Duce*, he became immersed in the publication of *FIAT*, spoke at meetings, and was consulted on all issues including the sponsorship of rallies, the boycotting of "immoral films," and the fight over Article 44 of the Irish Constitution. Fahey was a defender of Senator Joseph McCarthy, and was in communication with other radical right-wing figures in the United States in that period, as will be discussed later. One wonders if Coughlin became a kind of "role model" for Fahey. By 1948, the Irish professor had become "the activist priest" alerting the public to the political and moral evils of the day. Despite his flirtation with politics, however, Fahey remained primarily an academic throughout his life. Coughlin—the priest and politician; Fahey—the priest and professor. The former needed a rationale for his programs; the latter—a voice to express his convictions. Together they provided a generation of Americans with a "justification" for anti-Semitism.

Coughlin was "silenced"; Fahey was not. His books continue to be read in the United States, and can still be found in college, university and seminary libraries. One young seminarian who was enthusiastic about Fahey's writings summed up the pivotal role which the Irish priest had played in Coughlin's program. He wrote to Fahey from Baltimore, September 15, 1952: "Of course, I had heard all sorts of legends about how your original book had inspired Father Charles Coughlin's memorable crusade."[116]

[1]Sydney E. Ahlstrom, *A Religious History of the American People* (New Haven: Yale University Press, 1972), p. 920.

[2]See Charles J. Tull, *Father Coughlin and the New Deal* (Syracuse, New York: Syracuse University Press, 1965); Sheldon Marcus, *Father Charles E. Coughlin: The Tumultuous Life of the Priest of the Little Flower* (Boston: Little Brown and Company, 1973); and Alan Brinkley, *Voices of Protest: Huey Long,*

Father Coughlin, and the Great Depression (New York: Random House, 1983).

[3]With the exception of a few issues, *Social Justice* was available to me at the Doe Library, University of California, Berkeley. Several of the important missing issues are at St. Patrick Seminary, Menlo Park, California.

[4]Marcus, pp. 12-19. Cf. also Ruth Mugglebee, *Father Coughlin of the Shrine of the Little Flower* (New York: Garden City Publishing Co., 1933).

[5]Ibid., pp. 25-27; Mugglebee, pp. 164-165.

[6]Ibid., pp. 45-46, 82, 84; cf. also William V. Shannon, *The American Irish* (New York: Macmillan and Company, 1963), pp. 306-308, and David J. O'Brien, *American Catholics and Social Reform* (New York: Oxford University Press, 1968), pp. 153-154.

[7]*Newsweek* (September 12, 1936), as quoted in Marcus, p. 127.

[8]Marcus, p. 132.

[9]Gerald S. Brown, S.S., "The Reverend Charles S. Coughlin and the 1936 Election" (M.A. Thesis, University of Washington, 1971). See also Shannon, pp. 304, 313-314, and Marcus, pp. 132-137.

[10]Marcus, pp. 138-139; Shannon, p. 314.

[11]*Social Justice* (October 25, 1937): 1, 8-9. Cf. also Marcus, pp. 139-140; and Shannon, pp. 314-315.

[12]Marcus, pp. 144-145.

[13]See *Social Justice*, November 8-December 13, 1937. Cf. also Marcus, pp. 145-146, Shannon 314-315, and O'Brien, p. 157.

[14]Charles E. Coughlin, *A Series of Lectures on Social Justice* (Royal Oak, Michigan: Radio League of the Little Flower, 1935), pp. 17-18.

[15]Marcus, p. 67, from interview with Coughlin, April 11, 1970.

[16]Ibid., pp. 68-70. This effort can be contrasted with Fahey's scrupulous effort at moral justification when procuring two tires on the black market for a relative during World War II.

[17]Ibid., p. 69.

[18]*Detroit News* (January 17, 1934), as quoted in Marcus, p. 66.

[19]Coughlin, *Radio Sermons: October 1930-April 1931*, pp. 191-196.

[20]Ibid. See Chapters VIII, XIII, and XV.

[21]Coughlin, *A Series of Lectures on Social Justice*, pp. 17-18. An abbreviated version of the sixteen principles appeared weekly in *Social Justice*. *Fiat*, Trinity College, Dublin. Neither Trinity College nor the HGP Archives has a complete file.

[22]Coughlin, *Radio Sermons: October 1930-April 1931*, p. 100. See also Charles E. Coughlin, *Why Leave Our Own: 13 Addresses on Christianity and Americanism, January 8-April 2, 1939* (Published by author, 1939).

[23]Charles E. Coughlin, "Persecution—Jewish and Christian," *Addresses and Essays* (Royal Oak, Michigan: Radio League of the Little Flower, 1939), pp. 37, 39, 49. Coughlin used the expression four times on those three pages.

[24]*Social Justice*, December 7, 1936, p. 5, includes a picture of Hitler and the title "Foe of Communism." The caption reads: "A puritan in his personal life, Der Fuehrer Hitler made of defeated Germany a new united great nation.... The chancellor...is Europe's bitterest foe of Communism." See also *Social Justice* October 3, 1938, and April 3, 1939. Statements can be found where Coughlin "condemns" Nazism, but almost always with qualifications. Cf. also Marcus, pp. 149, 166-168.

[25]KCCJN, p. 5.

[26]Coughlin, *A Series of Lectures on Social Justice*, p. 16.

[27]*Social Justice*, June 7, 1937 headline: "Russian Revolution Financed by Bankers," p. 1; June 14, 1937, "Plotters of Revolution in Russia Turned to Bankers for Support," p. 1.

[28]Ibid., June 21, 1937, p. 2.

[29]Ibid., February 15, 1937, p. 2.

[30]Ibid., June 21, 1937, p. 2.

[31]Marcus, p. 254 in interview with Coughlin, April 11, 1970.

[32]*Social Justice*, June 20, 1938, p. 1. The buildup of anti-Jewish material began March 21, 1938.

[33]Ibid., July 18, 1938, p. 5. The one week in which an excerpt of *The Protocols* did not appear was September 5, 1938.

[34]Ibid., August 1, 1938, p. 5.

[35]Ibid., August 8, 1938, p. 5.

[36]Ibid., September 19, 1938, p. 7.

[37]Ibid., September 26, 1938, pp. 10-11.

[38]Ibid., October 1938, pp. 10-11. At the conclusion of Slomovitz's article there is an editorial note alerting readers to the forthcoming article by Ben Marcin: "Mr. Ben Marcin, whose research articles disclosing the untold 'story behind the story' of many a historical fallacy are already familiar to readers of *Social Justice*, has consented to comment on Mr. Slomovitz's article and the Protocols in next week's edition.... The informed reader cannot afford to miss 'The Truth About the Protocols' by Ben Marcin in *Social Justice*, October 3.—The Editor."

[39]Ibid., November 21, 1938, pp. 10-11.

[40]*Social Justice* (August 8, 1938), p. 5.

[41]E. Perrin Schwartz to Fahey, November 8, 1938, FP-HGP.

[42]Ibid.

[43]Marcus, p. 82. In the *New York Times*, April 21, 1942, Father Coughlin was quoted as stating: "Time and again I have said and here repeat that I am neither the editor, publisher nor owner of *Social Justice* Magazine. However, I do here and now publicly state that I, Father Charles E. Coughlin alone am responsible for and do control the magazine, its policies and contents." As cited in Marcus, pp. 214-215.

[44]D. O. Kelly to Fahey, November 17, 1938, FP-HGP. Although the signature on this letter is unclear, it is on Browne and Nolan Limited letterhead. A secretarial identification "DOK/JS" is included.

[45]Telephone interview with John Conway, November 1990.

[46]*Social Justice* (November 14, 1938), p. 8, as cited in MBCMW pp. 46-47.

[47]See "Persecution—Jewish and Christian," in *"Am I an Anti-Semite?"*, pp. 34-35.

[48]Ibid., p. 35.

[49]Ibid.

[50]Ibid., p. 36.

[51]Ibid., pp. 36-37.

[52]Ibid.

[53]Ibid.

[54]See MBCMW, pp. 88-90, 291-293.

[55]Coughlin, *"Am I an Anti-Semite?"*, pp. 47-55.

[56]Marcus, p. 161. Among the rebuttals and reflections on Coughlin's speech were two articles in the December 30, 1938 *Commonweal*: "Anti-Semitism in the Air" by John A. Ryan (pp. 260-262), and "The Jew and the Two Revolutions" by George N. Shuster (pp. 262-264).

[57]Coughlin, "Let Us Consider the Record," in *"Am I an Anti-Semite?"*, pp. 56-65.

[58]Ibid., pp. 61-62.

[59]Ibid., pp. 62-65.

[60]"Not Anti-Semitism but Anti-Communism," in *"Am I an Anti-Semite?"*, pp. 79-80.

[61]Interviews with Brother Benignus, C.S.Sp., Dublin, March 28, 1979, and with William Jenkinson, C.S.Sp., Berkeley, California, January 16, 1979.

[62]Coughlin, *"Am I an Anti-Semite?"*, p. 95.

[63]Ibid., p. 102.

[64]Ibid., pp. 103-104.

[65]*Social Justice* (December 12, 1938), p. 1.

[66]Ibid.

[67]Ibid., p. 7.

[68]Ibid., p. 5.

[69]Ibid., December 19, 1938, p. 7.

[70]Ibid.

[71]In addition to issues of *Social Justice* from November 1938 on, and the addresses published in *"Am I an Anti-Semite?"*, the booklet *Answer to Father Coughlin's Critics* by Father Coughlin's Friends (Royal Oak, Michigan: Radio League of the Little Flower, 1940), quotes Fahey extensively.

[72]*Social Justice* (February 6, 1939), p. 3.

[73]Marcus, p. 62. No other books were advertised in the pages of *Social Justice* as Fahey's were.

[74]Charles E. Coughlin to Denis Fahey, Cablegram, c. 1939-1940, FP-HGP (date unclear).

[75]Charles E. Coughlin to Denis Fahey, March 29, 1940, FP-HGP.

[76]Cora Quinlan to Denis Fahey, March 5, 1941, FP-HGP.

[77]Charles E. Coughlin to Hilaire Belloc, January 27, 1938, Boston College Archives.

[78]Charles E. Coughlin to Denis Fahey, March 5, 1941.

[79]*Social Justice* (January 23, 1939), pp. 1, 3.

[80]Ibid., July 24, 1939, p. 10.

[81]Ibid., July 3, 1939, p. 2.

[82]Ibid., November 14, 1938, p. 11. Emphasis added.

[83]Ibid., November 21, 1938, p. 23. Emphasis added.

[84]Ibid., November 14, 1938, p. 7. Emphasis added.

[85]Ibid., February 6, 1939, p. 3.

[86]Ibid., p. 1.

[87]Ibid., p. 3.

[88]Ibid., p. 3.

[89]Ibid., February 13, 1939, p. 5.

[90]Ibid.

[91]Ibid.

[92]Charles E. Coughlin to Denis Fahey, March 5, 1941, FP-HGP. Emphasis added.

[93]Ibid.

[94]Ibid. Emphasis added.

[95]Ibid.

[96]Ibid.

[97]Ibid.

[98]Ibid.

[99]Interviews with Holy Ghost Fathers Enda Watters, Michael McCarthy, Leo Layden and Desmond Byrne, HGP, Dublin, March 1979.

[100]MBCRS, pp. 230-233. In the chapter on "The Jewish Nation" Fahey once more emphasizes the leadership of Satan and the role of the Jews: "Now the world of which Our Lord speaks in the Gospel is the entire collection of forces marshalled by Satan against the Supernatural Life of Grace. It is therefore the naturalistic camp, of which Satan is the leader. *The Jews, under their rulers, entered the camp and led the others in the attack on the Supernatural Life in Person, Our Lord Jesus Christ.* They occupy a special place in that camp, it is true, because of God's loving preservation of them in spite of their obstinacy and pride, but in the conflict which divides the world into two opposing armies, there must not be any shadow of doubt about their being in the vanguard of visible opposition to the Supernatural"(pp. 181-182). Emphasis added.

[101]MBCRS, p. 136; KCON, p. 24.

[102]KCON, pp. 52-53.

[103]KCCJN, p. 5.

[104]Ibid., pp. 5-6.

[105]Charles E. Coughlin to Denis Fahey, May 27, 1953, FP-HGP.

[106]Ibid. Coughlin capitalizes the "M" and "B" in "the mystical body of Christ" in his letter to Fahey in 1953, whereas they were in lower case in his communication in 1941.

[107]Ibid.

[108]Ibid.

[109]Ibid.

[110]Ibid.

[111]Ibid.

[112]Interview with Michael O'Carroll, C.S.Sp., March 13, 1979.

[113]MBCRS, p. 155. Fahey quotes excerpts from Leo XIII: "Let Jesus be excluded and the human race is left without its greatest protection and illumination...." and from Pius XI: "No belief in God will in the long run be preserved true and genuine, if not supported by belief in Christ...." Fahey then concluded: "These principles of Pope Leo XII and Pope Pius XI apply

with greater force to the Jewish Nation and its leaders, then to others, for they have rejected greater graces and turned against God with direr ingratitude."

[114]An example of Fahey's occasional reliance on the Fathers of the Church is a quotation from a homily of St. Gregory the Great for the First Sunday in Lent, MBCRS, p. 150n: "Certainly the devil is the head of all wicked men and all wicked men are members of his head. Was not Pilate a member of Satan? Were not the Jews who persecuted Christ and the soldiers who crucified Him, members of Satan?" See also MBCRS, p. 152: "In his Commentary on St. Matthew, XXVI, 39, St. Thomas quotes the opinion of St. Jerome that Our Lord, by His Prayer in the Garden of Gethsemane, 'My Father, if it be possible, let this chalice pass from me,' asked to have the redemption of the world accomplished without the crime of the Jews, His own people, but bowed down to what His Father was permitting, namely, the abuse of their free will by that people, with all its dire consequences for Himself and for His Mystical Body, 'Nevertheless not as I will, but as thou wilt.'"

[115]In addition to Sydney Ahlstrom's statement above, see David H. Bennett, *Demagogues in the Depression: American Radicals and the Union Party, 1932-1936* (New Brunswick, New Jersey: Rutgers University Press, 1969), and Raymond Gram Swing, *Forerunners of American Fascism* (Freeport, New York: Books for Libraries Press, 1935).

[116]Joseph F. Tisch, Jr. to Fahey, September 15, 1952, FP-HGP. The editor of *Common Sense* who gave Fahey's book to Tisch was Conde McGinley.

CHAPTER VI

SIGNIFICANCE OF THE COUGHLIN-FAHEY CONNECTION FOR THE AMERICAN SCENE

Fahey's debut in the United States via Coughlin brought the Irish priest unexpectedly into the American limelight. With the cover of "The Mystical Body of Christ in the Modern World by Denis Fahey, C.S.Sp." printed on the front page of *Social Justice*, and heralded as the book of the year, if not the book of the decade, Fahey was given extraordinary publicity. Although circulation figures for *Social Justice* are not available for that year, Coughlin claimed there were nearly a million readers.[1] To receive such high praise from the "radio priest," and to have one's books made available through his publishing company assured ready acceptance among Coughlin's followers. Many of Fahey's new-found transatlantic admirers wrote to him; as always, he answered. Frequently these exchanges developed into ongoing correspondence. The variety of personalities from diverse backgrounds to whom Fahey wrote testify to his willingness to communicate with the famous, the infamous, and the little known.

This wider circle of followers found Fahey's writings instructive for their lives. Some were appreciative of his emphasis on the Kingship of Christ, and the Divine Plan for Order. Others gravitated to his writings on economics and ecology. Many, however, utilized only the sections which supported an anti-Semitic perspective. Particularly interesting in Fahey's voluminous correspondence are the letters from Protestants in the United States, individuals with whom he probably would not have communicated were they in Ireland.

Coughlin had been "silenced" in 1942. His defense of Hitler even after the United States declared war on Germany in 1941, his continued attacks on Roosevelt, and his accusation that Jewish intrigue was responsible for United States involvement in the war led to government investigations as to the possible collaboration of Coughlin with the enemy. Parallels of Coughlin's speeches to those of German propaganda broadcasts, comments that Hitler's persecution of the Jews in Europe was justified because the Jews had goaded the U.S. into the war, and other pro-Nazi statements led the Attorney General Francis Biddle to accumulate evidence regarding possible charges of sedition against him. Eventually the second class mailing privileges of *Social Justice* were revoked on the grounds that they had violated Section 3 of Title I of the Espionage Act of 1917: giving aid to the enemies of the United States by conveying false information.[2]

Biddle, however, did not want to give Coughlin the opportunity to become a "martyr" so enlisted the aid of Leo T. Crowley, a Catholic who was chair of the board of the Federal Deposit Insurance Corporation and also a friend of President Roosevelt. After being briefed, Crowley met with Archbishop Mooney in Detroit and informed him of the seriousness of the charges against Coughlin. Mooney was told that if he would order Coughlin to cease his non-religious activities, the "radio priest" would be dealt with leniently. Mooney agreed. Coughlin was informed and was obedient to the end. (See above, p. 188.)[3]

With the interruption in communication due to the war, and with Coughlin's "silencing," Fahey's further influence in America was delayed until the post World War II period. He was not forgotten, however, as is attested to by the correspondence of three Protestants of some public image in the United States: Reverend Gerald L. K. Smith, Senator Jack B. Tenney, and Mrs. Lyrl Clark Van Hyning. He also communicated at great length with Myron C. Fagan, Director of the Cinema Educational Guild. A cross section of American Catholics wrote to him including a critique from David Goldstein of Boston, Jewish convert to Catholicism.

Fahey provided a substantial group of Americans, both Catholic and Protestant, with a theological rationale for their anti-Semitic orientations. In many instances, it is questionable as to whether the readers understood Fahey's concepts in their more theological/philosophical forms. They imbibed his convictions, however, and believed that there was deep theological significance underlying the foundations for their anti-Jewish sentiments. Fahey also supplied the religio-political "radical right" with polemical material such as *The Rulers of Russia*. This booklet continued to serve their purposes during the McCarthy era in the 1950s and after.

Lastly, Fahey became a link between the French and Roman ultraconservative Catholic thought of the first part of the twentieth century with certain right-wing groups in America. Catholics in the United States, from the end of World War I to Vatican II, enjoyed the Neo-Thomistic revival and the cultural experiences related to that which harked back to "the thirteenth—greatest of centuries." Many were receptive to the ideas of Fahey and Coughlin regarding the Jews during that period. A key question to be explored is the possible relationship of anti-Semitic attitudes in the period 1930-1960 to the resurgence of interest among Catholics in the medieval period.

Correspondence with America

The Reverend Gerald L. K. Smith

Probably best known among the American Protestants with whom Fahey had some correspondence in the late 1940s and early 1950s was the Reverend Gerald L. K. Smith. This self-styled heir apparent of Senator Huey P. Long and the "Share the Wealth" program was known as the greatest rabble-rouser of the era. H. L. Mencken once described him as "the gustiest and the goriest, loudest and lustiest, the deadliest and damndest orator ever heard on this or any other earth...the champion boob-bumper of all epochs."⁴

After the defeat of the Union Party of Coughlin-Smith-Townsend fame in 1936, Smith continued in various political activities. He established himself as leader of the Christian Nationalist Crusade functioning out of St. Louis, Missouri, which published a monthly magazine entitled *The Cross and the Flag*. This periodical first appeared in March 1942, and was generally accepted as the successor to Coughlin's *Social Justice* which was being terminated at that time.⁵ Although Coughlin had no use for his former collaborator in later years, and apparently disliked him even when they were working together, Smith announced: "I shall defend the right of free speech and press for Father Charles E. Coughlin. The treatment that this minister of Christ is receiving at the hand of the blood-thirsty Reds is unbelievable."⁶

Exactly when Smith began communicating with Fahey is not clear. That he wrote to the Irish priest asking to distribute his book *The Mystical Body of Christ and the Reorganization of Society* is revealed in a letter from William J. O'Connor of Chicago to Fahey, with a cover letter from Pauline Wettrick, dated May 1, 1948. O'Connor, who distributed Fahey's books in Chicago and later in Seattle, warned the Irish author that the reason Smith wanted to make Fahey's books available was that he had lost his Catholic following. Smith was known to have exploited other mailing lists such as those of Huey Long and Father Coughlin. It appeared to Fahey's friends in Chicago that the book sales of the Irish priest would be hindered rather than helped if Smith became involved in their distribution.⁷

Gerald L. K. Smith wrote to Fahey December 6, 1948 on Christian Nationalist Crusade stationery, stating briefly that he had instructed that five hundred copies of the tract "Red Stars in Hollywood" be sent to Fahey. He added a postscript in his own handwriting: "M. Fagan was *very* happy with your letter."⁸ Fagan was also part of the rightist movement of that period.

Less than two weeks later, John Hamilton, an Associate Editor of *The Cross and the Flag*, wrote to Fahey stating that they had received his acknowledgement of the five hundred tracts of "Red Stars in Hollywood." A total of twelve hundred copies had been mailed to Fahey as of then. Hamilton claimed that he knew Fahey would make good use of them to fight "the Jewish forces of world wide Atheistic Communism." He emphasized: "The tract might well have been called Red Jew Stars in Hollywood, for most of them are Jews and several of the rest are married to Jews." Enclosed was a list of *The Cross and the Flag* recommended literature. Hamilton concluded with a word of appreciation for Fahey's work: "'The Mystical Body of Christ' was a great inspiration to me and lead [sic] me to a deeper spiritual life as well as a realization of the evil forces of International Jewry."[9] On the back of *The Cross and the Flag* stationery in red ink was printed the "10 high principles" of Christian Nationalism.

Whether Fahey agreed to let Smith distribute any of his books at that time is not clear. By May 3, 1949, however, Fahey was defending Smith's position to the *Maria Duce*. In a letter to one of the members of the Irish activist group regarding the reprinting of Myron Fagan's booklet *Moscow over Hollywood*, the Irish priest added in an important postscript:

> With regard to the mention of G. L. K. Smith in the pamphlet, if anybody questions the point, a letter can be printed saying: (a) that we understand that U.S.A. is a free *democratic* country and that the Cinema Education Guild is free to support any politician whose programme will help its cause; (b) the programme of G. L. K. Smith as taken from his paper *The Cross and the Flag* of [blank space] declares unflinchingly and unequivocally for the Rights of Christ the King. Are his detractors and smearers for Christ the King or against Him?
>
> The Judaeo-Communists tried to brand every man who stood for American nationalism and against Communism during the war as pro-Nazis.

That was part of the technique. Thus every really
national movement was paralyzed.
    We can print G. L. K. Smith's declaration
for Christ the King if necessary. I have it. [The
last sentence was added in Fahey's handwriting.] I
do not want to omit his name because of the nobility
of that declaration.[10]

There is a Smith newsletter from 1949 in the Fahey Papers,
but no further communication from the Protestant clergyman until
a letter dated March 31, 1952. At that time his request was specific: "I am interested in distributing your booklet entitled 'The
Rulers of Russia' in quantity. Please quote me a price per hundred,
per 500, per 1000." He then added: "You have done magnificent
work. You have been one of God's noblemen in bringing to the
world dangerous truth."[11]
    On May 30, 1952, Smith wrote to Fahey again, this time
mentioning "the throes of an intense political campaign." Apparently in answer to Fahey's inquiries regarding allegations that he
was anti-Catholic, Smith declared:

It is important that you never believe any reports
that come out accusing me of anti-Catholicism. The
chief attorney in our organization is not only a
Catholic, but a very prominent one and was for
some time President of the Catholic Lawyers Guild
of Chicago. His name is Maximillian St. George.
We have many Catholics in our organization, and I
have forfeited the support of quite a number of
Protestant bigots who insist on dividing Christians in
their battle against Stalinism and other forms of
Marxism.[12]

No further letters from Smith are available in the Fahey
Papers, but apparently the Protestant clergyman had convinced the
Irish priest, because The Rulers of Russia was advertised on the

"Price List of Crusading Literature" for the first time in the June 1952 issue of *The Cross and the Flag*. It continued to be one of Smith's recommended paperbacks until the Protestant clergyman's death in 1976.[13]

Michael O'Toole, Director of Regina Publications in Dublin, and a great admirer of Fahey, stated that the Irish priest believed Smith to be a rabble-rouser: "Father Fahey gave him courtesy, but really didn't give him any support."[14] O'Toole believed it was because Fahey did not want to get involved in politics. Considering the Irish priest's sponsorship of the *Maria Duce* campaign on Article 44 of the Irish Constitution, and his later warm concern for Senator Joseph McCarthy on the pages of *FIAT*, this seems unlikely.[15] He had been amply warned about Smith, however. That Fahey, despite his suspicions, should have been in communication at all, and allowed Smith to distribute his booklet, is notable. Smith clearly approved of Fahey's writings, and used them in succeeding decades.

Senator Jack B. Tenney

Senator Jack B. Tenney, described as a musician, composer, labor leader, attorney, and California legislator, was another notable with whom Fahey corresponded. Tenney was not a Catholic, but had attended Holy Cross Parochial School in Los Angeles, and spoke of this with pride in later years. While a member of the California Assembly in 1941, Tenney introduced the first resolution for an "interim committee on Un-American Activities." Elected to the California Senate in 1942, he became Chairman of the Committee on Un-American Activities, and continued to be involved in fact-finding, conducting hearings, and issuing reports through 1949. In March 1947 he testified before the U.S. House Committee on Un-American Activities in Washington, D.C. Charges of anti-Semitism against his committee work were first made about this period.[16]

On August 28, 1949, Fahey wrote to Tenney, apparently at the suggestion of Myron Fagan. The Senator mentioned in his reply that Fagan was a good friend of his who was to be commended for his courageous fight against Communism. Tenney stated that he was happy to furnish "extra copies of the Committee Report."[17] In a letter to Fahey December 6, 1949, Tenney acknowledged receiving $5.00 from the Irish priest for expenses, but returned it with the suggestion that it be donated to some anti-Communist refugee group. He then informed Fahey that he was forwarding multiple copies of "reports" (1947-1949) and bound copies of 1948-1949 reports for Fahey's personal use. These would account for "the very important California Legislative Reports" sent by Fahey to members of the Irish hierarchy in January 1950.[18]

Shortly after, Tenney requested that Fahey do some research for him regarding an Irish priest, Father Clarence Duffy, who wrote an article for a west coast Communist newspaper entitled "Why I, a Priest, Must Defend the Communists." Duffy was scheduled to make a series of addresses in the Los Angeles area, and Tenney wanted to discover if Duffy was a priest in good standing. Fahey did get some information to pass along to Tenney, although the Senator was able to get substantive facts from Edward R. Gaffney, Vicar General of New York, which information the Senator sent to Fahey in photo-static copy. The particulars are not important, but the liaison between Fahey and Tenney was indicative of the transatlantic efforts of anti-Communists to share information. Fahey was known as an ardent anti-Communist in Ireland who was more than willing to be of assistance to Americans. In a letter of February 15, 1950, Tenney stated: "I want you to know that I will consider it a privilege to assist you in any way possible, in the fine work you are doing!"[19]

The year 1952 was a banner year for Tenney. He accepted the nominations of the Constitutional and the Christian Nationalist parties for Vice-President as running mate to General Douglas MacArthur. The latter of the two parties was Gerald L. K. Smith's organization, and Tenney and Smith appeared jointly on political programs under the auspices of the Christian Nationalist Crusade.[20]

The last letters from Tenney to Fahey were written in September 1953, well after the tumult and shouting of the campaign were over. He stated that he had distributed several copies of Fahey's books to Catholic friends and had been meeting more and more people acquainted with Fahey's work.[21] Tenney wrote a letter of gratitude for a copy of *The Kingship of Christ and the Conversion of the Jewish Nation*. Although there is no evidence to prove that Fahey had a profound influence on Tenney, the Senator admittedly appreciated Fahey's insights, and recommended his works accordingly. Fahey's access to California legislative documents, particularly regarding Jews and Communists in Hollywood, was certainly facilitated by the relationship.

Mrs. Lyrl Clark Van Hyning

"We, the Mothers, Mobilize for America, Inc." was a political organization in Chicago which published a national monthly entitled *Women's Voice*. It was headed by Mrs. Lyrl Clark Van Hyning, an active participant in right-wing circles. She was named moderator of the convention which formed the Constitution Party in July 1952 in Chicago. That party subsequently allied with Smith's Christian Nationalist Party in the nominations of MacArthur and Tenney.[22]

In a flyer available through the *Women's Voice* at five cents a copy, Van Hyning described something of her own history as the daughter of a Mason—whose father had been a Mason, etc. back to Revolutionary days. Her husband was also a Mason, as were his ancestors. She had come to believe, however, that American Masons had been duped, and felt compelled to disseminate material regarding the machinations of the "Jewish Grand Orient Freemasonry" headed by "Bernard Manasses Baruch," and others who had infiltrated American politics. She was convinced of the truth of *The Protocols of the Elders of Zion*, and felt sure that it was the Freemasons who were responsible for the downfall of Father Charles E. Coughlin. Fahey's ideas were obviously compatible with her own.[23]

Van Hyning distributed Fahey's books from the office of *Women's Voice* on South Dearborn Street in Chicago. Fahey kept account of the books sent to various parts of the world (and the receipts received) in a small brown leather calendar book. Although others assisted him in filling orders, and some requests went directly to the publishers or were forwarded by Fahey to them, the calculation, from Fahey's chronological account, provides an estimate of the number of Fahey volumes requested by one Protestant distributor in approximately a two-year period. Total: 221 volumes with *The Rulers of Russia* (60), and *The Kingship of Christ and Organized Naturalism* (47) as the most popular. More than four years after Fahey's death, a letter was received from *Women's Voice* at the Holy Ghost College, Kimmage, Dublin which requested that *The Mystical Body of Christ in the Modern World* be reprinted.[24]

The services of Mrs. Van Hyning reached both coasts of the United States, as well as the Middle West. Joseph F. Tisch, Jr., Paulist seminarian in Baltimore, informed Fahey that the *Women's Voice* was one of two places to procure his books in the United States, and Dr. J. A. Slaughter, a dentist from Los Angeles, wrote to Fahey requesting a copy of *The Kingship of Christ and the Conversion of the Jewish Nation* which he had read about in *Women's Voice*.[25] Van Hyning's enthusiasm for Fahey's writings allowed the books of the Irish priest to reach a variety of sources. With the move of William J. O'Connor from Chicago to Seattle, Fahey was probably grateful to have the *Women's Voice* as a distributor in Chicago—even if the proprietors were Protestant!

Myron C. Fagan

Among the Catholics who were in contact with Smith, Tenney and others of the California "radical rightists" of the 1940s and 1950s, was Myron Coureval Fagan, National Director of the Cinema Educational Guild, who first wrote and introduced himself to Fahey on November 20, 1948. He explained to the Irish priest that he had delivered the "El Patio theater speech" which Gerald L.

K. Smith had printed under the title "Red Stars in Hollywood." He
noted: "He did this without my knowledge, but when a man does
a thing like this not for gain (in fact, at a loss) but to spread the
word of truth, he is to be honored for it, not censured."[26] Fagan
was delighted to hear that Fahey was interested in the speech, and
offered to be of any service to the Irish priest in his crusade
regarding films and plays in Ireland.

"Who Is Myron C. Fagan?" is the title of a leaflet in the
Fahey Papers. Fagan, included in *Who's Who in the Theater*, was
described as the author of forty-two stage plays, among them
"Nancy's Private Affair" and "The Little Spitfire". Mary Pick-
ford, Marie Dressler, Brian Donlevy, and many other "names"
were listed as those who had acted in his plays. The text of Jimmie
Fidler's Sunday evening broadcast of October 24, 1948, which
described Fagan's upcoming campaign, was printed on the leaflet.
The radio commentator's speech was used to publicize the validity
of Fagan's mission.

Writing to Fahey on December 18, 1948, Fagan shared his
joy with the Irish priest that the Cinema Educational Guild had
been organized on December 9 of that year. He added:

> On January 10th 250 Charter members are to
> meet and initiate a drive for one million members
> thruout [sic] America to blacklist and boycott all
> Red Stars, Writers, Directors and Producers—and
> drive the Louis B. Mayers, Warners, Schencks,
> Dore Schary and other Russian-born lovers of Stalin
> out of Hollywood. I will gladly put up your name
> for honorary—and honorable—membership. I'd love
> to have the spirit of Ireland, direct from Ireland,
> join us.[27]

On January 3, 1949, Fagan wrote to Fahey, in response to the
letter of encouragement he had received from the Irish priest.
Fahey's name would be presented at the charter members' meeting
for honorary membership "...and we fully appreciate the high

honor of having your name and your spirit with us. We know that it will make us find that much more favor with the Lord."[28]

Fagan then suggested that, should Fahey receive his communication in time, it would be appreciated if he would send a cablegram back to Fagan before the first meeting "...wishing us success and your blessing, it would be like a spiritual message from above."[29] Fahey complied. Fagan was delighted and he responded: "Your cablegram arrived in plenty of time. And when I read it to the members and announced that you had requested to be enrolled an honorary member, the Auditorium resounded with cheers and thunderous applause."[30]

Thus began the extended correspondence of Fagan and Fahey. The forty-two often lengthy handwritten letters from the Hollywood crusader to the Irish priest written between November 20, 1948 and October 2, 1952 give a regular account of his speaking tours, and his interpretation of the Communist affiliation of well known Hollywood personages. In addition, Fahey became a confidant to whom Fagan could express his spiritual aspirations as they related to his crusading ventures. On February 9, 1949, he wrote:

> Your welcome letter of the 4th Inst. is before me. I am perfectly agreeable to an arrangement for a printing of "Moscow Over Hollywood" by your friends. I, too, am not in it for the profit to be derived. I am turning all my royalties into the treasury of the Cinema Educational Guild to carry on this work to preserve Christian civilization, for without it this would be done for. However, I, for one, am fully confident that our Lord will strengthen our hands as we go on thru all the hardships to ultimate victory. We simply must bear our Cross as He did two thousand years ago with never a doubt in Allmighty [sic] God's inscrutable way of saving our souls.[31]

Fahey seemed to find in Fagan a kindred spirit. Both were fighting the "anti-supernaturalism" of Hollywood. A mimeographed letter which was sent to all members of the Cinema Educational Guild on the occasion of its second anniversary listed as one of its achievements the relationship to Fahey and the C.C.T.P.A.: "Rev. Denis Fahey and the top officials of Ireland's 'Catholic Cinema and Theatre Patrons Association' have PUBLICLY attested that C.E.G. is the Gibraltar upon which they built their fight against Communism."[32]

Fahey apparently shared some of his distress with Fagan regarding criticism he was receiving in Ireland, particularly in his altercations with Gabriel Fallon, literary critic of *The Standard*, who was openly opposed to Fahey's stand on films.[33] One section of Fagan's letter to Fahey in the spring of 1951 was later typed by Fahey on a separate sheet with the following heading:

> The following extract from a letter of March 20, 1951, is recommended to *The Standard* pro-Communist "Smearing School":

> I note what you say about meeting with opposition from sources of a surprising nature. My friend, that is the reason that the Reds have been so successful over here. Cohesion among the Reds is phenomenal. The bickering, throat-cutting, interferences, jealousies, back-stabbing, among the supposed enemies of Communism is both amazing and heartbreaking. You would be utterly astounded if I were to tell you the names of some of the individuals who through sheer greed and desire for personal glory and gain, *deliberately* help the Reds by creating obstacles for men like Senator McCarthy, Fulton Lewis, Jr., myself, etc. Only the knowledge that Our Lord in Heaven is ever sustaining me keeps me fighting. You can't know the obstacles I have to overcome. However, when the

clouds are blackest, beyond them I see The Saviour
beckoning me ever onward and my weariness leaves
me.

                    Myron C. Fagan[34]

These words were ones with which Fahey could obviously
resonate.

In August 1951, Fagan sent his Irish priest friend a copy of
a pamphlet "put out by Rev. Bob Schuler, of whom you have no
doubt heard." He then discussed the anti-Catholicism of some of
his right-wing allies. He stated that Schuler was not as viciously
anti-Catholic as he used to be. He then discussed how he had been
accused of being a "bigoted Catholic hater of all other Christian
Denominations, as well as Jews."[35] In his later letters to Fahey
there was a more Catholic emphasis.

Lastly, he shared with Fahey his awakening to Gerald L. K.
Smith's perceived anti-Catholicism:

> I am also enclosing a document of interest to
> you. The Masons are really going all-out on an
> anti-Catholic campaign. And they have very strange
> bed-fellows—but, upon careful analysis, not so
> strange: Gerald L. K. Smith, who had previously
> been charged with anti-Jew, anti-negro, and anti-
> Catholicism (the latter of which he had denied to
> me), has been uttering veiled poison against
> Catholicism. I think Jack Moffett can enlighten
> you. However, the man who can best confirm (or
> refute) it is Father Coughlin of Detroit.[36]

Fagan added, possibly with a sense of disappointment: "I just
became aware of Smith's more or less secret hatred of Catholicism
in 1950, but had no convictions until recently, when the 'School'
matter became an issue in California."[37] Smith's letter to Fahey on
May 30, 1952 which had denied any anti-Catholicism, and resulted
in Fahey's permission for Smith to distribute *The Rulers of Russia*,

preceded Fagan's reflections by only a few months. Had Fagan shared his concerns about Smith earlier, Fahey might have evaluated the situation differently.

Michael O'Toole and others recall Fahey speaking glowingly of Fagan and his admirable work against the Communists in Hollywood.[38] Fahey referred to Myron C. Fagan in a letter in 1949: 'He has been extremely decent and he is fighting a good fight.'[39] The mutual admiration between Fahey and Fagan allowed their efforts to transcend national boundaries. The crusade against Communism had to be "supernatural and supranational"; both of these men had sincerely committed their lives to that cause.

The Diversity of Fahey's Correspondents

The correspondence between Fahey and people in the United States is substantial: 217 letters from fifty-eight people, mostly in the post-World War II period. In addition to those discussed above, there is correspondence from Gertrude M. Coogan of Chicago, author of *Money Creators*, to whom Fahey was indebted for advice on monetary issues;[40] from Paquita de Shishmareff, author of *Waters Flowing Eastward*, published under the pseudonym "L. Fry"—and from many of her coterie in southern California who were active in a group known as "Our Lady's Crusaders";[41] and from Sister Margaret Patricia McCarran of the College of the Holy Names in Oakland, daughter of Senator Patrick McCarran of Nevada. She wrote to Fahey with gratitude for a copy of *The Kingship of Christ and the Conversion of the Jewish Nation*, and stated that she still had his volume of *The Kingship of Christ* which had been given to her by Father Coughlin.[42] Some correspondence was initiated by Fahey. He wrote to *The Tidings*, newspaper of the Archdiocese of Los Angeles, to inquire about the relations of Emmett Lavary and Gene Kelly to Communist Front organizations, and had questions regarding Myron C. Fagan's accusation against William H. Mooring, Motion Picture Editor of the paper.[43] When Fahey desired information, he did not hesitate to inquire of the person at the pinnacle of power. A letter from J. Edgar Hoover, Director of the U.S. Federal Bureau of Investigation in Washington, D.C., thanked Fahey for his letter of June 3, 1951, together with the enclosures. Hoover then stated that the policy of the Bureau did not allow for sharing their files, which were only available for official use. He added: "No inference should be drawn that we do or do not have data in our files concerning the organizations you mentioned." Unfortunately, a duplicate of the letter Fahey sent to Hoover is not available.[44]

When Robert H. Williams first wrote to Fahey in 1946, he was a speech writer for Upton Close of Hollywood, California. He had received a copy of *The Rulers of Russia* from Fred Roemheld of Detroit. Williams asked Fahey if he would send photostatic copies of the much publicized "British White Paper" to them. Fahey responded affirmatively. On December 28, 1946, Williams replied: "I promised one to Congressman Wood, head of the House Committee on Un-American Activities."[45] Some pamphlets of the U.S. House Committee on Un-American Activities are in the Fahey Papers; one lists Richard M. Nixon of California as a committee member.[46] Williams later established the *Williams Intelligence Summary* on which Fahey heavily relied. They exchanged substantial material in the years 1946-1951. Williams assured Fahey that the Irish priest has many friends in America.[47]

Williams' effort to obtain copies of the "British White Paper" was not an isolated incident. W. H. Kelly of Mishawaka, Indiana, who was in a graduate research program in the Political Science Department at the University of Notre Dame, wrote to Fahey requesting the same.[48] The Irish priest had become an "authority" on Communism in the United States.

Supplying Libraries and Bookstores

Fahey's books were not unknown in college and university libraries. Elizabeth Nugent, who taught English literature at Seton Hall University in South Orange, New Jersey, wrote to tell Fahey that she was putting the titles of several of his books on their acquisition list.[49] Fahey's cousin, Sister Mary Adria Redding, B.V.M. , wrote with news of the family, and also requested a copy of his book on mental prayer. She mentioned that Marquette University in Milwaukee, where she was studying for the summer, had some of his books, but not all.[50]

Eighteen-year-old Lawrence S. Brey, who was studying for the priesthood at St. Francis Seminary in Milwaukee, wrote to Fahey in the autumn of 1945 to say that he had been introduced to *The Rulers of Russia* and *The Mystical Body of Christ in the Modern World* by Father Coughlin. "Both of these writings help me greatly in understanding the great world problems of today in which the Mystical Body is under so much attack." Brey then continued:

I am deeply interested in the great Christian movement carried on by yourself and Fr. Coughlin. I will try to devote much of my time and effort in the years to come to such a great cause. One tragic fact, however, is that there are many clergy who are not fighting as they should for the Church, and some who, perhaps through misguidance, yet at times deliberatly [sic], tend to obstruct militant Catholicism. We are all waiting for Fr. Coughlin's freedom to come again to America's aid....What we need in this country, ay, in this world, is many more Francos to bring back the Christian order of things, which [order] our enemies at this moment are snatching away.

I keep your book on my desk at the seminary. I hope I will never have to part with it.[51]

There were those who believed that high school students could benefit from Fahey's books. Mrs. Joseph Gregg, who was part of William O'Connor's group in Chicago, and who wrote to the Irish priest to encourage him not to deal with Gerald L. K. Smith, reported that the boys at St. Philip's and De La Salle High Schools were studying his smaller books. "We are quietly infiltrating the boys schools—thank God and a few friends." In a postscript she reminded Fahey: "You can tell Smith you have a Chicago outlet."[52]

The commitment of people to advertising and distributing Fahey's books was impressive. William J. O'Connor, mentioned above, a medical technician from Chicago, disseminated Fahey's material. He shared this task with a group which became a kind of "sodality." They were daily communicants and boasted of a few converts, and kept in touch with other Fahey promoters such as Gertrude M. Coogan and Lyrl Clark Van Hyning.[53]

In 1948 O'Connor moved to Seattle because of his wife's health. They experienced some financial reversals. However, on the eve of St. Patrick's Day, March 16, 1950, O'Connor wrote to Fahey on "The Book House" stationery—and continued to write on that letterhead thereafter. Whether he was the proprietor, part-owner, or an employee is not clear. He mentioned that the *Williams Intelligence Newsletter* had referred to *The Rulers of Russia*, and had given O'Connor's name, so he was receiving inquiries and orders.[54] The continued enthusiasm of Fahey's friends included sending snapshots of themselves and their families, and seeing themselves as part of his program to promote the Kingship of Christ.

Devotion to Our Lady of Fatima was popular at that time, and several of these groups—including "Our Lady's Crusaders" in California—encouraged the practices associated with it. Agnes Stanton Bolt, R.N., of Cleveland had "personalized" stationery headed with advice for her friends, including the recommendation to read *The Scapular* of New York City, *Our Lady of the Cape*, from Cap-de-la-Madeleine, Canada, and *The Tablet* of Brooklyn. Also on the letterhead was the quotation: "Our Lady of Fatima said it: 'If My requests are heard Russia will be converted and there will be peace.'" Bolt told Fahey that she had just finished sending off two thousand of the book lists to priests scattered through Canada, and had printed up another two thousand to send in the near future.[55]

Letters from American Missionaries in China

Word of Fahey's books even reached American missionaries in China, both Catholic and Protestant. J. L. Beal wrote to the Irish priest from the Catholic Mission, Sung Yang, Chekiang, China, October 23, 1940 stating that through the kindness of Father Coughlin he had read *The Rulers of Russia*. Beal informed Fahey that he had written an article about the booklet in their monthly publication entitled *China*, and encouraged readers to procure a copy. He also made arrangements to receive *The Mystical Body of Christ in the Modern World* in exchange for a number of Mass intentions.[56]

From Kuling, China, Fahey received a letter from Hugh W. White, who wanted to order the book "proving that Jews established the Soviet and are still conducting the system." White informed Fahey that he was a Protestant missionary, of the 'Southern' Presbyterian Church of the United States, and was doing his best to rally the Christians and the patriots of the world. He believed that his best work was in establishing *The China Fundamentalist*. He sent Fahey a copy.[57] Former students recalled that Fahey received mail from all over the world and frequently brought it to class to share with them. A letter from an American Southern Presbyterian missionary in China which included a copy of *The China Fundamentalist* must have been one of the extraordinary days.

This sampling of correspondence to Fahey from Americans indicates the diversity of personalities who appreciated his work. Most of them, however, shared his basic thesis regarding the enemies of the Kingship of Christ. There are only a few letters from priests[58] and there is no indication that Fahey ever wrote to any members of the American Catholic hierarchy.

A Challenge Accepted: Royal Oak and Dublin

One voice from the Catholic community in the United States which responded in a unique way to the Coughlin-Fahey stance was the Jewish convert to Catholicism, David Goldstein of Boston. As Director of the "Catholic Campaigners for Christ: Apostolate to the Man in the Street," Goldstein authored several volumes, among them *The Campaigners for Christ Handbook*, and *Autobiography of a Campaigner for Christ.*[59] Goldstein, who was raised a Jew, became involved in the Socialist movement and from that experience was eventually converted to Catholicism.[60] Fahey sent him a copy of *The Mystical Body of Christ in the Modern World* (first edition), December 16, 1936, with a copy of the review it received in the London *Jewish Chronicle*. He requested that Goldstein send him two copies of the *Campaigners for Christ Handbook*, one for himself, and one "for a Jewish correspondent who wrote to me attacking my book on the same lines as the review in *The Jewish Chronicle*."[61]

Goldstein's response to Fahey's letter mentioned above reads in part:

> If I may venture an opinion, with no intention to offend, I believe the use of the Protocols, which you say you did not use in the study of the growth of opposition to our Lord, left an opening for a comeback on the part of the reviewer. You used the Protocols that are of very doubtful authenticity. To say that the Jewish protest against them does not carry conviction to serious minded persons, and name Nesta Webster as one of them, is a weakening factor in a in a [sic] thesis you work out that has, no doubt, a very sound foundation.[62]

The early draft included Goldstein's suggestion that it would be better to put the second copy of the handbook in the public library rather than give it to the Jewish critic. "He impresses me as argumentally impregnable." That section was crossed out, and Goldstein replaced it with the following: "I hardly think giving your Jewish critic my book will win him. This is said because your book is not likely to impress any Jew favorably as it will non-Jews."[63]

Fahey did not accept Goldstein's advice. On February 12, 1937, he wrote to thank "the campaigner for Christ" for his excellent book just received, and added: "I shall have the pleasure in recommending the book, because of its extrinsic excellence." He still intended, however, to send the second copy to the Jewish correspondent "...with a courteous reply to his rather unkind one. It may do some good." In a postscript, Fahey quoted from *The Kingship of Christ according to the Principles of St. Thomas Aquinas*: "Just as Our Lord's Sacred Heart is wrung in a special manner by His own nation's rejection of Him, so every effort and every prayer for the conversion of the Jews appeal to Him, too...." To assure Goldstein of his sincerity he added: "For years, I say at least one mass for the conversion of the Jewish nation."[64] Fahey was incapable of understanding that his approach was hostile to, and painful for the Jews.

When Coughlin's anti-Semitic tirade against the Jews began in the fall of 1938, Goldstein was one of the few who tried to analyze the fallacy of Coughlin's argument based on Fahey.[65] Goldstein composed a seven-page single-spaced article entitled "Royal Oak and Dublin Challenge Accepted." He sent a copy to Fahey with a cover letter which stated:

> I regret very much that duty, as I see it, obligates me to take issue with your book in a public way as I shall do next week. I would have much preferred to have communicated with you privately about the matter in detail. This I did regarding one matter, as you will very likely recall, when you

favored me with a copy of your book a couple of years ago. I then said that the "protocols" alone were enough to ju[s]tify the hostility expressed by the Jewish Chronicle against you and the contents of the book.[66]

Goldstein feared that the extensive publicity given by Coughlin to Fahey's errors was having an adverse effect. Therefore "in the interest of Catholic truth" he felt compelled to furnish the public with "the true status of things dealt with in the book." He then offered his analysis of Coughlin:

Father Coughlin is an able speaker and ardent worker, but intellectually irresponsible when he leaves the sphere of religion proper and enters into economics and politics. His tendency, I regret to say, is to out-demagogue the demagogues. It gets the publicity, the front page in the papers, but it means dealing unfairly with the enemy and awakening a fanatical spirit among some of the laity. It is my studied opinion that the matter he uses, and the manner in which he sometimes presents it, make him a liability rather than an asset to the Church.[67]

He concluded his letter to Fahey with the statement: "Frankly, my opinion is that a statement regarding the errors your book has disseminated is due the public."[68] This is probably the most straightforward statement anyone ever made to the Irish priest regarding his writings, and his relationship to Coughlin.

The article by Goldstein was a careful analysis of the sections of Fahey's book quoted by Coughlin in his radio broadcasts in November 1938. He stated clearly that, not only were the *Protocols* forged, but that no such document existed as the one cited from *Documentation Catholique* by the "American Secret Service," as confirmed by Chief Frank J. Wilson of the United States Secret Service in Washington. According to Wilson, there was no knowledge of any such memorandum "in the memories of members of the service from 1916-1919."[69] This statement quoted from the New York *Times*, was also referred to by Msgr. John A. Ryan in his *Commonweal* article refuting Coughlin.[70]

Goldstein then discussed the errors in Fahey's "Jewish lists," as well as the whole episode of the "British White Paper." These he classified as "historical rumor." That such an abridgement of this latter document existed was hardly proof that Jews in the British government were attempting to deceive the public. Goldstein added: "The world did not have to see a British White Paper to learn that, for the same thing had been said a thousand times in a thousand different ways...."[71]

The Jewish convert seemed to sense, however, that Fahey's anti-Semitic orientation was not identical with Coughlin's. He stated: "Dr. Fahey's book is unfortunately, and very likely unintentionally, offensive to Jews...."[72] Goldstein cited as an example the number of references to Marx and Engels as Jews, and suggested that this was equivalent to describing "renegade ex-Catholics as 'Hitler the Catholic,' ... 'the Catholic Margaret Sanger'. He then discussed the Protestant heritage of both Marx and Engels.[73]

Goldstein's final comment expresses his sadness "to see such a sublime title attached to a book against which the contents rebels, a book dedicated 'to the Immaculate Heart of Mary,' the Lily of Israel, whose people it offends."[74] This book which "has misguided Royal Oak and its supporters" was doubly painful to Goldstein, because it emanated from a member of the Congregation of tbe Holy Ghost and the Immaculate Heart of Mary, "a religious society that owes its united existence to Venerable Father Libermann, a convert from Judaism."[75] Although Goldstein's clear and careful article, which discussed not only the factual errors but also Jewish sensitivities, was in the Fahey Papers, it is notable that none of Goldstein's letters were to be found there.

A copy of this article was sent to the Apostolic Delegate, the Most Reverend Ameleto Cicognani, in Washington, D.C. with a cover letter from Goldstein indicating that he regretted the fact that he felt morally obligated to respond to Coughlin:

> To repeat what I said today in a letter to Archbishop Mooney, I say regret, because my mind and heart have been so deliberately set upon the positive side of Catholic educational work, that I have only dealy [dealt] incidentally with Communism during the past few years. Besides, any one who takes issue publically [sic] with the work of Father Coughlin is subject to insults from fanatical and anti-clerical Catholics whom he stirs up to the point of gross uncharitableness.[76]

Lastly, Goldstein wrote to Coughlin, sending the article, and assuring him that a copy had been sent to Fahey. The second paragraph in this brief note probably captured the response of many persons in the United States in the aftermath of Coughlin's anti-Semitic discourses during that period:

> I deeply regret to find myself in conscience bound to take issue with you. Mainly because you are a priest, one God has gifted with admirable propaganda skills that might be used to further the pro-Catholic cause instead of intensifying the anti-Judaic spirit of our time.[77]

Not all Fahey's mail from America was "fan mail." The Irish priest continued to use his "Jewish lists" and other questionable material. Goldstein's thorough critique never caused Fahey to revise his earlier statements. He was satisfied to quote from Goldstein's *Campaigners for Christ Handbook*, and his autobiography on less controversial issues of the day. If Fahey believed that Maritain was incapable of having an objective view of the Jewish question because his wife was Jewish, there is the strong possibility that he came to the same conclusion about Goldstein's evaluation.

Conclusions

Fahey had indeed become a significant person to a substantial number of Americans in the period 1938-1954 after his introduction to the United States by Coughlin. Two further questions, however, remain: (1) Why was Fahey's work so acceptable to Americans, both Catholics and Protestants, during that era? (2) What is the meaning of the Coughlin-Fahey relationship to the United States when viewed in its historical context?

The acceptability of Fahey's work was, in part, because of Coughlin's recommendation. On a deeper level, however, it served a need, as did Coughlin's speeches, for those who were searching for someone to "blame" for the untoward events of the period between the World Wars. Communist scares, the overt prejudice revolving around the Al Smith campaign, the depression, and the rise of fascism in Europe all contributed to enlarging the fears of ordinary Americans. Fahey's efforts to describe where history had "gone wrong" beginning with the Jews on Calvary, and tracing their involvements to the present provided a rationale which "explained" a world out of control. The Irish priest provided an easy answer when discouraged people were grasping for a clue and Coughlin popularized his ideas through his radio broadcasts.

Although the "radio priest" emphasized Fahey's thesis on the Bolshevik Revolution, those who purchased Fahey's books and explored his ideas found that he spoke to many of their needs. Fahey prided himself that he was dealing with the real problems of people. He was something of an Irish Populist with his concern for farming and the land, his suspicions about big city life and the dangers of corruption from modern inventions like the cinema, and advertisements of immodest apparel. His emphasis on the linkage between the international financiers and the manufacture of manure was a typical example of his conviction that just as all the good in the world emanated from the order within the Mystical Body of Christ, so all the evil somehow flowed from the body of Organized

Naturalism controlled by Jews and Freemasons, Bolsheviks and bankers.[78] The distress of the Irish priest over land and money was not limited to Ireland.[79]

Among Coughlin's most faithful listeners were Irish Catholics of every generation in America. Many of them experienced a new "self-esteem" in terms of their Catholic identity when the Detroit priest's popularity was on the rise. That an Irish American priest could draw such a following, and mesmerize so many listeners, both Catholic and Protestant, on Sunday afternoons was a new phenomenon: a Catholic radio evangelist of enormous power. Their pride was compounded, therefore, when Coughlin called forth as his authority one who was not a German exegete, or a French philosopher, but an Irish theologian named "Professor Denis Fahey, one of the most outstanding scholars in Ireland...a professor of philosophy at Blackrock Seminary, Dublin."[80] The solidarity which many Irish Catholics felt with the citizens of their homeland across the sea provided an openness to Fahey's ideas.

In addition, Fahey appealed to a certain piety in people, particularly the Irish. At a time when some scholars among Catholics were caught up in the Neo-Thomistic revival, Fahey's thesis and his crusade mentality, cloaked in a Thomistic framework, were welcomed by those who wanted to have their more simplistic religious world affirmed. It might be suggested that Fahey became for some "the poor person's Maritain." He had all the scholarly credentials; he could quote Latin and French sources to prove his points. The rigid dichotomy in his world view, however, and his preoccupation with the enemies of Christ and their relationship to diabolical elements, allowed him to feed a distorted view of Christianity to the English-speaking world.

French and Roman influences had been powerful for Fahey in his formative years, both at Chevilly, and at the *Séminaire Française* in Rome. During that troubled era in the church, an alliance had been forged between integralist theology and right-wing politics. Such a combination would not seem unnatural to Fahey. His later leadership in the formation of the *Maria Duce* which provided a religio-political outlet for those who were on the "radical right" in Ireland grew out of the intellectual and political components to which he had been exposed in his earlier years.

It was not unusual, therefore, that Fahey's work received considerable acceptance from rightist elements in the United States. In the process, he became a link in the transmission of French and Roman conservative right-wing thought to America. The possibility of being a vehicle for communication was enhanced by the fact that the Irish priest wrote in English. His writings, therefore, became available to Coughlin, Smith, Tenney and others who would not have devoted extended time to reading books in French, Latin or German. Fahey, drawing largely on French and Roman ultraconservatives, found himself championed by "radical rightists" in both Ireland and America.

In the United States during the years 1880-1924, Jewish-Christian relations were strained by prejudice. A new kind of racial anti-Semitism grew out of social Darwinism and the emphasis on purity of race. Fear that America as a nation would be "polluted" by Eastern European Catholics, Orthodox and Jews, was related primarily to ethnic, cultural and racial dimensions, although religious factors were certainly a consideration.

With the aftermath of World War I, new fears emerged among those comfortably established in America, particularly apprehensions that the United States would be infiltrated by the Communists. The closure of immigration in 1924 allayed some of those fears, and allowed for experiences of acculturation and assimilation; the immigrants of the late nineteenth and early twentieth centuries began to blend into the American scene. Although racial tensions vis-à-vis Blacks, Hispanics, and Asians (especially the Japanese-Americans during World War II) continued to be problematic, the antagonism toward the racially swarthy Mediterranean and East European immigrants began to subside by the 1930s. Coughlin's stance toward the Jews evolved, as noted earlier. In 1934 he welcomed Jews into the National Union for Social Justice. Although he was not devoid of anti-Semitic utterances in the 1934-1938 period (particularly the 1936 campaign), it was not a total preoccupation for him.

Coughlin's overt anti-Semitic crusade which began in 1938, however, was cast in a different mold. In accepting Fahey's thesis, the "radio priest" was not just concurring with the Irish theologian's theory regarding Jewish involvement in the Bolshevik Revolution; he was affirming that that activity took place within a particular theological framework. To publicize *The Mystical Body of Christ in the Modern World* and *The Kingship of Christ* as "proofs" for his statements regarding the Jews and Communism was to affirm a theological justification; it was to remove the question from a racial setting and return it to the religious spectrum.

In the 1920-1940 period, American Catholicism enjoyed the experience of "innocence." It dwelt, as has been stated, on "the thirteenth, the greatest of centuries," the revival of Gothic architecture, Gregorian chant, and Neo-Scholasticism. In examining Jewish-Christian relations in the Middle Ages, however, one becomes aware of the decrees of the Church Councils in the twelfth and thirteenth centuries, which include some of the most harsh ordinances against the Jews in ecclesiastical history.[81] Joshua Trachtenberg in *The Devil and the Jews: The Medieval Conception of the Jews and Its Relation to Modern Antisemitism* contends that Christians in the medieval period actually considered the Jews to be the devil.[82] If Baptism was that ritual in which one renounced Satan and all his works and pomps, the unbaptized person in medieval times was sometimes perceived as still "possessed" by the devil.

Catholics gloried in the positive aspects of the high Middle Ages. Although the relationship is complex, it seems that one can suggest that a negative by-product of the Neo-Thomistic revival and the concurrent interest in the Middle Ages was that the attitudes toward Jews in medieval times were filtered, if only by a kind of "osmosis," into various aspects of contemporary church life and thought in the 1930's. The stance of the Christian toward the Jew in the Middle Ages came alive in the work of Denis Fahey, however subconsciously. Coughlin, who also imbibed the thirteenth-century emphasis in his own studies, accepted Fahey's "theology of history" and used it to further his own anti-Semitic thrust, extending it further to include "the mystical body of Satan." In a sense, for both Fahey and Coughlin, "the Jews" became "the devil" again.

Catholics and Jews had often come to the United States in the same waves of immigration, and had endured the difficult years of arrival together. There was competition and some hostility, but there was give-and-take in the political sphere, a strong sense of family, *joie de vivre*, and a common fear of the Nativist enemy. It was in the Coughlin era, however, that the real polarization of Catholics and Jews emerged in twentieth century America. Father Coughlin was an important Irish American Catholic priest. There were "theological" implications when he spoke of diabolical conspiracies. To associate Jews with hidden relationships and mysterious events related to the Mystical Body of Christ was to view the problem not primarily as a socio-cultural, political, economic or racial concern, but to emphasize that it was a religious matter. In Fahey's system it was described as the body of "Organized Naturalism" which was awaiting the Natural Messias who was probably the "Jewish Messias" and who could well be the Anti-Christ; in Coughlin's words, it was part of the "mystical body of Satan." In adopting Fahey's scheme, Coughlin attempted to give theological respectability to his own unredeemable ideas. The "radio priest" tried to dignify his message with a deformed Christian theology. The result was that the original message, which was meant to be "Good News," became a source of suffering for Jews in America and around the world. It also proved destructive for some Christians whose vision of Christianity was deprived, and whose understanding of Judaism was distorted. Coughlin's silence was welcomed by many in the summer of '42.

[1]Marcus, p. 182 states: "In its August 3, 1936 issue, *Social Justice* claimed a circulation of one million. It is probable that this was an exaggeration, although the figure has been used by some social scientists. N.W. Ayer and Son, Inc., stated that the circulation of the journal was 228,678 in 1940 and 184,929 in 1941. These are the only two years for which circulation figures were available."

[2]See Marcus, Chapter IX.

[3]Ibid., see especially pp. 216-217.

[4]David H. Bennett, p. 125. See also *Current Biography 1943*, ed. Maxine Block (New York: H.W. Wilson Co., 1943), p. 707.

[5]Marcus, pp. 105, 113, 117, 125, 137. In an interview with Sheldon Marcus on April 11, 1970, Father Coughlin denied that he was allied with either Smith or Townsend. Coughlin reacted: "Smith was a viper...a leech...who was anti-Christian, anti-Semitic and anti-God. I had no more of a relationship to him than I had to Spartacus and the gladiators" (p. 105). Pictures of Coughlin, Smith and Townsend with arms joined, even on the front page of *Social Justice* (July 27, 1936), with the headline "Forces Unite" are among the facts which prove Coughlin's statement to Marcus otherwise. See also D.H. Bennett, p. 12 and Marcus, p. 116.

[6]*Current Biography 1943*, p. 709. See also *The Cross and the Flag* (February 1952), p. 23 for Smith's praise of Coughlin some years later.

[7]William J. O'Connor to Fahey, n.d., unsigned; cover letter Pauline Wettrick to Fahey, May 1, 1948, FP-HGP.

[8]Gerald L.K. Smith to Fahey, December 6, 1948, FP-HGP.

[9]John W. Hamilton to Fahey, December 18, 1948, FP-HGP.

[10]Fahey to Joris, May 3, 1949, FP-HGP.

[11]Gerald L.K. Smith to Fahey, March 31, 1952, FP-HGP.

[12]Ibid., May 30, 1952.

[13]*The Cross and the Flag* (June 1976), memorial issue for Gerald L.K. Smith, advertised *The Rulers of Russia* on its "Literature List Prepared Under the Direction of Gerald L. K. Smith for the Christian Nationalist Crusade," p. 28.

[14]Interview with Michael O'Toole, Dublin, September 18, 1980.

[15]*Fiat* (Dublin: *Maria Duce*, n.d.), No. 32, featured a picture of Senator Josephy McCarthy and an extended article. Headline reads: "Senator McCarthy fearlessly faces the menace of Communism—but is opposed by 'anti-Communists,'" p. 2.

[16]*Jack B. Tenney: California Legislator* (Los Angeles, California: Oral History Program, University of California, Los Angeles, 1969), I, pp. iv, xi.

[17]Jack B. Tenney to Fahey, January 4, 1950, FP-HGP.

[18]Ibid., December 6, 1949.

[19]Jack B. Tenney to Fahey, January 4, 1950, January 6, 1950, and February 15, 1950. FP-HGP.

[20]"Extremist Literature," Collection 50, Department of Special Collections, University of California, Los Angeles.

[21]Jack B. Tenney to Fahey, September 17, 1953, FP-HGP.

[22]Harry and Bonaro Overstreet, *The Strange Tactics of Extremism* (New York: W. W. Norton and Company, Inc., 1964), p. 214. Cf. also Ralph Lord Roy, *Apostles of Discord: A Study of Organized Bigotry and Disruption on the Fringes of Protestantism* (Boston: Beacon Press, 1953), pp. 16-17. Referring to the two nationalist conventions rallying delegates in Chicago in the summer of 1952, Roy stated: "The more important caucus was organized by Mrs. Lyrl Clark Van Hyning. . . . Mrs. Van Hyning had announced her 'Holy Crusade' in February—'to witness to our faith in God and our Republic.'"

[23]"Is Masonry World Jewry?" n.n., n.d., but in the text the author refers to her father-in-law as Charles Van Hyning. FP-HGP.

[24]Violet Waggoner of *Women's Voice* to "Holy Ghost College," Kimmage, Dublin, October 1, 1958. FP-HGP.

240

[25]Joseph F. Tisch, Jr. to Fahey, September 15, 1952, and J.A. Slaughter to Fahey, January 13, 1954, FP-HGP.

[26]Myron C. Fagan to Fahey, November 20, 1948, FP-HGP.

[27]Myon C. Fagan to Fahey, December 18, 1948, FP-HGP.

[28]Ibid., January 3, 1949.

[29]Ibid.

[30]Ibid., n.d., but sometime after January 10, 1949.

[31]Ibid., February 9, 1949.

[32]Mimeographed letter of the C.E.G. from Myron C. Fagan, P.O. Box 8655, Cole Branch, Hollywood, 46, California, n.d.

[33]Myron C. Fagan to Fahey, March 30, 1951, FP-HGP.

[34]Ibid.

[35]Ibid., August 24, 1951. This was the first statement in Fagan's letters where he clearly identified himself as a Catholic. Some believed that he was a Jewish convert to Christianity. According to Harvey Schecter, Director of the ADL Office, Los Angeles, Fagan was never Jewish, and his wife was Catholic. Telephone interview with Millie Marcus, May 11, 1982.

[36]Ibid., October 2, 1952.

[37]Ibid.

[38]Interview with Michael O'Toole, Dublin, September 18, 1980.

[39]Fahey to Joris, May 3, 1949, FP-HGP.

[40]In the preface to MBCRS, Fahey stated: "I am under particular obligation to Miss G. M. Coogan, writer of *Money Creators* and *Lawful Money Lectures*, for guidance and instruction on the subject of finance. If this book proves helpful to others in understanding the relation of money to the real order of the world, it is in great part owing to Miss Coogan's kindness. She not only assisted me with books and advice, but spurred me on to the effort required to help the poor on the one hand and to enlighten the bewildered on the other"

(xiii-xiv). In a letter to Fahey April 4, 1945, Coogan ordered sixteen copies of Fahey's book (presumably MBCRS), for the clergy. She informed Fahey that she had written to Bishop John F. Noll of Fort Wayne, Indiana, who was a personal friend of hers, asking if she could review Fahey's book for *Our Sunday Visitor* which "has national distribution and is the one Catholic paper most suited for review of your book."

[41]This group included D. J. Lauzon (Mrs. Charles J. Schreiber), and her husband who were leaders in "Our Lady's Crusaders" in Reseda, California. Mr. Schreiber was also Director of the "Christian Patriotic Rally" at another address in Reseda. The motto of this latter group was "Undivided loyalty to Christianity and Sovereign America...." After Fahey's death, Schreiber wrote to "the Reverend Superior" at Kimmage, March 25, 1954: "We know that you too must feel the loss of Father Fahey, but here in America his friends were legion and have not yet fully realized our tremendous loss." FP-HGP.

[42]Sister Margaret Patricia McCaran to Fahey, July 21, 1953.

[43]Reverend William E. North to Fahey, August 11, 1949; William H. Mooring to Fahey, October 13, 1949; ibid., July 17, 1951, FP-HGP.

[44]J. Edgar Hoover to Fahey, June 23, 1951, FP-HGP.

[45]Robert H. Williams to Fahey, November 19, 1946; December 28, 1946. Leo Reardon, who was a top aide for Coughlin, became associated with Upton Close after the demise of *Social Justice* in 1942 (Marcus, p. 255).

[46]*Spotlight on Spies* (Washington, D.C.: Committee on Un-American Activities, U.S. House of Representatives, stamped "For release March 25, 1949).

[47]Robert H. Williams to Fahey, August 23, 1951, FP-HGP.

[48]W.H. Kelly to Fahey, March 25, 1953, FP-HGP.

[49]Elizabeth Nugent to Fahey, June 27, 1953, FP-HGP.

[50]Sister Mary Adria Redding, B.V.M. to Fahey, August 4, 1940, FP-HGP.

[51]Lawrence S. Brey to Fahey, October 7, 1945, FP-HGP.

[52]Mrs. Joseph Gregg to Fahey, April 9, 1948.

[53]There are twenty letters from William J. O'Connor to Fahey during the years 1946-1953, FP-HGP.

[54]William J. O'Connor to Fahey, February 10, 1949, FP-HGP.

[55]Agnes Stanton Bolt, R.N. to Fahey, July 13, 1949, FP-HGP.

[56]J. L. Beal to Fahey, October 23, 1940, FP-HGP.

[57]Hugh W. White to Fahey, October 10, 1938, FP-HGP.

[58]Father Edward F. Brophy, Precious Blood Rectory, Long Island, New York, who was distressed about conditions in the church and in the country, wrote five letters to Fahey. He also sent copies of letters he had written to *The Tablet* (Brooklyn), *Our Sunday Visitor* (Huntington, Indiana), *The Catholic News* (New York City), and *The Catholic Digest* (St. Paul, Minnesota), requesting to review Fahey's books. On May 15, 1953, he ordered fifty copies of KCCJN.

There is only one letter in the Fahey Papers from Father Joseph Diesz (May 21, 1943), but references to him in many letters indicate that he was an important liaison person to the people and groups with whom Fahey corresponded. He was the celebrant of the memorial liturgy for "American Friends of Father Denis Fahey, C.S.Sp." at St. Patrick's Cathedral in New York, arranged by Thomas Kavanagh.

[59]David Goldstein, *The Campaigners for Christ Handbook* (Boston: T.J. Flynn, 1934); and *Autobiography of a Campaigner for Christ* (Boston: Catholic Campaigners for Christ, 1936)

[60]Goldstein, *Autobiography*, Chapters I-VI. See also review by O'Brien Atkinson, *America* (November 21, 1936), 56:165.

[61]Fahey to David Goldstein, December 16, 1936, Goldstein Papers, JJB-BC. There are no Goldstein letters in the Fahey Papers, but there are carbon copies of the Jewish convert's communication with Fahey in the Goldstein Papers in Boston.

[62]David Goldstein to Fahey, January 23, 1937, Goldstein Papers, JJB-BC.

[63]Ibid.

[64]Fahey to David Goldstein, February 12, 1937, Goldstein Papers, JJB-BC.

[65]Others, in addition to Msgr. John A. Ryan and George Shuster, who tried to refute Coughlin as mentioned above were members of the Catholic Worker movement.

[66]David Goldstein to Fahey, December 7, 1938, Goldstein Papers, JJB-BC.

[67]Ibid.

[68]Ibid.

[69]David Goldstein, "Royal Oak and Dublin Challenge Accepted" (mimeographed article), pp. 2-3, FP-HGP. Note on p. 1 in Fahey's handwriting: "From David Goldstein, Astor P.O., Boston, Mass."

[70]Ryan, *Commonweal* (December 20, 1938): 260. The *New York Times* mentioned Fahey on November 28, 1938 (8:2) as the source of Coughlin's material on the Russian Revolution. Those statements were denied the following day by Alexander Kerensky (20:3).

[71]Goldstein, "Royal Oak and Dublin Challenge Accepted," p. 6.

[72]Ibid.

[73]Ibid.

[74]Ibid., p. 7.

[75]Ibid.

[76]David Goldstein to Amaleto Cicognani, December 8, 1938, Goldstein Papers, JJB-BC.

[77]David Goldstein to Coughlin, December 11, 1938, Goldstein Papers, JJB-BC.

[78]Denis Fahey,C.S.Sp., *The Church and Farming*, Chapter III: "Cartesian Philosophy in Action—Artificial Manures."

[79]Examples of Fahey's efforts to include American material in *The Church and Farming*: "Joint Pastoral of the Archbishops and Bishops of Quebec, Canada on the Rural Problem in Relation to the Social Doctrine of the Church" (pp. 29-59); statistics on soil erosion in the United States (p. 90); quotations from

Manifesto on Rural Life, published by Bruce Publishing Company of Milwaukee for the National Catholic Rural Life Conference in the U.S. (p. 209).

[80]Coughlin, *"Am I an Anti-Semite?"*, p. 62.

[81]The following is a summary of some canons from church councils in the twelfth and thirteenth centuries:

> Jews not permitted to be plaintiffs, or witnesses, against Christians in the courts, 3rd Lateran Council, 1179, Canon 26.
>
> Jews not permitted to withhold inheritance from descendants who had accepted Christianity, 3rd Lateran Council, 1179, Canon 26.
>
> The marking of Jewish clothes with a badge, 4th Lateran Council, 1215, Canon 68.
>
> Construction of new synagogues prohibited, Council of Oxford, 1222.
>
> Compulsory ghettos, Synod of Breslau, 1267.
>
> Christians not permitted to sell or rent real estate to Jews, Synod of Ofen, 1279.

From A. Roy Eckardt, *Elder and Younger Brothers: The Encounter of Jews and Christians* (New York: Charles Scribner's Sons, 1967), pp. 12-14. Eckardt cites Raul Hilberg's comparisons of Canon Law with Nazi anti-Jewish measures in the 1930s. See *The Destruction of European Jews* (New York: Harper and Row, 1961), pp. 5-6.

[82]Joshua Trachtenberg, *The Devil and the Jews: The Medieval Conception of the Jews and Its Relation to Modern Anti-Semitism* (New Haven: Yale University Press, 1943), xii. The following statement of Trachtenberg is particularly relevant to this study: "If it is possible for demagogues to sow the seeds of disunion and discord, to stir fanatical emotions and set neighbor against neighbor, it is because the figure of the 'demonic' Jew, less than human, indeed, antihuman, the creation of the medieval mind, still dominates the folk imagination."

BIBLIOGRAPHY

Primary Sources: Archives

Archives of the Irish Province of the Holy Ghost Congregation, Holy Ghost Provincialate (HGP), Temple Park, Dublin, Ireland. Denis Fahey, C.S.Sp. Papers. Approximately 2,700 pages of documents in the Fahey Papers are relevant to this study including his *Apologia Pro Vita Mea*, correspondence, notebooks, class notes, papers, clippings, early drafts of books and articles.

Archives of the Irish Province of the Society of Jesus, 35 Lower Lessen Street, Dublin, Ireland. Edward Cahill, S.J. Papers.

Boston College Archives, Chestnut Hill, Massachusetts. Hilaire Belloc Papers.

Denis Fahey, C.S.Sp. Papers. Fahey Homestead, Kilmore, Golden, County Tipperary, Ireland.

Department of Special Collections, University Research Library, University of California, Los Angeles: "Extremist Literature," Collection 50; "Jack B. Tenney: California Legislator," Oral History program—transcript, 4 vols.

Holy Ghost Missionary College Library, Kimmage, Dublin. Collection of approximately two hundred books which were annotated by Fahey and were in his room when he died. They have been kept in a special section of the library.

John J. Burns Library, Boston College, Chestnut Hill, Massachusetts.

Primary Sources: Books

Belloc, Hilaire. *The Jews*. Boston: Houghton Mifflin Company, 1922.

Billot, Louis, S.J. *De Ecclesia Christi*. 2 vols. Roma: S.C. de Propaganda Fide, 1903.

Cahill, Edward, S.J. *Freemasonry and the Anti-Christian Movement*. Dublin: M.H. Gill and Son, Ltd., 1930.

Clinchy, Everett Ross. *All in the Name of God*. New York: The John Day Company, 1934.

Coogan, Gertrude. *Money Creators*. Chicago: Money Press, Inc., 1935.

246

Coughlin, Charles E. *"Am I an Anti-Semite?": 9 Addresses on Various "ISMS" Answering the Question.* Royal Oak, Michigan: Radio League of the Little Flower, 1939.

_____. *Eight Lectures on Labor, Capital and Justice.* Royal Oak, Michigan: Radio League of the Little Flower, 1934.

_____. *Father Coughlin's Radio Discourses.* Royal Oak, Michigan: Radio League of the Little Flower, 1932.

_____. *Father Coughlin's Radio Sermons: October 1930-April 1931—Complete.* Baltimore: Knox and O'Leary, 1931.

_____. *Father Coughlin on Money and Gold: Three Pamphlets.* New York: Arno Press, 1974.

_____. *Money! Questions and Answers.* Royal Oak, Michigan: National Union for Social Justice, 1936.

_____. *The New Deal in Money.* Royal Oak, Michigan: Radio League of the Little Flower, 1933.

_____. *Sixteen Radio Lectures.* Royal Oak, Michigan: Charles E. Coughlin, 1938.

_____. *Why Leave Our Own? 13 Addresses on Christianity and Americanism: January 8-April 2, 1939.* Royal Oak, Michigan: Charles E. Coughlin, 1939.

Deschamps, Nicholas, S.J. *Les Sociétés Secrètes et la Société.* 3 vols. Paris: Oudin Frères, 1882.

Fahey, Denis, C.S.Sp. *The Church and Farming.* Cork: The Forum Press, 1953.

_____. *The Kingship of Christ according to the Principles of St. Thomas Aquinas.* Dublin: Browne and Nolan Ltd., 1931.

_____. *The Kingship of Christ and the Conversion of the Jewish Nation.* Dublin: Regina Publications, 1953.

_____. *The Kingship of Christ and Organized Naturalism.* Cork: The Forum Press, 1943.

_____. *Mental Prayer according to the Principles of St. Thomas Aquinas.* Dublin: M.H. Gill and Son, 1927.

_____. *Money Manipulation and the Social Order.* Dublin: Browne and Nolan Ltd., 1944.

_____. *The Mystical Body of Christ in the Modern World.* Dublin: Browne and Nolan Ltd., 1935.

_____. *The Mystical Body of Christ and the Reorganization of Society.* Cork: The Forum Press, 1945.

_____. *The Rulers of Russia.* Dublin: Holy Ghost Missionary College, 1938. (Third edition rev. and enlarged 1939).

_____. *The Rulers of Russia and the Russian Farmers.* Kimmage, Dublin: Holy Ghost Missionary College, 1948.

Fagan, Myron C. *Red Treason in Hollywood.* Hollywood, California: Cinema Educational Guild, Inc., 1949.

Father Coughlin: His "Facts" and Arguments. New York: General Jewish Council, 1939.

Father Coughlin's Friends. *An Answer to Father Coughlin's Critics.* Royal Oak, Michigan: Radio League of the Little Flower, 1940.

[Ford, Henry]. *The International Jew.* 4 vols. Dearborn, Michigan: *The Dearborn Independent*, 1920-1921.

Goldstein, David. *Autobiography of a Campaigner for Christ.* Boston: Campaigners for Christ, 1936.

_____. *Campaigners for Christ Handbook.* Boston: T.J. Flynn and Company, 1934.

Joyce, James. *A Portrait of the Artist as a Young Man.* London: Granada Publishing Company, 1977. (First published 1916.)

Kurth, Godefroid. *The Church at the Turning Points of History.* Trans. Rt. Rev. Victor Day. Helena, Montana: Naegele Printing Company, 1918.

_____. *Les Origines de la Civilisation Moderne.* 2 vols. Paris: Victor Retaux, Libraire-Editeur, 1898.

_____. *The Workingmen's Guilds of the Middle Ages.* Intro. Denis Fahey, C.S.Sp. Trans. Denis Fahey, C.S.Sp. and Stephen Rigby. Dublin: Regina Publications, 1943.

Lunn, Arnold. *Now I See.* New York: Sheed and Ward, 1945.

Maritain, Jacques. *The Things That Are Not Caesar's.* London: Sheed and Ward, 1930.

_____. *Three Reformers: Luther—Descartes—Rousseau.* London: Sheed and Ward, 1947. (First published 1928.)

_____. *Integral Humanism.* Notre Dame: University of Notre Dame Press, 1973. (First published 1936.)

Mugglebee, Ruth. *Father Coughlin—the Radio Priest of the Shrine of the Little Flower: An Account of the Life, Work and Message of the Reverend Charles E. Coughlin.* Intro. Robert E. Rogers. Garden City, New York: Garden City Publishing Company, 1933.

Niebuhr, Reinhold. *Moral Man and Immoral Society.* New York: Charles Scribner's Sons, 1932.

Théotime de St. Just. *La Royauté Sociale de N.S. Jésus-Christ d'après le Cardinal Pie.* Paris: Société et Librairie S. François d'Assise, 1925.

Thomas Aquinas. *Summa Theologica.* 3 vols. New York: Benziger Brothers, 1947.

Walsh, James J. *The Thirteenth, Greatest of Centuries.* New York: Catholic Summer School Press, 1907.

Webster, Nesta. *Secret Societies and Subversive Movements.* N.p.: Christian Book Club of America, n.d. (First published 1924.)

248

_____. *World Revolution: The Plot against Civilization.* Boston: Small, Maynard and Company, 1921.

Primary Sources: Articles

"Anti-Semitism Is Part of the Coughlin Campaign." *Christian Century* 56 (May 24, 1939): 661.

Bennett, John Coleman. "After Liberalism—What?" *Christian Century* 50 (November 8, 1933): 1403-1406.

Bulletin de la Congrégation. Paris: Holy Ghost Congregation, 24 (Avril 1920): 605.

"Cardinal Mundelein Repudiates Coughlin's Anti-Semitism." *Christian Century* 55 (December 21, 1938): 1563.

Comerford, F., C. S. Sp. "Late Fr. Denis Fahey, C. S. Sp. An Appreciation." N.p. , n.d. Reprinted from *The Tipperary Star* by the Catholic Central Library, Merrion Square, Dublin.

The Cross and the Flag. St. Louis, Missouri: Published by Gerald L. K. Smith, 1942-76. Vols. 6:7-7:5; 35:1-12.

Fahey, Denis, C.S.Sp. "Causes of the Rending of Christendom." IER 63 (March 1944): 185-190.

_____. "Father Libermann's Faith." *The Missionary Annals of the Holy Ghost Fathers* 5 (February 1923) 2: 28-30.

_____. "Human Personality and Individuality." IER 59 (April 1942): 339-348.

_____. "The Introduction of Scholastic Philosophy into Irish Secondary Education." IER 22 (August 1923): 177-193.

_____. "Latin and the Supernatural." IER 23 (February 1924): 189-205.

_____. "The Metaphysics of Suarez." IER 23 (April 1924): 289-415; (May 1924): 485-500.

_____. "Nationality and the Supernatural." IER 21 (March 1923): 261-174.

_____. "Ockhamism or Nominalism and the Undermining of the Unity of Christendom." IER 62 (July 1943): 51-56.

_____. "Our Real Life." IER 27 (November. 1926): 490-502; 27 (December 1926): 611-629; 29 (June 1927): 600-616; 30 (July 1927): 41-53.

_____. "St. Thomas: Official Metaphysician of the Catholic Church." IER 25 (March 1925): 273-290.

_____. "The Twenty-Four Theses of St. Thomas." IER 23 (June 1924): 614-627; 24 (July 1924): 35-55.

_____. "The Value of Scholastic Philosophy in Modern Conditions." IER 22 (November 1923): 480-499.

"Father Coughlin and the Jews." *Commonweal* 29 (December 9, 1938): 169-170.

"Father Coughlin and the Jews." *Commonweal* 29 (December 30, 1938): 268-270.

"Father Coughlin and the Press." *Commonweal* 29 (December 16, 1938): 213-214.

Masterson, Edward, S.J. "Are the Metaphysics of Suarez in Opposition to Those of St. Thomas?" IER 23 (January 1924): 41-54.

_____. "The Twenty-Four Theses of St. Thomas." IER 24 (September 1924): 268-290.

Parsons, Wilfrid, S.J. "Father Coughlin and Social Justice." *America* 53 (May 18, 1935): 129-131.

Ryan, John A. "Anti-Semitism in the Air." *Commonweal* 29 (December 30, 1938): 260-262.

Shuster, George N. "The Jew and the Two Revolutions." *Commonweal* 29 (December 30, 1938): 262-264.

Troy, Michael, C.S.Sp. "Reverend Denis Fahey, C.S.Sp.: Towards a Critical Analysis of His Published Works." Reprint from *Tomorrow's Laborers*. Dublin: Kimmage Manor, 1954.

Primary Sources: Government Documents

Great Britain. Foreign Office White Paper, "Russia, No. 1 (1919), A Collection of Reports on Bolshevism in Russia." Library, Trinity College, Dublin.

U.S. Congress. House of Representatives. Committee on Un-American Activities. *Spotlight on Spies*. Pamphlet prepared and released by Committee, March 25, 1949.

Selected Secondary Sources: Books

Abell, Aaron I. *American Catholicism and Social Action: A Search for Social Justice, 1865-1950*. Garden City, New York: Doubleday and Company, 1960.

Ahlstrom, Sydney E. *A Religious History of the American People*. New Haven: Yale University Press, 1972.

Altholz, Josef L. *The Church in the Nineteenth Century*. New York: Bobbs-Merrill, 1967.

Bell, Daniel, ed. *The Radical Right: The New American Right*. New York: Doubleday and Company, 1963.

Bennett, David H. *Demagogues in the Depression: American Radicals and the Union Party, 1932-1936*. New Brunswick, New Jersey: Rutgers University Press, 1969.

Blau, Joseph L., and Salo W. Baron *The Jews in the United States, 1790-1840: A Documentary History*. 3 vols. New York: Columbia University Press, 1966.

Brinkley, Alan. *Voices of Protest: Huey Long, Father Coughlin, and the Great Depression.* New York: Random House, 1983.

Broderick, Francis L. *Right Reverend New Dealer: John A. Ryan.* New York: Macmillan and Company, 1963.

Carter, Paul. *The Decline and Revival of the Social Gospel: Social and Political Liberalism in American Protestant Churches, 1920-1940.* Ithaca, New York: Cornell University Press, 1956.

Crosby, Donald F., S.J. *God, Church and Flag: Senator Joseph R. McCarthy and the Catholic Church, 1950-1957.* Chapel Hill, North Carolina: University of North Carolina Press, 1978.

Curry, Lerond. *Protestant-Catholic Relations in America: World War I to Vatican II.* Lexington, Kentucky: University of Kentucky Press, 1972.

Dolan, Jay P. *The American Catholic Experience.* New York: Doubleday and Company, 1985.

Eckardt, A. Roy. *Elder and Younger Brothers: The Encounter of Jews and Christians.* New York: Charles Scribner's Sons, 1967.

Ernst, Eldon G. *Moment of Truth for Protestant America: Interchurch Campaign following World War One.* Missoula, Montana: Scholars' Press, 1972.

Glanz, Rudolf. *Jew and Irish: Historic Relations and Immigration.* New York: Alexander Kohut Memorial Foundation, 1966.

Glazer, Nathan, and Daniel P. Moynihan. *Beyond the Melting Pot: The Negroes, Puerto Ricans, Jews, Italians and Irish of New York City.* Notre Dame, Indiana: University of Notre Dame Press, 1969.

Glock, Charles Y., and Rodney Stark. *Christian Beliefs and Anti-Semitism.* New York: Harper and Row, 1966.

Gwynn, Stephen. *The History of Ireland.* Dublin: Talbot Press, 1924.

Halsey, William M. *The Survival of American Innocence: Catholicism in an Era of Disillusionment, 1920-1940.* Notre Dame, Indiana: University of Notre Dame Press, 1979.

Handlin, Oscar, and Mary F. Handlin. *Danger in Discord: Origins of Anti-Semitism in the United States.* New York: Anti-Defamation League, 1948.

Heller, James G. *Isaac M. Wise: His Life, Work, and Thought.* New York: Union of American Hebrew Congregations, 1965.

Hennesey, James. *American Catholics: A History of the Roman Catholic Community in the United States.* New York: Oxford University Press, 1981.

Herberg, Will. *Protestant—Catholic—Jew: An Essay in American Religious Sociology.* Rev. ed. Garden City, New York: Doubleday and Company, 1960.

Higham, John. *Strangers in the Land: Patterns of American Nativism: 1860-1925.* New York: Atheneum, 1974.

251

Hilberg, Raul. *The Destruction of European Jewry*. Chicago: Quadrangle Press, 1961.

Hoehn, Matthew, ed. *Catholic Authors: Contemporary Biographical Sketches*. 2 vols. Newark, New Jersey: St. Mary's Abbey, 1952.

Jeansonne, Glen. *Gerald L. K. Smith: Minister of Hate*. New Haven: Yale University Press, 1988.

Kaplan, Mordecai M. *Judaism as a Civilization: Toward a Reconstruction of American Jewish Life*. New York: T. Yoseloff, 1957.

Keogh, Dermot. *The Vatican, the Bishops, and Irish Politics, 1919-1939*. New York: Cambridge University Press, 1986.

Kernan, William C. *The Ghost of Royal Oak*. New York: Free Speech Forum, 1940.

Koren, Henry J. *The Spiritans: A History of the Congregation of the Holy Ghost*. Pittsburgh: Duquesne University Press, 1958.

Larkin, Emmet. *The Historical Dimensions of Irish Catholicism*. New York: Arno Press, 1976.

Learsi, Rufus [Israel Goldberg]. *The Jews in America*. Cleveland: World Publishing Company, 1954.

Lyons, F. S. L. *Ireland since the Famine*. Great Britain: Collins/ Fontana, 1973.

Marcus, Sheldon. *Father Coughlin: The Tumultuous Life of the Priest of the Little Flower*. Boston: Little, Brown and Company, 1973.

Marty, Martin E. *Righteous Empire: The Protestant Experience in America*. New York: Dial Press, 1970.

May, Henry. *The End of American Innocence: A Study of the First Years of Our Own Time, 1912-1917*. New York: Franklin Watts (New Viewpoints), 1964.

McManners, John. *Church and State in France: 1870-1914*. London: SPCK, 1972.

Miller, Robert Moats. *American Protestantism and Social Issues, 1919-1939*. Chapel Hill, North Carolina: University of North Carolina Press, 1958.

Myers, Gustavus. *History of Bigotry in the United States*. New York: Capricorn, 1960.

Nolte, Ernst. *Three Faces of Fascism: Action Française, Italian Fascism, National Socialism*. New York: Holt, Rinehart and Winston, 1963.

O'Brien, David J. *American Catholics and Social Reform: The New Deal Years*. New York: Oxford University Press, 1968.

O'Dea, Thomas F. *American Catholic Dilemma: An Inquiry into the Intellectual Life*. New York: Sheed and Ward, 1958.

Ong, Walter J., S.J. *American Catholic Crossroads*. New York: Macmillan, 1959.

_____. *Frontiers in American Catholicism: Essays on Ideology and Culture*. New York: Macmillan, 1957.

252

Overstreet, Harry and Bonaro. *The Strange Tactics of Extremism*. New York: W.W. Norton and Company, 1964.

Partin, Malcolm O. *Waldeck-Rousseau, Combes, and the Church: the Politics of Anti-Clericalism, 1899-1905*. Durham, North Carolina: Duke University Press, 1969.

Reardon, Bernard, ed. *Roman Catholic Modernism*. Stanford, California: Stanford University Press, 1970.

Ribuffo, Leo P. *The Old Christian Right: The Protestant Far Right From the Great Depression to the Cold War*. Philadelphia: Temple University Press, 1983.

Rischin, Moses. *The Promised City: New York's Jews, 1870-1914*. Cambridge, Massachusetts: Harvard University Press, 1962.

Roy, Ralph Lord. *Apostles of Discord: A Study of Organized Bigotry and Disruption on the Fringes of Protestantism*. Boston: Beacon Press, 1953.

Ruether, Rosemary Radford. *Faith and Fratricide: The Theological Roots of Anti-Semitism*. New York: Seabury Press, 1974.

Shannon, William V. *The American Irish*. New York: Macmillan, 1963.

Smith, H. Shelton, Robert T. Handy, and Lefferts A. Loetscher. *American Christianity*. 2 vols. New York: Charles Scribner's Sons, 1960, 1963.

Spivak, John. *Shrine of the Silver Dollar*. New York: Modern Age Books, 1940.

Stokes, Anson Phelps, and Leo Pfeffer. *Church and State in the United States*. Rev. New York: Harper and Row, 1964.

Strong, Donald Stuart. *Organized Anti-Semitism in America: The Rise of Group Prejudice during the Decade 1930-1940*. Washington, D.C.: American Council on Public Affairs, 1941.

Swing, Raymond Gram. *Forerunners of American Fascism*. Freeport, New York: Books for Libraries Press, 1935.

Thomson, David, ed. *France: Empire and Republic, 1850-1940*. New York: Harper and Row, 1968.

Trachtenberg, Joshua. *The Devil and the Jews: The Medieval Conception of the Jew and Its Relation to Modern Antisemitism*. New Haven: Yale University Press, 1943.

Tull, Charles J. *Father Coughlin and the New Deal*. Syracuse, New York: Syracuse University Press, 1965.

Van Kaam, Adrian, C.S.Sp. *A Light to the Gentiles*. Milwaukee: Bruce Publishing Company, 1959.

Weber, Eugen. *Action Française: Royalism and Reaction in Twentieth Century France*. Stanford, California: Stanford University Press, 1962.

Whyte, J. H. *Church and State in Modern Ireland, 1923-1970*. New York: Barnes and Noble, Inc., 1971.

Selected Secondary Sources: Articles

Catholic Encyclopedia. New York: Encyclopedia Press, Inc., 1908. "Deschamps, Nicholas," by J. F. Sollier, p. 478.

Dru, Alexander. "From the *Action Française* to the Second Vatican Council." *Downside Review* 81 (July 1963) 264: 226-245.

Encyclopedia of Judaism. New York: Macmillan, 1971. "Sombart, Werner," pp. 134-135.

"Fagan, Myron C." *Who Was Who in Hollywood: 1912-1976.* Vol. 2. Detroit: Gale Research Company, 1976, pp. 792-793.

Handy, Robert T. "The American Religious Depression, 1925-1935." *Church History* 29 (March 1960): 3-16.

Hennesey, James, S.J. "Leo XIII's Thomistic Revival: A Political and Philosophical Event." *Journal of Religion* 58 (Spring 1978): 5185-5197.

Higham, John. "Social Discrimination against Jews in America, 1830-1930." *The Jewish Experience in America.* Vol. 5. Ed. and intro. Abraham J. Karp. New York: KTAV Publishing House, Inc., 1969, pp. 349-381.

Judaism. Special Issue: "Interfaith at Fifty." Vol. 27, No. 3 (Summer 1978).

Kennedy, Thomas P. "Essay on Church Building." *A History of Irish Catholicism.* Ed. Patrick J. Cornish. Dublin: Gill and Macmillan, 1970.

McCool, Gerald A., S.J. "Twentieth Century Scholasticism." *Journal of Religion* 58 (Spring 1978): 5198-5221.

McGrath, Fergal, S.J. "The University Question." *A History of Irish Catholicism,* V. Ed. P. J. Cornish. Dublin: Gill and Macmillan, 1971.

Modras, Ronald. "Father Coughlin and Anti-Semitism: Fifty Years Later." *The Journal of Church and State* 31 (Spring 1989):231-247.

O'Brien, David J. "American Catholics and Anti-Semitism in the 1930's." *The Catholic World* 204 (February 1967): 270-276.

O'Brien, Gerald J. "Anti-Modernism: The Integralist Campaign." *Continuum* 3 (1965): 187-200.

"Smith, Gerald L. K." *Current Biography* 1943. Ed. Maxine Block. New York: H.W. Wilson Company, 1943, pp. 707-710.

Unpublished Thesis

Brown, Gerald L., S.S. "The Reverend Charles E. Coughlin and the 1936 Election." M.A. Thesis, University of Washington, 1971.

Personal Interviews

Aherne, John, C.S.Sp. Dublin, Ireland. September 18, 1980.

Barry, Sean, C.S.Sp. Blackrock College, Dublin. March 13, 1979.

Benignus, Brother, C.S.Sp. Holy Ghost Missionary College, Kimmage, Dublin. March 20, 1979.

Blair, Leonard P. Archivist, Archdiocese of Detroit. Telephone interview, March 16, 1972.

Bloom, Jack. Dublin Hebrew Congregation, Dublin, Ireland. March 10, 1979.

Byrne, Desmond, C.S.Sp. Holy Ghost Provincialate, Templeogue, Dublin. March 3, 1979.

Chisholm, John, C.S.Sp. Our Lady of Templeogue Convent, Tereneure, Dublin. March 11, 1979.

Curtin, Maurice, C.S.Sp. Holy Ghost Missionary College, Kimmage, Dublin. March 19, 1979.

Daley, John, C.S.Sp. Holy Ghost Missionary College, Kimmage, Dublin. March 5, 1979; Holy Ghost Provincialate, Templeogue, Dublin, September 17, 1980.

Duff, Frank. Consilium House, Dublin. March 19, 1979.

Fahey, Denis. Kilmore, Golden, County Tipperary. September 16, 1980.

Fahey, Mary Jo. Dublin. September 17, 18, and 20, 1980.

Fahey, Nellie McGrath. Kilmore, Golden, County Tipperary. September 16, 1980.

Fallon, Gabriel. Holy Ghost Provincialate, Templeogue, Dublin. March 22, 1979.

Galvin, Seamus, C.S.Sp. Holy Ghost Provincialate, Templeogue, Dublin. August 30, 1980.

Good, Hermann. Dublin Hebrew Congregation, Dublin. March 10, 1979.

Hurley, James, C.S.Sp. Rockwell College, Cashel, County Tipperary. September 16, 1980.

Jenkinson, William, C.S.Sp. Berkeley, California. January 16, 1979.

Kavanagh, Thomas. New York City, Telephone interview, May 4, 1979.

Kelly, Bernard, C.S.Sp. Holy Ghost Missionary College, Kimmage, Dublin. March 7, 1979.

Kennedy, Denis, C.S.Sp. Blackrock College, Dublin. March 13, 1979.

Keogh, Dermot. Trinity College, Dublin. August 26, 1980.

Layden, Leo, C.S.Sp. Holy Ghost Provincialate, Templeogue, Dublin. February-March 1979; August-September, 1980.

Macken, Thomas, C.S.Sp. Holy Ghost Missionary College, Kimmage, Dublin. March 19, 1979.

Marcus, Mildred. Anti-Defamation League, Los Angeles, California. Telephone interview, January 4, 1982.

McCarthy, Michael, C.S.Sp. Holy Ghost Provincialate, Templeogue, Dublin.
February-March 1979; August-September 1980.

McGann, James, C.S.Sp. Holy Ghost Provincialate, Templeogue, Dublin.
August 31, 1980.

Moran, Theresa. Dublin. September 18, 1980.

Murtagh, Frank. Dublin. March 20, 1979.

Nolan, Peter, C.S.Sp. Holy Ghost Provincialate, Templeogue, Dublin.
September 3, 1980.

O'Carroll, Michael, C.S.Sp. Blackrock College, Dublin. March 13, 1979.

O'Sullivan, Donal, C.S.Sp. Holy Ghost Provincialate, Templeogue, Dublin.
September 13, 1980.

O'Toole, Michael. Dublin. September 18, 1980.

Ryan, Patrick, C.S.Sp. Holy Ghost Provincialate, Templeogue, Dublin.
August 28, 1980.

Sheridan, Farrell, C.S.Sp. Holy Ghost Missionary College, Kimmage, Dublin.
March 19, 1979.

Tuohy, Josie Fahey. Kilmore, Golden, County Tipperary. September 16, 1980.

Watters, Enda, C.S.Sp. Holy Ghost Provincialate, Templeogue, Dublin.
February-March 1979; August-September 1980; Berkeley, California,
January 29, 1981.

INDEX

262